MARK N. SWANSON is Harold S. Vogelaar
professor of Christian–Muslim studies and
interfaith relations at the Lutheran School
of Theology at Chicago.

The Popes of Egypt

2

The Coptic Papacy in Islamic Egypt

The Popes of Egypt

A History of the Coptic Church and Its Patriarchs
from Saint Mark to Pope Shenouda III

Edited by Stephen J. Davis and Gawdat Gabra

Volume Two

The Coptic Papacy
in Islamic Egypt
(641–1517)

Mark N. Swanson

The American University in Cairo Press
Cairo   New York

Copyright © 2010 by
The American University in Cairo Press
113 Sharia Kasr el Aini, Cairo, Egypt
420 Fifth Avenue, New York, NY 10018
www.aucpress.com

Dar el Kutub No. 3057/07
ISBN 978 977 416 093 6

Dar el Kutub Cataloging-in-Publication Data

Swanson, Mark
        The Coptic Papacy in Islamic Egypt, 641–1571 / Mark Swanson.—Cairo: The American
University in Cairo Press, 2010
        p.   cm.
        ISBN 978 977 416 093 6
        1. Christianity—Biography
        927.71

1 2 3 4 5 6   15 14 13 12 11 10

Designed by Sebastian Schönenstein
Printed in Egypt

Contents

Editors' Introduction

T he Arab conquest and the ensuing period of Islamic rule led gradually to the Arabization and/or Islamization of many territories in the eastern Mediterranean and North Africa. Over time, Christianity disappeared completely in some regions, but in other areas, Christians survived as small minorities. Egyptian Christians, also known as the Copts, were prominent among these survivors, and today they represent the largest Christian community in the Middle East. This volume, as described by its author, is about the early story of their survival, from the seventh to the sixteenth century.

Despite its shortcomings, the eight-volume *Coptic Encyclopedia* (1991) is undoubtedly the most important reference tool for the history and culture of the Copts during the medieval Islamic era.[1] At the time of its preparation and publication, however, only a handful of scholars were equipped for the task of researching topics related to Copto-Arabic literature. Indeed, the responsibility for producing approximately five hundred entries on such topics fell primarily to three scholars: Samir Khalil Samir, René-Georges Coquin, and Aziz S. Atiya.[2]

Fortunately, there has been an appreciable upsurge in scholarship on Arabic-speaking Christian communities in Egypt since that landmark publication, and Mark Swanson has been instrumental in documenting recent advances in the field.[3] Therefore, it is not surprising that Swanson— an expert in the early Christian–Muslim encounter, Copto-Arabic literature, and the history of the Egyptian Christian community in the Middle Ages— should be ideally situated to produce the volume *The Coptic Papacy in Islamic Egypt*. In addition to his access to scholarship on Arabic Christian literature and theology, Swanson also draws on recent research in a range of other fields, including Coptic art, Arabic papyrology, and Islamic historiography. This allows him to analyze in detail important changes that took place not only in the public arena between Coptic popes and Muslim rulers, but also within the Christian community between the clergy and laity. In doing so, he takes into consideration religious, social, political, and economic factors that shaped the contours of church leadership during this period. Framed for both the scholar and the general reader, Swanson's book most importantly tells an engaging story—the story of the Copts' survival under Islamic rule in Egypt.

The Coptic Papacy in Islamic Egypt is the second of three volumes in the AUC Press series entitled The Popes of Egypt: A History of the Coptic Church and Its Patriarchs from Saint Mark to Pope Shenouda III. The authors of these volumes have dedicated much of their careers to the study of Egyptian Christianity and are intimately familiar with the material culture and institutional life of the Coptic Church from years of living and working in Egypt. Volume One, *The Early Coptic Papacy*, published in 2004, focuses on the history of the Alexandrian patriarchate from its origins to the rise of Islam in the seventh century. Its author, Stephen J. Davis, is Professor of Religious Studies at Yale University, with special expertise in the history of Christianity in late antiquity. The present Volume Two focuses on the period from the rise of Islam to the Ottoman conquest. Its author, Mark Swanson, an expert in the Arabic Christian history and literature, is the Harold S. Vogelaar Professor of Christian–Muslim Studies and Interfaith Relations at the Lutheran School of Theology at Chicago (LSTC). Volume Three focuses on the developments from the Ottoman era to the present day. Forthcoming under the title *The Emergence of the Modern Coptic Papacy*, it is co-authored by two leading scholars in the field. The first, Magdi Girgis (Ph.D., Cairo University), is a specialist in Coptic documentary sources during the Ottoman period and author of *An Armenian Artist in Ottoman Egypt: Yuhanna al-Armani and His Coptic Icons* (AUC Press, 2008). The second, Nelly van Doorn-Harder, is a professor in the Department of Religion at Wake Forest University who has published books in both Islamic studies and modern Coptic history. Serving as associate editor for this third and final volume is Michael Shelley, currently the Dean and Vice President for Academic Affairs and Director of the Center of Christian–Muslim Engagement for Peace and Justice at LSTC.

As editors of the series, we want to express our thanks to the American University in Cairo Press, and especially to Mark Linz and Neil Hewison for their commitment to this project. The publication of this series is in large part a testament to their professional vision and dedication.

Stephen J. Davis and Gawdat Gabra, co-editors

Author's Preface

In Volume I of this three-volume set, Stephen J. Davis wrote a "discursive history" of the early Egyptian papacy, aiming to show "how the Alexandrian patriarchate was rhetorically and socially 'constructed'" in the centuries before the Islamic conquest. His work paid careful attention to how the popes were represented (or how they represented themselves), and how "such discourses actually *shape* the church's understanding of itself and its leaders."[1]

Such a "discursive historical" method provides a fresh and promising approach to the study of the Coptic Orthodox patriarchs who led their community as Egypt was absorbed into the "new world order" of the *Dar al-Islam*. As is the case with other treatments of the Coptic Orthodox church and its leadership under Muslim rule, the Arabic compilation usually known as the *History of the Patriarchs* will be a chief source for this study. What may be new in the present study is that I intend to take seriously recent research that clarifies the history of composition of the *History of the Patriarchs*, especially the work of David W. Johnson and Johannes den Heijer.[2] They and their predecessors have enabled us to discern within this standard reference a series of compositions by a variety of authors, many of whom were contemporaries of the patriarchs they portrayed.

The analyses of Johnson, den Heijer, and their predecessors provide the present study its framework. Each of its nine chapters relates to a particular source or section of the *History of the Patriarchs*, as summarized in the table on page xii.

Having sorted out the sources, it is possible to ask questions such as: With what understanding of history does each author work? What "strategies of representation" (Davis) of the patriarchs can we discern in each author's portrayals? What do these writings reveal about Christian life and identity in a land no longer under Christian rule? What do the identities and

Chapter	Title Patriarchs	Dates	Author of Source Material in the *History of the Patriarchs*
One	**Continuity and Reinvention** Benjamin I (#38)– Simon (#42)	640–700	George "the Archdeacon" (wrote in Coptic)
Two	**Patient Sufferers** Alexander II (#43)– Michael I (#46)	704–767	John "the Deacon" (wrote in Coptic)
Three	**Crisis of Cohesion** Menas I (#47)– Shenoute I (#55)	767–880	John "the Writer" (wrote in Coptic)
Four	**Saints and Sinners** Michael II (#56)– Shenoute II (#65)	880–1046	Michael al-Damrawi, Bishop of Tinnis (wrote in Coptic)
Five	**Transitions** Christodoulos (#66)– John VI (#74)	1046–1216	Mawhub ibn Mansur ibn Mufarrij and continuators (wrote in Arabic)
Six	**Chaos and Glory** Cyril III (#75)	1216–1250	Yuhanna ibn Wahb (wrote in Arabic)
Seven	**Marginalized Patriarchs** Athanasius III (#76)– Gabriel IV (#86)	1250–1378	Anonymous continuators (wrote in Arabic)
Eight	**A Burst of Holiness** Matthew I (#87)	1378–1408	Anonymous author of the Life of Matthew (wrote in Arabic)
Nine	**Humility in Action** Gabriel V (#88)– John XIII (#94)	1409–1524	Anonymous continuators (wrote in Arabic)

interests of the authors tell us about patterns of leadership and patronage in the church, and their changes with the passage of time?

While the *History of the Patriarchs* provides the framework for the present study, it is, of course, not its only primary source. For the period under consideration here we have some additional material: other *Lives* of popes (sometimes written by contemporaries), homilies and canonical collections coming from the popes themselves, and a variety of churchly literature produced by close associates or opponents.

The present volume is by no means a comprehensive history of the Coptic Orthodox Church in the Middle Ages.[3] Discoveries in Coptic archaeology and art history, Copto-Arabic literature, Arabic papyrology, and various other fields are taking place at such a pace that any attempt to offer such a history is beyond both my competence and my capacity to keep up.[4] At the same time, I at least attempt to be attentive to significant discoveries in these fields, in the hope that the picture of the Coptic Orthodox papacy that emerges from a close reading of literary representations will be illumined by results and insights coming from other disciplines.[5]

Some readers will find the story of the Coptic Orthodox papacy from the Arab conquest to the Ottoman conquest to be mainly one of loss and decline. Certainly, the Christian population of Egypt decreases over the course of the story from the vast majority of all Egyptians to a small minority. One can seek the reasons for this decline, making it the center of one's inquiry. However, I believe that this story can be read and told in another way: as a remarkable narrative of *survival*, in which Coptic Christian identity was continually reconstructed and maintained in the midst of strong pressures for accommodation to and assimilation with the dominant Arabic–Islamic culture. This volume is the story of that survival.

Technical Notes

Among the discoveries of Johannes den Heijer is the fact that the *History of the Patriarchs* exists in both a 'primitive' recension and a later 'Vulgate' recension.[6] In the present work I have used accessible published texts of the 'Vulgate' recension, in the awareness that some details may have to be reassessed as the 'primitive' recension becomes better known and more accessible.[7]

Arabic words and names are transcribed without macrons or sublinear dots, but the reader who knows Arabic should have no difficulty in deciphering them.

For much of this volume, I have made use of published English translations of primary sources, when available, unless I have stated otherwise.[8] Accordingly, I normally make reference to the page number of the English translation when this differs from that of the Arabic text—as is the case with the Cairo, Société d'Archéologie Copte edition of the *History of the Patriarchs* [*HPEC*]. (I trust those who wish to check the Arabic text to find their own way to it.) When quoting the English translation of the *History of the Patriarchs* found in *HPEC*, I have privileged ease of reading over technical information by (a) eliminating the frequent Greek or Arabic equivalents given in parentheses; (b) eliminating the parentheses around English words added for readability; (c) substituting a proper name in square brackets for "he" or "him" followed by that name in parentheses; (d) placing Arabic words (written, as usual in this book, without special symbols) in italics. In the notes these changes shall be indicated with a statement of the form, "Translation slightly modified."

All dates are given in the Common Era. The dates given after the name of a patriarch or ruler (caliph, sultan) are the dates during which that person was *in office*. (Only in the case of four saints treated in Chapter Eight do I provide dates of *birth*.) It should be noted that the dates given in this volume for each patriarchate are sometimes uncertain, with the greatest uncertainty affecting the dates of the patriarchs of the last third of the seventh century (see Chapter One): a discrepancy of up to four years may be found between commonly used reference works.[9] Throughout this volume I have used the dates provided in the detailed tables found as an appendix in Wadi' Farajallah Zakhari, *Babawat al-Kanisah al-Mu'allaqah*,[10] which differ only very slightly from those provided by Otto Meinardus in his classic volume, *Christian Egypt, Ancient and Modern*.[11]

Acknowledgments

This book has been more than five years in the writing, and over that time my debts to friends and colleagues have piled up. In the first place, I want to thank my publishers and editors. Mark Linz and Neil Hewison of the AUC Press have been both supportive and exceedingly patient. Steve Davis is not only a great personal and scholarly friend, but a model editor: his responsiveness to queries and feedback on drafts of chapters have been unfailingly prompt, encouraging, and insightful. Gawdat Gabra has, over the years, lured me into a variety of projects—all of which have contributed to my ongoing education in Coptic Church history.

Other friends and societies have similarly participated in my education in matters Coptic, both showing me great hospitality and giving me challenging assignments: the faculty and students of the Evangelical Theological Seminary in Cairo; Samir Khalil Samir, sj, a mentor for more than two decades; Hany Takla and the members of the St. Shenouda the Archimandrite Coptic Society; Stephen Emmel and the Board of the International Association of Coptic Studies; Betsy Bolman and William Lyster, who drew me in to projects sponsored by the American Research Center in Egypt; Nelly van Doorn-Harder, who regularly challenges me to think about contemporary realities; and all the members of the Asdiqa' al-Turath al-'Arabi al-Masihi (Friends of the Arabic Christian Heritage) in Cairo, of which it was my great joy to be a member while living in Cairo between 1992 and 1998.

Libraries are critical to a project like this, and I have been privileged to use some fine ones. In Cairo, I must mention the library of the Evangelical Theological Seminary (where friends always make me feel at home); the Franciscan Centre for Christian Oriental Studies (where Wadi Abullif, ofm, is unfailingly generous with expertise and resources); and the Netherlands-Flemish Institute (one of several places where my path has crossed that of

Han den Heijer, whose research is so foundational to this book). In St. Paul, Minnesota, my colleagues at the Luther Seminary Library were always helpful; Sally Sawyer, in particular, tracked down the most obscure interlibrary loan requests with delight. Nearby, I spent many fruitful hours at the Wilson Library of the University of Minnesota; the John Ireland Library of the Saint Paul Seminary School of Divinity; and the Alcuin Library of St. John's University, Collegeville. In Chicago, I have the great good fortune to live within blocks of magnificent collections: at the Regenstein Library of the University of Chicago; and at the JKM Library, housed on the campus of the Lutheran School of Theology at Chicago and staffed by wonderful colleagues.

Chapter Eight would have been much poorer had it not been possible to consult a number of unpublished manuscripts. I had access to a copy of the *Life of Marqus al-Antuni*, MS Monastery of St. Paul, Hist. 115, as part of the American Research Center in Egypt's Cave Church at the Monastery of St. Paul conversation and publishing project, which was funded by the United States Agency for International Development. I am deeply grateful to my colleagues Gawdat Gabra and Samiha Abd el-Shaheed Abd el-Nour, to ARCE, and to the monks of the monastery, especially the manuscript librarian Fr. Yohanna. In addition, Gawdat Gabra supplied me with a photocopy of the *Life of Ibrahim al-Fani* in the context of the Monastery of St. Paul project, while Hany Takla provided me with a copy of the *Life of Anba Ruways*.

Much of the planning for this volume was done, and the first four chapters written, during a sabbatical leave granted me by Luther Seminary, St. Paul, Minnesota. I thank the Seminary Board and my colleagues there, as well as Thrivent Financial for Lutherans for a sabbatical grant that allowed for a research trip to Egypt.

Many friends and colleagues have read or listened to parts of this book. Students in an LSTC graduate seminar in the spring of 2007 read and critiqued Chapters One through Four, while LSTC colleagues devoted a faculty colloquy in the fall of 2008 to Chapter Six. I presented material from Chapter Five at the Eighth Conference on Arab Christian Studies (Granada, September 2008) and material from Chapter Eight at the Annual Meeting of the American Academy of Religion (Chicago, November 2008), while parts of Chapters Five, Seven, and Eight began as presentations at the annual conferences of the St. Shenouda the Archimandrite Coptic Society (Los Angeles, 2002–2008). In addition, my friend and colleague Michael Shelley, my wife Rosanne Swanson, and my father Theodore Swanson have carefully and uncomplainingly read the drafts that I've regularly placed before them. Steve Davis and Yoni Moss have read the entire text with close attention. Wadi Abullif, Sharbel Iskandar Bcheiry, Gawdat Gabra,

Adel Sidarus, Hany Takla, Jos van Lent, and Ugo Zanetti have all responded generously to appeals for help on particular points. I am grateful to all these readers, audiences, and authorities. Obviously, any mistakes in the book are solely my own responsibility.

Pressures of time made the tasks of compiling a bibliography and an index seem quite monumental—and it was a great blessing that Yonatan Moss of Yale University was willing to take them on. I offer my heartfelt thanks to him, as well as to the AUC Press for support of his precise work. Noha Mohammed and her associates at the AUC Press have done a magnificent job of copyediting, proofreading, and design.

My wife Rosanne has been a conversation partner, reader, and constant source of encouragement throughout this project—which has corresponded with a busy season of our lives, as our children Carl, Hannah, and Rebekah grew to adulthood; as we made a move from St. Paul to Chicago; and as Rosanne herself completed her Ph.D. and assumed new teaching and administrative responsibilities. Rosanne has somehow held us—and me— together during all of this. It is to her, with love, that I dedicate this book.

Abbreviations

**The editions of the *History of the Patriarchs*
used in this volume are cited as follows:**

PO 1.4   B.T.A. Evetts, ed., *History of the Patriarchs of the Coptic
              Church of Alexandria*, II, *Peter I to Benjamin I (661)*,
              in Patrologia Orientalis, vol. 1, fasc. 4 (Paris: Firmin-
              Didot, 1904), 381–519.

PO 5.1   B.T.A. Evetts, ed., *History of the Patriarchs of the Coptic
              Church of Alexandria*, III, *Agathon to Michael I (766)*,
              in Patrologia Orientalis, vol. 5, fasc. 1 (Paris: Firmin-
              Didot, 1910), 1–215.

PO 10.5   B.T.A. Evetts, ed., *History of the Patriarchs of the Coptic
              Church of Alexandria*, IV, *Mennas I to Joseph (849)*, in
              Patrologia Orientalis, vol. 10, fasc. 5 (Paris: Firmin-
              Didot, 1915), 357–551.

HPEC 2.1   Yassa 'Abd al-Masih and O. H. E. Burmester, eds.,
              *History of the Patriarchs of the Egyptian Church, known
              as the History of the Holy Church, by Sawirus ibn
              al-Mukaffa', bishop of al-Asmunin*, Vol. II, Part I, *Khaël
              II—Shenouti I(AD 849–880)* (Cairo: Société d'Archéologie
              Copte, 1943).

HPEC 2.2   Aziz Suryal Atiya, Yassa 'Abd al-Masih, and O. H. E.
              Burmester, eds., *History of the Patriarchs of the Egyptian
              Church . . . ,* Vol. II, Part II, *Khaël III—Shenouti II (AD
              880–1066)* (Cairo: Société d'Archéologie Copte, 1948).

HPEC 2.3   Aziz Suryal Atiya, Yassa 'Abd al-Masih, and O. H. E.
                Khs-Burmester, eds., *History of the Patriarchs of the*
                Egyptian Church . . . , Vol. II, Part III, *Christodoulus—*
                Michael (AD 1046–1102) (Cairo: Société d'Archéologie
                Copte, 1959).

HPEC 3.1   Antoine Khater and O. H. E. Khs-Burmester, eds.,
                History of the Patriarchs of the Egyptian Church . . . ,
                Vol. III, Part I, *Macarius II—John V (AD 1102–1167)*
                (Cairo: Société d'Archéologie Copte, 1968).

HPEC 3.2   Antoine Khater and O. H. E. Khs-Burmester, eds.,
                History of the Patriarchs of the Egyptian Church . . . , Vol.
                III, Part II, *Mark III—John VI (AD 1167–1216)* (Cairo:
                Société d'Archéologie Copte, 1970).

HPEC 3.3   Antoine Khater and O. H. E . Khs-Burmester, eds.,
                History of the Patriarchs of the Egyptian Church . . . , Vol.
                III, Part III, *Cyril II—Cyril V (AD 1235–1894)* (Cairo:
                Société d'Archéologie Copte, 1970).

HPEC 4.1–2   Antoine Khater and O. H. E. Khs-Burmester, eds.,
                History of the Patriarchs of the Egyptian Church, known
                as the History of the Holy Church, according to MS. arabe
                302 Bibliothèque Nationale, Paris, foll. 287v–355r, Vol.
                IV, 2 parts, *Cyril III—Cyril V (AD 1216–1243)* (Cairo:
                Société d'Archéologie Copte, 1974).

                          Other primary sources:

HCME   B.T.A. Evetts, ed., *The Churches and Monasteries of*
(ed. Evetts)   *Egypt and Some Neighbouring Countries, Attributed to*
                Abu Salih, the Armenian (Oxford: The Clarendon
                Press, 1895; reprint ed. Piscataway, NJ: Gorgias Press, 2001).

HPYusab   Samu'il al-Suryani and Nabih Kamil, eds., *Tarikh al-aba'*
                al-batarikah li-l-Anba Yusab usquf Fuwwah ([Cairo]:
                [Coptic Institute of Higher Studies], [c. 1987]).

L.Ibrahim   The *Life of Ibrahim al-Fani* as recorded in MS Monastery
                of St. Antony, Hist. 75.[1]

L.Marqus	The *Life of Marqus al-Antuni* as recorded in MS Monastery of St. Paul, Hist. 115.
L.Ruways	The *Life of Anba Ruways* as recorded in MS Paris, Bibliothèque Nationale, arabe 282, ff. 82r–151r.
Maqrizi, Suluk, i–ii	Taqi al-Din Ahmad ibn 'Ali al-Maqrizi, *Kitab al-suluk li-ma'rifat duwal al-muluk*, vols. 1 (in 3 parts) and 2 (in 2 parts), ed. Muhammad Mustafa Ziyadah (Cairo: Lajnat al-Ta'lif wa-l-Tarjamah wa-l-Nashr, 1934–1942).
Maqrizi, Suluk, iii–iv	Taqi al-Din Ahmad ibn 'Ali al-Maqrizi, *Kitab al-suluk li-ma'rifat duwal al-muluk*, vols. 3 (in 3 parts) and 4 (in 3 parts), ed. Sa'id 'Abd al-Fattah 'Ashur (Cairo: Dar al-Kutub, 1970–1973).
Synaxarion (ed. Basset)	René Basset, ed., *Le Synaxaire arabe jacobite (rédaction copte)*, Patrologia Orientalis 1.3, 3.3, 11.5, 16.2, 17.3, 20.5 (Paris: Firmin-Didot, 1907–1929).
Synaxarion (Cairo ed.), i–ii	*Kitab al-Sinaksar: al-Jami' akhbar al-anbiya' wa-l-rusul wa-l-shuhada' wa-l-qiddisin al-musta'mal fi kana'is al-karazah al-marqusiyyah fi ayam wa-ahad al-sanah al-tutiyyah*, 2 vols. (Cairo: Maktabat al-Mahabbah, n.d.).
Synaxarion (ed. Forget), i–ii	Jacobus Forget, ed., *Synaxarium Alexandrinum*, 2 vols., Corpus Scriptorum Christianorum Orientalium Ser. III, 18–19 (Beirut: E Typographeo catholico, 1905).

Secondary sources, text and monograph series, encyclopedias:

BSSOr	*Bibliotheca sanctorum orientalium. Enciclopedia dei santi: Le chiese orientali*, 2 vols., ed. J. Nadal Cañellas and S. Virgulin (Rome: Città Nuova, 1998–1999).
The Cambridge History of Egypt, i	Carl F. Petry, ed., *The Cambridge History of Egypt*, Vol. 1, *Islamic Egypt, 640–1517* (Cambridge, UK and New York: Cambridge University Press, 1998).

CE   *The Coptic Encyclopedia*, 8 vols., ed. Aziz Suryal Atiya
            (New York: Macmillan, Toronto: Collier Macmillan Canada,
            and New York: Maxwell Macmillan International, 1991).

CMR1   *Christian-Muslim Relations: A Bibliographical History*,
            Vol.1 (600–900), ed. David Thomas and Barbara Roggema,
            HCMR 11 (Leiden and Boston: Brill, 2009).

CSCO   Corpus Scriptorum Christianorum Orientalium (Louvain)

Davis,   Stephen J. Davis, *The Early Coptic Papacy: The Egyptian*
The Early   *Church and Its Leadership in Late Antiquity*, The Popes of
Coptic Papacy Egypt, Vol. 1 (Cairo and New York: The American
            University in Cairo Press, 2004).

Den Heijer, Johannes den Heijer, *Mawhub ibn Mansur ibn Mufarrig et*
Mawhub   *l'historiographie copto-arabe: Étude sur la composition de*
            l'Histoire des Patriarches d'Alexandrie, CSCO 513 =
            subsidia 83 (Louvain: E. Peeters, 1989).

EI (new ed.) *The Encyclopedia of Islam* (new edition), 13 vols., ed.
            H. A. R. Gibb et al. (Leiden: Brill, 1954–2008).

Graf, *GCAL*, Georg Graf, *Geschichte der christlichen arabischen Literatur*,
i–v   5 vols., Studi e Testi 118, 133, 146, 147, 172 (Vatican
            City: Biblioteca Apostolica Vaticana, 1944–1953).

HCMR   The History of Christian-Muslim Relations (Leiden)

Nakhlah,   Kamil Salih Nakhlah, *Silsilat Tarikh al-babawat batarikat*
Silsilah   *al-kursi al-Iskandari*, 5 fascicles, 2nd edition (Cairo: Dayr
(2nd ed.)   al-Suryan, 2001). [The first four fascicles were origi-
            nally published, with different pagination, between
            1951 and 1954.]

PO   Patrologia Orientalis (Paris)

One

Continuity and Reinvention

Benjamin I (#38, 623–662)
Agathon (#39, 662–680)
John III of Samannud (#40, 680–689)
Isaac (#41, 690–692)
Simon (#42, 692–700)

Succession and Innovation

Seven patriarchs are portrayed in wall paintings around the altars of the principal church at the Monastery of St. Antony in the eastern Egyptian desert, where the saint often considered the "father of monasticism" lived for over forty years.[1] Following a pattern common in Coptic churches, the church has three sanctuaries, each with its own altar, along its eastern wall. In the sanctuary to the north (left as one faces the front of the church), one finds within a niche a painting of the founder of the Egyptian church and its first patriarch, St. Mark the Evangelist. Opposite this, in the sanctuary to the south, there is another niche containing a wall painting of Athanasius "the Apostolic," the great champion of the faith of Nicaea and Antony's biographer. Above him, along the eastern and the southern walls of the sanctuary, are pictured a number of patriarchs who stand serenely in a row: first Severus of Antioch, then to his left the Alexandrian patriarchs Dioscorus, Theophilus, and Peter Martyr. Next to Peter stands one other patriarch. The inscription recording his name has been damaged, but the name appears to begin with B and to end with N:[2] in all probability, this is Benjamin, anti-Chalcedonian patriarch of Alexandria at the time of the Arab conquest of Egypt.

It is exalted company in which Benjamin finds himself, and this suggests that the planner of this painted program, dated to AD 1232/1233,[3] intended to make it clear that Benjamin was a true successor of St. Mark, a confessor of the faith of Nicaea, a father of his church even from exile (like Athanasius, Dioscorus, Theophilus, and Severus before him), and one worthy of honor akin to that of martyrdom (such as those of Mark and Peter).[4]

Stories told about Benjamin shortly after his death emphasize and expand on such a description. A small fragment of a Coptic *Life* of Benjamin, preserved in a single parchment page in Paris,[5] relates how the patriarch one day entered a monastery church (probably that of the Monastery of St. Macarius) in which there was a painted program not dissimilar from that at the Church of St. Antony: on the one side of the church, the great Egyptian monastic founders Antony, Paul, Macarius, and Pachomius were pictured; on the other, the Alexandrian patriarchs Mark, Peter Martyr, Athanasius (who is pictured as seated upon a cherub along with his friend and defender Pope Liberius of Rome), Cyril, and Dioscorus. As Benjamin approached the images to kiss them before celebrating the liturgy, they gave forth a sweet-smelling oil and called out, "You are holy, O King and Lord, and your saints!" The cherub flapped its wings for joy, and the "angel of the altar" called out, "Worthy, worthy, worthy, the archbishop who will today celebrate the Holy Anaphora!"[6] The saints' and angels' welcome makes it clear that Benjamin is a true monk, priest, and confessor of the faith, a genuine heir of the great Alexandrian patriarchs.

As we examine the sources that record the lives of the (anti-Chalcedonian) patriarchs of the Egyptian church during the early years of Islamic rule, we repeatedly meet with an emphasis on the ways in which they—often over against competitors—stand in true continuity with their sainted predecessors. At the same time, we will find that the sources tell a story of the shaping of something *new*, something for which we can confidently use the expression 'Coptic Orthodox Church': a specifically Egyptian church, freed from increasingly problematic ties to Constantinople, creating its distinctive forms of life and witness within the "new Islamic world order."[7] It is a story in which the patriarchs are intimately involved, through their actions (so far as they are known to us) and in the way that they are depicted, since these depictions tell us much about how the Coptic Orthodox Church as a whole is being understood and imagined. It is, perhaps, not surprising that the principal history of the medieval Coptic Orthodox Church is called the *History of the Patriarchs*: the patriarchs serve as an instantiation—one might even say as "icons"—of the community as a whole.

Earning the "Crown of Exile"

The section of the *History of the Patriarchs* dedicated to the period from the Arab conquest to the death of Patriarch Simon in AD 700 is translated from a Coptic source written by one George (*Jirjah* in Arabic) the Archdeacon.[8] We are fortunate in this; George informs us that he was the spiritual son of Patriarch John III (#40), and scribe to Patriarch Simon (#42). He is therefore a contemporary, and sometimes an eyewitness, of many of the events that he describes.

George's account does not actually begin with the Arab conquest of Egypt, but rather many years earlier, in the aftermath of the Council of Chalcedon in the second half of the fifth century AD.[9] He tells the story of patriarchs who steadfastly confess "the orthodox faith" before rulers, bear persecution patiently, and tend their orthodox flock even from exile. They are confronted with heretics on all sides, but through gentle persuasion are able to win many back. In Patriarch Benjamin (#38, 623–662), George has considerable material for elaborating all these themes.

Benjamin had come to the patriarchal throne during the Sassanid Persian occupation of Egypt (619–629), and saw the expulsion of the Persians by the Byzantines under the emperor Heraclius.[10] Any sense of liberation from the Persian yoke was short-lived. Heraclius was determined to find a solution to the theological quarrel that had been creating division within the empire for much of the previous two centuries: whether one must speak of one nature *(physis)* or of two natures in Jesus Christ, the incarnate Word. The two-nature formula had been promulgated as dogma at the Council of Chalcedon in 451, with imperial support; however, the formula was seen as an inadmissible innovation by many of the staunchest supporters of Patriarch Cyril of Alexandria, whose "one nature of the incarnate Word" formula remained a touchstone of Christological orthodoxy for many Christians, especially in Egypt and Syria. The emperor's attempt at unity involved a carefully calibrated balance of pressure and theological compromise: an attempt was made to address the legitimate concerns about Christ's unity raised by the one-nature Christologians through the Monoenergist (one-*activity*) and Monothelite (one-*will*) doctrinal proposals, while leaving the politically untouchable two-*natures* language of Chalcedon intact.[11]

The man chosen to implement this policy in Egypt was Cyrus, metropolitan of Phasis in the Caucasus (whence his Arabic title, "al-Muqawqas"), who was appointed Chalcedonian patriarch of Alexandria (in 631) with the authority to impose the imperially approved Christological formulations on the Egyptian church. Benjamin, as a staunch successor of patriarchs who had endured maltreatment and exile for the sake of the confession of the one nature of Christ the incarnate Word, was obliged to flee, and for ten years he managed to evade imperial agents by taking refuge with the monks of Upper Egypt. At the end of that period, Byzantine control of Egypt was swept away by the Arab Muslim armies under the command of 'Amr ibn al-'As: the stronghold of Babylon at the base of the Delta (today's Old Cairo) fell to the Arabs in the spring of 641, and the city of Alexandria surrendered to them in September 642.[12]

Benjamin, as we shall see, was soon ready to return from his long period of hiding from his opponents. His steadfast resistance to imperial coercion, however, earned him a place in the imagination of later Copts alongside earlier confessors such as Athanasius (five times banished from his see), Severus (who spent twenty years in Egypt, exiled from his see in Antioch), and Theodosius (who spent nearly thirty years in exile in Constantinople). When the *History of the Patriarchs* relates Benjamin's death, we are told that precisely these three patriarchs came to accompany his soul, which was borne aloft by the holy angels.[13] Like them, he had earned the "crown of exile."[14]

The Church in a "New World Order"

The Arab conquest of the Eastern Byzantine provinces and the Sassanid Persian empire had taken place with remarkable rapidity: the first major invasion of Byzantine territory took place in 633, and by 648 the ancient Christian heartland of Egypt, Palestine, Syria, and Iraq was in Arab hands. This rapid conquest posed enormous challenges to the conquerors, who had little experience of the complex administrative systems that had been developed in the ancient lands of the Fertile Crescent, whether of water management, the ordering of trade and commerce, or the gathering of taxes. They were, therefore, quite happy to leave in place the social and bureaucratic structures that enabled economies to function and produce wealth in a sustained, uninterrupted way.[15] Civil servants carried on as before but under new management, and in fact for decades continued to keep official records in the traditional languages of their guilds. Existing Christian and Jewish religious communities were granted a considerable measure of autonomy, in exchange for their fundamental acquiescence in the "new world order"and payment of taxes. The heads of these religious communities became the primary points of contact between their communities and the Arab Muslim authority.[16]

Once in control in Egypt, 'Amr shrewdly determined that the anti-Chalcedonian patriarch Benjamin should be recalled to Alexandria and allowed to resume his public role as head of the community that claimed the allegiance of the great majority of Egyptians.[17] Given guarantees of safe passage, Benjamin emerged from hiding and returned to Alexandria. There, in about 644, he met with 'Amr, who gave him leave to resume the administration of his community, which was given a considerable degree of latitude to tend to its own affairs, with the usual expectations in return. For Benjamin's patriarchate, the *History of the Patriarchs* mentions financial obligations in passing: the new governor 'Abd Allah ibn Sa'd (whom the caliph 'Uthman appointed in 645 to replace 'Amr) reorganized the financial bureaus and regulated the collection of the *kharaj* (land tax); the *History of the Patriarchs* remembers him as a "lover of money."[18] It is under Benjamin's successor Agathon that we hear the first mention of *jizyah* (the term that eventually came to be understood as the poll tax assessed on individual non-Muslims, as opposed to the *kharaj*, which was assessed on land).[19] Agathon was forced to pay the *jizyah* for his clergy, as well as other exactions intended to finance the Arab naval buildup in the Mediterranean (that 'Abd Allah had very effectively begun).[20] In the new Islamic order in Egypt, the patriarch would increasingly serve—and suffer—as the point at which revenue was transferred from the Christian community to the Muslim ruling class.

Our sources reveal that the Copts had a complex mix of attitudes toward the Arab conquerors;[21] by the time of Patriarch Simon (#42, 692–700), the coming of the Muslims was being absorbed into anonymous End-Time scenarios![22] At first, however, at least some members of the anti-Chalcedonian community saw their regained autonomy as a liberation.[23] One early source reports Benjamin as offering up the following prayer:

> "I give you thanks, my savior Jesus Christ, that you have made me worthy once again to see the liberty [*parrhesia*] of the Orthodox faith, the flourishing of the holy churches, and the destruction and elimination of the godless heretics."[24]

The language of "destruction and elimination of the godless heretics" is, of course, hyperbolic. While the imperially sanctioned Chalcedonian community lost its position of privilege with the Byzantine defeat, and remained for many decades without a patriarch after the death of Cyrus (in Constantinople in 643) and the departure from Egypt of his successor Peter III,[25] it continued to claim the loyalties of a number of high civil servants, who at times did their utmost to promote the welfare of their community at the expense of the anti-Chalcedonians.[26] Rivalry between Chalcedonians and anti-Chalcedonians would be a continuing feature of Egyptian church history for a long time to come. Furthermore, the schisms within the anti-Chalcedonian ranks that had so complicated Egyptian church life in the late fifth and sixth centuries did not simply go away.[27] We continue to hear of *akephaloi*, "Phantasaists," Gaianites, Barsanuphians, and others in sources such as the *History of the Patriarchs*.[28] However, the prestige that Benjamin had gained as a staunch confessor of the faith in the face of Chalcedonian persecution no doubt strengthened his hand as he set about the task of consolidating the "orthodox" Church.

All the indications in our sources are that he set about this task energetically, seeking to bring back into the fold those church leaders who had
given in to Chalcedonian inducements or pressure under Cyrus and
to rebuild the anti-Chalcedonian hierarchy that Cyrus had specifically
targeted.[29] He also began a campaign to reclaim,[30] repair, and build
churches and monasteries.

These activities of rebuilding the "infrastructure of the Church and, when
possible, of winning back the various "heretics" to it, continued under
each of his successors. Agathon, for example, "was occupied all his days
in providing for the ordination of priests who were worthy of the laying on
of hands;"[31] John III was remembered for bringing Chalcedonians back into
the "orthodox" fold.[32] And Simon "chose spiritual men, brilliant in their
deeds, deeply learned in the scriptures and in wisdom and sciences,
and ordained them bishops over every place."[33] At one point during his
patriarchate, sixty-four bishops gathered in synod.[34]

One building project of particular significance was the rebuilding of the
cathedral church of St. Mark, which had been destroyed by fire during the
fighting between the Byzantines and the Arabs in Alexandria. For Patriarch
Benjamin and his successors, this church and its relics were of the greatest
significance, as they provided a sacred setting for the regular reenactment of
their claim (over against that of the Chalcedonians, for example) to continuity
with St. Mark, evangelist and first patriarch of Alexandria. This claim is
clearly asserted in the *History of the Patriarchs*: George the Archdeacon
reports that St. Mark himself appeared to Patriarch Benjamin in a vision,
saying, "O my beloved, make a place for me with thee, that I may abide
therein."[35] George also describes how the relic of the head of St. Mark—
a precious possession of the Coptic Church throughout the period covered
in this book[36]—was miraculously saved from theft and delivered to the
patriarch.[37] Benjamin then provided a reliquary for St. Mark's head and
gathered funds for the project of rebuilding his church, which was actually
completed and provided with a sizable endowment under Patriarch John
III.[38] John's final act as patriarch was to recite the liturgy in the church, and
he was buried in the tomb that he had prepared for himself there (and was
later joined by many of his successors).[39]

Relationships with Rulers

We have already pointed out that, in the new order of affairs in Egypt, the
patriarch had become the chief point of contact between his community
and the Arab Muslim authority. Naturally, then, the existing accounts of
the Coptic patriarchs of the Islamic period show a great deal of interest

in the relationship between the patriarch and the highest governmental authority in the land, be he governor, caliph, or sultan.

George the Archdeacon wants to make plain to his readers that the first (and exemplary) encounter between a Muslim governor of Egypt and a Coptic patriarch was one of the greatest mutual courtesy and respect. He tells the story of the meeting of Patriarch Benjamin with 'Amr ibn al-'As as follows:

> And Amr, when he saw the patriarch, received him with respect, and said to his companions and private friends: "Verily in all the lands of which we have taken possession hitherto I have never seen a man of God like this man." For the Father Benjamin was beautiful of countenance, excellent in speech, discoursing with calmness and dignity.
>
> Then Amr turned to him, and said to him: "Resume the government of all thy churches and of thy people, and administer their affairs. And if thou wilt pray for me, that I may go to the West and to Pentapolis, and take possession of them, as I have of Egypt, and return to thee in safety and speedily, I will do for thee all that thou shalt ask of me." Then the holy Benjamin prayed for Amr, and pronounced an eloquent discourse, which made Amr and those present with him marvel, and which contained words of exhortation and much profit for those that heard him; and he revealed certain matters to Amr, and departed from his presence honoured and revered.[40]

This story is very well known in present-day Egypt; it is regularly retold, and often amplified upon, in the context of discussions about "national unity" (that is, Christian–Muslim solidarity within the one Egyptian state).[41] It is remarkable in that there is nothing in the account to suggest that 'Amr is other than a Christian prince.[42] He not only requests prayers, but he listens to the patriarch preach a sermon and speak words of prophecy! This picture is certainly idealized. George the Archdeacon wrote his history sometime after the death of Patriarch Simon in AD 700, that is, more than half a century after the event, and perhaps had the need to remind his readers of what governor–patriarch relations *ought* to be like, and to provide documentation of a precedent to which appeal could be made.

The first major conflict between governor and patriarch related by the *History of the Patriarchs* comes considerably later, when in the course of the Second Muslim Civil War the caliph Marwan (683–685) successfully defeated his rival's forces in Egypt (684) and appointed his son 'Abd al-'Aziz as governor (685–705). The new governor's relationship with the Coptic patriarch John III began badly when John was falsely accused (by Theophanes, Chalcedonian governor of Mareotis) of behaving arrogantly toward the governor.[43] John was arrested and fined 100,000 dinars, although that sum was eventually reduced to 10,000 dinars, which the Coptic notables of Alexandria undertook to pay—establishing a pattern that would often be repeated. Once the negotiations had been finalized, John was summoned before the governor, who "raised his eyes to him" and "saw him as if he were in the similitude of an angel of God."[44] With this, George the Archdeacon's view of the paradigmatic pattern of governor–patriarch relations was reestablished.

'Abd al-'Aziz did, in fact, come to be actively interested in church affairs, and in general treated the Copts well.[45] This is reflected in a variety of Coptic literary texts, including, for example, an account of a religious debate between (the anti-Chalcedonian) Patriarch John, a Chalcedonian Christian, and a Jew in the governor's presence.[46] John, as is to be expected in the Coptic account, confounds his opponents, who convert to the creed of the patriarch. Then 'Abd al-'Aziz enters the conversation, asks a number of questions about Christian claims about Christ's divinity and the reality of his crucifixion, but is soon reduced to silence by the force of the patriarch's arguments.[47] The governor concludes by conceding that the Christian faith is the true one and ordering that the patriarch be held in honor![48] While the content of this sample of "the monk in the emir's *majlis*" literature is more typical of the eighth or ninth century than the seventh,[49] its portrayal of a wise and witty patriarch, able to best his opponents in debate, reconcile heretics to the true faith, and earn the admiration of the governor, fits well with what we find elsewhere.[50]

The most extensive portrayal of the relationship between a patriarch and the governor 'Abd al-'Aziz is found in the contemporary Coptic *Life* of the patriarch Isaac by Mena, who near century's end became bishop of Nikiu (Pshati). According to Mena, Isaac's holiness shines through to the governor (who sees the power surrounding the patriarch as he stands at the altar, celebrating the sacrament)[51] and to his wife (who sees bands of angels about the patriarch as he visits their palace in Hulwan).[52] All the same, the patriarch has enemies who scheme at his downfall. Mena tells a delightful story about a time that the governor's advisors persuaded 'Abd al-'Aziz to test the patriarch's friendship by inviting him to eat with him while forbidding him from making the sign of the cross over his food, as was his practice.[53] The governor's Christian secretaries were perturbed, but not the patriarch. He was seated among a great assembly of notables, and a tray of dates was placed before him.

> Straightaway he stretched out his right hand . . . and said
> to the king, "From which place would you like me to eat?
> This place or that place? Here or there?" . . . The king
> answered and said to him, "Eat from whichever part you
> want," and when they had finished eating the dates, the king
> let the archbishop leave.[54]

It was only later that 'Abd al-'Aziz realized that Isaac, in asking "This place or that place? Here or there?" had unostentatiously traced the sign of the cross over the dates! Rather than erupting in fury, the governor marveled at the patriarch's wisdom.[55]

An area where the Coptic patriarch could easily get into trouble with the Muslim authorities was that of foreign relations: the patriarch of Alexandria had the responsibility of consecrating bishops for the churches in Nubia and Ethiopia, neither of which had been subjected to Arab rule, and which were occasionally actively hostile to the Muslim authority in Egypt. While the Muslim authorities in Egypt sometimes found the patriarch to be useful in their diplomatic dealings with Nubian or Ethiopian kings, *direct* contacts between the patriarch and foreign ecclesiastical or secular authorities could look suspicious, and were readily exploitable by the patriarch's enemies.

Both Mena's *Life of Isaac* and the *History of the Patriarchs* make reference to a particular case during Isaac's brief term as patriarch, when he intervened by letter in a quarrel between the Christian kingdoms of Makouria (Nubia) and Abyssinia.[56] Isaac's enemies seized on the occasion to accuse Isaac of conspiring to create an anti-Arab alliance, and 'Abd al-'Aziz had the patriarch arrested and brought before him. According to the *History of the Patriarchs*, Isaac was saved on this occasion through the perspicacity of his secretaries, who had foreseen such a danger and, through careful editing, had ensured that Isaac's letters were politically blameless.[57]

Again according to the *History of the Patriarchs*, a yet more serious situation arose during the patriarchate of Isaac's successor Simon, who, we are told, trod very delicately throughout his term in office: "this holy man Simon was striving all his life to prevent difficulties between the Christians and the Muslims, so that none might suffer loss through him."[58] When he was approached by an "Indian" (Ethiopian?) envoy who asked that he consecrate a bishop for his church, he responded: "I cannot ordain a bishop for you without the command of the Amir, who is governor of the land of Egypt. Go to him. . . ."[59] When a Gaianite bishop consecrated a bishop for the envoy without the governor's permission, it was Simon who was called before the governor, who, before the truth of the matter came out, threatened to kill him and the bishops, and to tear down the churches, in recompense for the patriarch's presumed dealings with an enemy power.[60]

Another regular point of contact between governors and the Church had to do with the appointment of new patriarchs. According to the *History of the Patriarchs*, the patriarchs Benjamin (#38), Agathon (#39), and John of Samannud (#40) had all been trained by their predecessors and were enthroned after their deaths with a minimum of delay. Later, however, the selection of a new patriarch becomes more complex, in part because of questions as to who among the Christians had a role in his selection, but also because of the role that the Muslim ruler came to play in the process. In the *History of the Patriarchs* this first becomes apparent in the selection of Isaac (#41) during the governorship of 'Abd al-'Aziz.[61] It appears from our sources that after the death of John of Samannud, the leading bishops of Lower and Upper Egypt wanted to consecrate a successor without the involvement of the governor, and were prepared to rush their candidate, the deacon George of Sakha, through ordination to the priesthood (on a Sunday) and then consecration as patriarch (in mid-week), so as to present 'Abd al-'Aziz with a *fait accompli*.[62] The maneuver failed due to the scrupulousness of the archdeacon of Alexandria, who refused to participate in these uncanonical proceedings; the bishops and their candidates were then summoned to Misr to appear before the governor.[63] According to the *History of the Patriarchs*, 'Abd al-'Aziz *commanded* the bishops to appoint the monk Isaac, whom John III had foreseen should succeed him.[64] When Isaac died less than three years later, 'Abd al-'Aziz once again summoned the bishops and their candidates to Misr, where the Syrian monk Simon emerged as a surprise consensus candidate. When 'Abd al-'Aziz asked the bishops about their strange choice of a non-Egyptian, they replied: "the matter belongs to God, *and in the second place to thee*."[65] The role of the governor in appointing a new patriarch had been conceded, as had been the role of the new capital in church affairs.

The complexities of the relationship between the patriarchs of Alexandria and civil authorities had always been part of the story of the Egyptian church, but, for the most part, troublesome emperors (for example) were far away, in places like Constantinople. With the Arab conquest this aspect of the story of the Church becomes much more intimate, with regular face-to-face encounters and verbal exchanges between patriarch and governor (or caliph, or sultan), who often felt it his prerogative to intervene in the affairs of the Church. An important element in the portrayal of the patriarch throughout the period covered in this volume is how he comports himself in this difficult relationship. In the stories of the patriarchs of the period AD 644–700 we already see a number of typical elements in this portrayal: the monastic serenity that evokes admiration; steadfast patience in the face of arbitrary violence; and quick and disarming wit in negotiating situations fraught with danger. These patterns are no doubt idealized; but in seeing how Coptic historians depicted their patriarchs, we get an idea of how they pictured their Church, and themselves.

A Sacred Geography

When the Arabs conquered Egypt in the 640s, they found a landscape regularly marked with areas of sanctified space. Churches and monasteries dotted the landscape, many of them commemorating particular holy men and women; some of these were sites of annual festivals and destinations for local or international pilgrimage.[66] In addition, several sites had been identified as way stations on the route of the Flight of the Holy Family into Egypt.[67]

An important aspect of the history of the Coptic Church in the period covered in this volume is its tending of sacred space, even as a non-Christian authority took power and exerted ever-increasing cultural influence in the land. A major role was played in this process by the patriarchs, beginning with Benjamin. Upon resuming open authority in the Egyptian church, he set himself to rebuilding monasteries and churches, including (as we have seen) initiating the project of rebuilding the cathedral church of St. Mark.[68]

Benjamin is strongly connected to the desert monastic settlements of Kellia (called "al-Muna" in the Arabic sources) and Scetis ("Wadi Habib") to the south of Alexandria; he passed through them in his flight from Cyrus,[69] and later, upon his restoration to authority, set himself to rebuilding them. The *History of the Patriarchs* includes a précis of a book that has also come down to us in its entirety, *The Book of the Consecration of the Sanctuary of Benjamin*, perhaps written by Benjamin's successor Agathon.[70] It relates how Benjamin agreed to the request of monks coming from "the holy land" of Scetis to go to the Monastery of St. Macarius in order to consecrate a new sanctuary that had been built there.[71] The consecration is related in the most awe-inspiring terms, as Benjamin is addressed by a seraph, encounters St. Macarius himself, and sees the finger of the Lord anointing the walls of the new sanctuary;[72] in all this, Isaiah 19:19 is fulfilled: "In that day there will be an altar to the Lord in the midst of the land of Egypt."[73]

Miraculous details aside, the account of Benjamin's journey to the Monastery of St. Macarius is an important witness to the close connection that this particular monastery would have with the patriarchate over the coming centuries. The monastery had already served as a refuge for exiled patriarchs from the time of Theodosius on, and under the Arabs the connection between the monastery and the patriarch would become firmer: most of the patriarchs from the mid-eighth to the mid-eleventh century would come from the Monastery of St. Macarius,[74] and even later the monastery claimed a role in consecrating the patriarch.[75]

A shrine that had attracted pilgrims from throughout the Mediterranean world in the fifth and sixth centuries was that of St. Mena in Mareotis, to the southwest of Alexandria.[76] If, however, the attribution of the Coptic *Encomium on St. Menas*[77] to Patriarch John III is correct, then we see the concern of this very active patriarch for the shrine, which had been largely destroyed by the Persians in 619. The *Encomium* reads like a defense of anti-Chalcedonian rights to the shrine (perhaps necessary at a time that Theophanes the Chalcedonian was governor of the region)[78] as well as an invitation to pilgrimage (the income from which would undoubtedly have helped John finance his building and charitable projects).[79]

A network of shrines that would come to be of great importance to the Coptic Orthodox Church was the itinerary of the Holy Family during its 'Flight into Egypt' from the murderous wrath of King Herod, as mentioned briefly in the Gospel of St. Matthew (2:14–15). While the history of the development of this itinerary is fairly opaque,[80] it is clear that the city of Hermopolis (Coptic Shmun, Arabic al-Ashmunayn) was identified as a Holy Family site already by the late fourth century.[81] The *Vision of Theophilus*— perhaps a sixth-century text, though attributed to an earlier patriarch (Theophilus, #23, 385–412)—identifies Tell Basta in the eastern Delta as the Holy Family's point of entry into Egypt, and the town of Qusqam (and the nearby monastery known as Dayr al-Muharraq), some twenty miles south of Hermopolis, as the southernmost point in the Holy Family's journey.[82] The *Homily on the Rock*—from the sixth or seventh century, but attributed to the patriarch Timothy Aelurus (#26, 455–477)—promoted the site, thirty miles to the north of Hermopolis, of Jabal al-Tayr.[83] Through the attribution of authorship, the authority of revered patriarchs was being claimed for these pilgrimage sites.

The tradition continued to be elaborated, as more and more sites were integrated into the Holy Family's itinerary. One text that claims to go back to the first century of Islamic rule is a *Homily on the Entry of the Holy Family into Egypt* attributed to Zacharias of Sakha, consecrated bishop when Simon was patriarch (692–700). Unfortunately, the homily exists only in Arabic translation in manuscripts not older than the fourteenth century AD. They give an elaborate itinerary for the Holy Family's sojourn including the Delta, Scetis, and the vicinity of the capital (al-Fustat or Cairo).[84]

In all of this, we may see a desire to tend the Egyptian Christian 'sacred geography'. The *Consecration of the Sanctuary of Benjamin* assures its readers that an "altar to the Lord" *did* exist in the land of Egypt, in fulfillment of Isaiah 19:19, in shrines that could be described as "the Paradise of God, the meeting place of the angels, the joy of the saints, the place of the repose of the righteous."[85] The developing Holy Family traditions reinforced a sense of Egypt as a "holy land"—not just in its desert fastnesses, but also in its towns, roads, and boat landings along the Nile. The construction of a Christian Egyptian 'sacred geography', existing as a network of churches, shrines, and monasteries, would in centuries to come (and to the present day) help to sustain a Coptic Christian culture and sense of rootedness, even as Arabization and Islamization made their inexorable progress in the country as a whole.

Two

Patient Sufferers

Alexander II (#43, 704–729)
Cosmas I (#44, 729–730)
Theodore (#45, 730–742)
Michael (Kha'il) I (#46, 743–767)[1]

Coming to the End-Time?

The whole world is beset with misfortunes one on top of
another and is running the risk of coming to the end-time
which will destroy all things, on account of our many sins
up to now.[2]

O
ne of the most remarkable documents that we have from the hand
of a medieval Egyptian patriarch[3] is a paschal letter of Patriarch
Alexander II announcing the date of Easter for the year 724.[4]
Writing with theological sophistication in elegant Greek,[5] Alexander
explicitly claims the legacy of Athanasius and Cyril and expounds
the Christology of Severan/Theodosian "orthodoxy" over against "the
Chalcedonian perversion" on the one side, or "the Manichaean insanity of
the docetists" (that is, the Julianists) on the other.[6] At the same time, the
patriarch insists on the reality of the Incarnation of the Word of God, and
of the crucifixion of the incarnate one, in a way that would surely resonate
in a special way with Christian readers familiar with Islamic criticisms of
those fundamental Christian doctrines.[7] And while tactful, the letter does
not avoid addressing present difficulties: toward its end, the patriarch prays
that God may "gentle the hearts of those who oppress us, and abate the
disturbing storms that lower over us."[8]

The "misfortunes" that Patriarch Alexander saw the Church experiencing
"one on top of another" were varied in nature. Some of the most acutely
painful developments for Christians, not only in Egypt but throughout the
Umayyad empire, had to do with milestones in the empire's development of a

confident and assertive Islamic self-identity. Some of these milestones had already been passed in the last decade of the seventh century, under the caliph 'Abd al-Malik (685–705). His construction of the Dome of the Rock (completed 692) on the site of the Temple in Jerusalem, from which height it overshadowed the Church of the Resurrection, sent shock waves through Christian communities.[9] So did 'Abd al-Malik's replacement of Byzantine-model coins (bearing the image of the cross) with epigraphic ones bearing Islamic creedal statements.[10] Another milestone—one that had immediate impact on many members of the Christian elite—was 'Abd al-Malik's decision to make Arabic (rather than the variety of regional languages) the official language of state record-keeping, a decision that was implemented in Egypt in 705.[11]

If Patriarch Alexander thought it possible that the world might be "coming to the end-time which will destroy all things," he was not alone; a number of Christian writers were interpreting current events as the opening act of the drama of the End.[12] An apocalypse written at the end of the seventh century, but attributed to the fourth/fifth century monastic leader Shenoute, "predicts" that the "children of Ishmael" will "rebuild the Temple which is in Jerusalem," after which the Antichrist will appear.[13] Another Coptic apocalypse, written about the same time as Alexander's paschal letter but attributed to Patriarch Athanasius,[14] "foresees" a nation that "will destroy the gold on which there is the image of the Cross of Our Lord" and mint instead "their own gold with the name of a beast written on it, the number of whose name is six hundred and sixty-six."[15] If earlier Egyptian Christians had been tempted to see Islamic rule as a passing phenomenon, like that of the Persians at the beginning of the seventh century, that was no longer possible after the reign of 'Abd al-Malik. For some Christian writers, the most plausible explanation of God's agonizingly mysterious ways in history was that God was about to bring history itself to its End.

Bearing Trials Patiently

We find a different conception of history, however, in the section of the *History of the Patriarchs* that covers the first two-thirds of the eighth century. For these years the Arabic compilation translates the Coptic account of John (Yuhannis), a monk, deacon, and eventually bishop who describes himself as the spiritual son of Abba Musa (Moses), bishop of Awsim (or Wasim) in Giza.[16] With Abba Musa he was a companion of Patriarch Michael I (#46, 743–767), and in the *Life* of that patriarch regularly reminds his readers that he was an eyewitness to the events he relates.

For John the Deacon (as I shall call him here), the task of writing church history was always to explicate

the good and the evil, and the trials which befell the saints and
shepherds of the flock of the Lord Christ, and the troubles
which they underwent for the sake of the Church and the
orthodox people at the hands of the secular governors at
all times, not only in Egypt, but also at Antioch and Rome
and Ephesus.[17]

John's account of "trials . . . and troubles . . . at the hands of the secular
governors" is set within a firm theological framework: "the Lord Christ did
not cease to govern the Church."[18] As John works to make abundantly plain,
God remains in control of history.[19] The suffering of the Christian people
may be, in part, a result of their sins,[20] and Satan is certainly active in the
world, stirring up strife wherever he can.[21] But God hears the prayers of
the righteous and has pity on them,[22] while the arrogance of rulers will
inevitably earn them divine retribution.[23] In the meantime, the vocation
of the shepherds of the Church is to bear trials and tribulations patiently,
with courage and with unceasing prayer.[24]

Trials and tribulations were not slow in coming to Patriarch Alexander,
who was made patriarch in the same year (AD 704) that Governor 'Abd
al-'Aziz died (and just a year before the death of his brother, the caliph 'Abd
al-Malik).[25] Now the Church would enter (according to John) a period
marked by a succession of oppressive caliphs (with the notable exception of
Hisham, 724–743), governors, and financial administrators.

The task of the governor of Egypt was a delicate one. The Umayyad
caliph in Damascus expected a regular flow of revenue from the rich agricultural province. Yet, at the same time, the governor was dependent militarily
upon locally rooted soldiers who received salaries from locally raised funds,
and who grew restive if their expected payments were missed.[26] In addition,
Egypt was on the front line of the struggle against Byzantium as far as
sea-power was concerned: ships were constructed in ports such as Alexandria,
and were to a large extent manned by Egyptian Christian conscripts.[27]

The maximization of revenues (as well as the provision of other resources
of material and manpower) involved an intricate calculus: over-taxation,
or ruling with too heavy a hand, could (and on occasion did) lead either to
economic stagnation or to out-and-out rebellion.[28] It is not surprising that
a governor who was successful from the caliph's point of view would be seen
as oppressive from the point of view of those who paid the taxes and provided
the manpower. For the author of the *Apocalypse of Athanasius*, for example,
the various measures adopted in the 710s and 720s to maximize revenue
collection—including census ("they will count the men"), cadastre ("they

will measure the whole earth"), and restrictions on movement ("they will chase the strangers")[29]—are catalogued among the sufferings of the end-time: "Woe to the earth and its inhabitants!"[30]

The Account of John the Deacon

At the beginning of John's account, commencing even before Alexander became patriarch, Governor 'Abd al-'Aziz—under whom the Copts had fared well—gave his son al-Asbagh responsibility for Egypt's financial affairs. Al-Asbagh, who his father hoped might one day become caliph, is the first "hater of the Christians" in John's narrative: he investigated the Christian community closely, was the first to take the *jizyah* from the monks, and added to the financial obligations of the bishops.[31] But, as John reports, "the Lord Jesus Christ did not long respite al-Asbagh, and in a short time hurried him out of the world."[32] Al-Asbagh's arrogance is made plain with an anecdote typical of John's history: at a church in Hulwan, al-Asbagh spat on an icon of the Virgin and Child, demanding, "Who is Christ that you worship him as a God?" The answer came that night in a dream in which he was bound in chains and brought naked before Christ enthroned in glory: "*This* is Jesus Christ. . . ." He was then stabbed in his side by one of the armed host gathered about the throne, and his soul was received by demons. Al-Asbagh woke from his dream, but only long enough to relate it to his father before falling into a deep fever, from which he did not recover.[33] This is the first of a number of stories of this sort related by John the Deacon, which remind his readers that the desecration of holy objects or places is dangerous, and that God's power can flash forth at any time, in judgment as well as for salvation.[34]

The next governor of Egypt was the caliph's son 'Abd Allah ibn 'Abd al-Malik (704–708), who may possibly have been as grasping in fact as he is pictured in the *History of the Patriarchs*, where it is reported that he would not allow someone to be buried until the *jizyah* had been collected on his behalf.[35] The new caliph al-Walid (705–715) replaced him (although John sees this as *the Lord*'s vengeance)[36] with Qurrah ibn Sharik (709–714) who, if not remembered fondly in Christian sources, appears to have been a capable administrator.[37] John reports that both 'Abd Allah and Qurrah mistreated Patriarch Alexander and made financial demands upon him that forced him to undertake fundraising tours, first in the Delta (to pay 'Abd Allah), then in Upper Egypt (to pay Qurrah): "many trials came to the holy father, but he endured them patiently."[38]

Qurrah died in an outbreak of plague in 714, but John's narrative pattern of government oppression, patriarchal patience, and divine retribution continues. Succeeding governors and financial administrators continued to seek ways of enhancing revenue and controlling the movement of persons (in order to prevent people from becoming tax fugitives or from avoiding corvée labor).[39] Caliphal policies that impacted the Christian community are noted, including the policies of 'Umar II (717–720) that encouraged conversion to Islam ("but God . . . destroyed him swiftly")[40] or the icono-clastic edict of Yazid II (720–724) ("but the Lord Jesus Christ destroyed him").[41] The caliph Hisham (724–743) is judged to be a "God-fearing man according to the method of Islam,"[42] but his chief tax official *(sahib al-kharaj)* 'Ubayd Allah ibn Habhab (c. 724–734) raised taxes and made use of forced labor in such manner as to set off the first Coptic tax revolt in the eastern Delta in 725.[43] It was put down with great violence and afterward, according to John, 'Ubayd Allah would have humiliated Patriarch Alexander by branding him, had not the patriarch's prayers to be removed from this world been answered.[44]

After the fifteen-month reign of Cosmas I (729–730), the ascetic Theodore (730–742) was made patriarch. John tells us almost nothing about the patriarch himself, simply that "the Church was growing, without adversaries or internal divisions, all his days."[45] In spite of that rosy report, John's basic plot line—of "trials and troubles at the hands of the secular governors" and of divine judgment—continues. The *sahib al-kharaj* 'Ubayd Allah continued his oppressive policies; we know, for example, that he resettled three thousand Qaysi Arabs from Syria in the margins of the eastern Delta, thus beginning a process of demographic change in the region and accelerating processes of Arabization and Islamization.[46] But 'Ubayd Allah was banished—modern historians would say "transferred"—to North Africa in 734 since, according to John, "God would not suffer him."[47] His son al-Qasim (734–741) was, in John's report, a lover of luxury who found new ways of extorting money from the Church, but divine judgment fell on him when he and a favorite concubine refused to dismount from their horses as they entered the great church at the Monastery of St. Shenoute: the concubine and her mount fell down dead, and al-Qasim was thrown down in something like an epileptic fit.[48] Even then, al-Qasim did not repent of his evil ways, and (John tells us) his sins brought years of drought, famine, and plague upon the country[49] before "God took away the government" from him and he was led off to imprisonment and torment.[50]

John the Deacon was a contemporary and companion of the next patriarch, Michael I (743–767), and John's history is full of detail about particular incidents. He gives a full account, for example, of the choice of Michael as a compromise candidate for patriarch, after the electors had deadlocked between the northern bishops and the Alexandrian clergy on the one hand, and the clergy of Misr and Upper Egypt on the other.[51] In the course of the negotiations, the Alexandrian clergy's claim that it was their prerogative to choose their bishop was rebuffed, with the key contributions toward a solution being made by Bishop Musa of Awsim in Giza—all of which points to the growing weight of Misr and environs as opposed to Alexandria.[52] As usual, the cooperation and approval of the governor, now Hafs ibn al-Walid al-Hadrami, was required before the monk Michael of the Monastery of St. Macarius could be proclaimed the "new Mark."[53]

Even before Michael was made patriarch of the 'orthodox,' the Chalcedonians had been able, after a long vacancy, to install for themselves a patriarch, Cosmas I (742–768). Cosmas moved quickly to reclaim some churches for the Chalcedonian community,[54] and even challenged the anti-Chalcedonians' claim to the shrine and pilgrim destination of St. Menas in Mareotis. The matter was settled—by Muslim officials—in favor of the anti-Chalcedonians.[55] In addition to saving the shrine of St. Menas for the anti-Chalcedonians, Michael was able, during his reign, to restore the Church of St. Mark in Alexandria and to build other churches outside the city.[56]

In the previous chapter we noted the delicate situation in which the patriarchs were placed with regard to foreign contacts. Michael appears to have trodden carefully, deciding not to intervene in a quarrel between the Antiochian patriarch John and his bishops,[57] and only reluctantly cooperating with the Nubian king Abraham in deposing the aged bishop of Dongola.[58] A little later, the governor 'Abd al-Malik ibn Marwan ibn Musa arrested Michael when he discovered that Michael had been corresponding with the new Nubian king Cyriacus. When a Nubian army invaded Egypt, however, the governor turned to Michael for assistance in persuading Cyriacus to withdraw his forces.[59] As usual, the Muslim authority in Egypt looked on the Coptic patriarch's relationship with Christian powers to the south with suspicion, but at the same time found the patriarch useful once actual hostilities were threatened.

Much of the drama in John the Deacon's biography of Michael is supplied by his description of how Michael, his most loyal followers, and the Christian community as a whole were caught up in the chaos that engulfed Egypt as the Umayyad empire declined and fell to the new 'Abbasid power. One blow to the Church took place when Hafs ibn al-Walid and his force of non-Arab Muslims (the Hafsiyyah) briefly took control of Egypt in 744–745: Hafs proclaimed that converts to Islam would be exempted from the *jizyah*, which, according to John, induced twenty-four thousand Christians to renounce their faith.[60] A brief period of peace for the Church followed under

Hawtharah ibn Suhayl al-Bahili, sent by the caliph Marwan II to reassert Umayyad control over Egypt. However, with the advance of the 'Abbasid forces in the east, the Umayyads soon found themselves in desperate need of funds, and a new governor, 'Abd al-Malik ibn Musa, moved to call all sectors of the society to strict financial account.[61] According to John, when Michael could not pay what was demanded of the Copts, he and his companions were placed in stocks and put in prison, although they were released after seventeen days with permission to go on a fund-raising tour of Upper Egypt.[62]

Worse was yet to come. As Umayyad control of the east collapsed, Marwan fled to Egypt; almost simultaneously, a Christian-led tax revolt broke out in the marshy Bashmur region of the Delta.[63] The *History of the Patriarchs* tells us that Patriarch Michael, seen as somehow responsible for the revolt, was arrested and imprisoned. In captivity, he and a few faithful companions were frequently beaten and more than once were just moments away from execution.[64] This state of affairs lasted until Marwan was finally hunted down and killed in August 750 by the 'Abbasid forces under Salih ibn 'Ali and Abu 'Awn.[65]

Through all this complex and often painful sequence of events, John would have his readers know that it is *God* who has control over human history. John makes it clear that it was God who raised up the 'Abbasids and gave them victory over Marwan,[66] even causing the level of the Nile to drop so that their troops could cross in pursuit of the fleeing Umayyads,[67] since "when the Lord desired to take vengeance upon them, he endured them no longer."[68] Once the 'Abbasids had taken power, however, "they forgot that it was God who had given them the government."[69] Familiar patterns of oppressive taxation reasserted themselves at the same time that the 'Abbasids implemented their policy of exempting converts from payment of the *jizyah*— a fateful move that led to many conversions.[70] Michael ended up spending a great deal of time in the capital, seeking tax relief on church lands. But God continued to punish tyrants: "God did not endure" the 'Abbasids, "but raised up wars against them from every side,"[71] "destroyed" the 'Abbasid caliph al-Saffah (d. 754),[72] and "requited" his generals "for the evil which they had done in the land of Egypt."[73] John's history ends as it began, with the rise and fall of tyrannical rulers—in the midst of which the patriarch serves his Church with holy patience.

Patriarchs and Martyrdom

At one point in John the Deacon's narrative, he describes the imprisoned patriarch Michael and his companions as "martyrs without bloodshed."[74] The language of martyrdom is no new thing in the history of the portrayal of the patriarchs. We recall that George the Archdeacon, in his account of the "orthodox" patriarchs during the controversy over Chalcedon down to the first decades of Islamic rule, could say of embattled patriarchs— Benjamin, in particular—that they had earned "crowns": if not the crown of martyrdom *per se*,[75] then the crown of victory,[76] of patience,[77] or of exile.[78] In the meantime, Benjamin's brother Menas had undergone real martyrdom, resisting torture and accepting death by drowning rather than saying that "the council of Chalcedon is good."[79]

It is also George the Archdeacon who tells the story of how the relationship between governor 'Abd al-'Aziz and Patriarch John III got off to a very bad start, when John was falsely accused of insolent behavior toward the governor and fined one hundred thousand dinars, to be extracted by any method necessary.[80] The story, as George tells it, is full of familiar echoes for those with ears to hear them. Standing before an accomplished torturer, John speaks the typical language of the martyrs:

> "Do therefore whatever it pleases thee to do. My body is in thy hands, but my soul and body are both in the hands of my Lord Jesus Christ."[81]

John is spared the torments typical of Coptic martyrdoms through a divine intervention: that same night, the governor's wife was troubled and sent a message to the patriarch's jailer:

> "Take heed that thou do no harm to that man of God, the patriarch, whom they have delivered to thee; for great trials have befallen me on account of him this night."[82]

For George's biblically literate readers, these words call to mind those of the wife of Pontius Pilate: "Have nothing to do with that righteous man, for I have suffered much over him today in a dream."[83] The confrontation between 'Abd al-'Aziz and Pope John III could be read in the light of the confrontation between the Roman procurator and Jesus Christ.[84]

The history that follows George's, that of John the Deacon, is likewise permeated with the language of martyrdom. The pages that he dedicates to Patriarch Alexander II tell us little about his policies as patriarch;[85] rather, all emphasis is on his sufferings: twice was he arrested and forced to beg for funds; he was on the brink of being executed, was deserted by friends, imprisoned in fetters, manhandled, reviled, and seized for branding. And yet he bore all this with Christlike patience, courage, and prayer.[86] The same can be said for Patriarch Michael and his companions, in particular the saintly Bishop Musa of Awsim, as they got caught up in the death throes of Umayyad rule. On one occasion Michael was savagely beaten on the head, but—as is typical of contemporary martyrdom accounts—suffered no harm from it.[87] He gladly bared his neck for the swordsman, although Governor Hawtharah called off his execution at the very last minute.[88] Later, Michael and Musa were summoned to appear before Marwan. Their disciples fled (as had Jesus's in the Gospels).[89] The venerable old monk Musa was severely beaten, but received it with thanksgiving and with prayer "to make him worthy to suffer for the Church of God."[90] In the meantime, Michael was hauled before the caliph and accused of disloyalty.

> So when Marwan heard these accusations, his interpreter said to the father patriarch: "Art thou the patriarch of Alexandria?" For that was Marwan's question. Abba Michael answered: "Yea, I am thy servant." And I heard him say this, because I was near him. So Marwan said to him: "Tell me, art thou the chief of the enemies of our religion?" Then the holy patriarch answered and said: "I am not the chief of wicked men, but of good men; and my people do not work evil, but they have been ruined by troubles, so that they have even been forced to offer their children for sale." After that, I did not hear another word from his mouth.[91]

Michael's silence before his accusers again echoes details of the biblical passion narrative.[92] Marwan responded to what he took as Michael's insolence by ordering that his beard be plucked out, though true to Coptic martyrological form (in which mangled bodies are regularly restored to wholeness),[93] it grew back with miraculous speed, "more comely than before."[94]

Patriarch Michael's loss of his beard was not the end of the story. On later occasions, he was forced to stand before the caliph for an entire day (which he did, with his arms outstretched in prayer);[95] he and his faithful companions prepared for death as Marwan's officers argued over what sort of death-by-torture they should be put to;[96] and they were imprisoned without room to turn around or eat.

> And our father's sadness on our account was greater than his care for himself; but he encouraged us with the word of God and the holy canons of our ancient fathers. So not one of us hid anything from the others, but we were all one soul, as Paul says, awaiting the end; and we prayed God to send it quickly, that

we might lay down our lives for the people, rather than that one of them should perish. When the father discoursed to us, he spoke a spiritual language like the music of a harp, while the breath of life came forth from his mouth with spiritual praises; and he persevered in fasting and in prayer day and night.[97]

Finally, the Umayyads were defeated: "when the Lord desired to take vengeance upon them, he endured them no longer."[98] Although Michael "the chosen martyr"[99] and his companions were nearly burned alive while still in prison, they were saved at the last moment, John reports, when a mighty voice caused their tormentors to flee in terror.[100]

The presentation of patriarchs as (near-) martyrs that we find in the eighth-century patriarchal histories of George the Archdeacon and John the Deacon may well fit in with a growing popularity of the literature of the martyrs among Egyptian Christians of the time. While Coptic martyrdom texts are notoriously difficult to date, at least one scholar has suggested that it was only after the year AD 700 that texts which had been used in local cults were "copied and gathered on a large scale, thus becoming a major genre in Coptic literature."[101]

John's history itself gives examples of interest in the martyrs. Among the many edifying anecdotes that adorn his history is the story, well-known in a number of versions in the Christian east, about the beautiful nun who saved herself from sexual violation by offering her own neck for a demonstration of the miraculous powers of a sword-stopping salve in her possession. One of Marwan's soldiers took the bait, and unintentionally beheaded the maiden.[102] At another point in the history, when Patriarch Michael and Bishop Musa were being tormented by Marwan's officers, the martyrs Sergius and Bacchus rode across the Nile on horseback and taunted Marwan.[103]

When John the Deacon wrote his history, the martyrs appear to have been playing an ever-increasing role in the piety of ordinary Egyptian Christians. In the cult of the martyrs, some Christians may have found the patrons that were not available to them in the entourage of arbitrarily oppressive governors and tax officials; in the stories of the martyrs, they found examples of how believers should bear adversity. John the Deacon holds up patriarchs Alexander II and Michael I as *living* martyrs who embody characteristics that belong to the Church as a whole:[104] patience in suffering, fervency in prayer, and trust in God who—perhaps in spite of all appearances —remains in control of history, and will bring vengeance upon his enemies.

Patriarchs and Sainthood

It is no surprise that John the Deacon, who can portray the patriarchs whose reigns he chronicles as living martyrs, also names and portrays them as saints.[105] For John, however, it is not enough to assert the sanctity of the individual patriarch. Integral to the story of certain patriarchs is an account of the saints who flourished "during the days of his life."[106] The patriarch is a saint who facilitates sanctity.

Because of this, John's biography of Patriarch Alexander II is incomplete without a listing of some of the saints who lived in his time: Matthew "the Poor," remembered for both his healing powers and his severity in judgment;[107] the monks of the Monastery of St. Shenoute, especially Abba Seth, at whose grave healings took place; and the clairvoyant and visionary monks of the Wadi Habib (Scetis), with special note of the *hegumenos* John and his disciples Abraham, George, and Epimachus.[108] (It is worth noting that the Monastery of St. Shenoute and the monasteries of the Wadi Habib—the Monastery of St. Macarius in particular—occupy key places in the sacred geography of Egypt, as John the Deacon describes it.)[109] A similar list of saints may be found at the end of John's biography of Patriarch Michael I, with a concentration on the virtues of the bishops: the same Epimachus mentioned earlier (but now bishop of al-Farama, Pelusium), who effectively cursed a Chalcedonian; John of Sarsana, who cast out demons; Cyrus of Tanah, whose mantle was not burned by pagans' fire; Zacharias of Atrib, who wept continuously and gave alms; Stephen of Shutb, who induced a newborn to defend his widowed mother from a charge of adultery; Hesychius, "who spoke of divine matters"; Paul of Akhmim, who saved a woman from a sorcerer who regularly turned her into a donkey;[110] Cyrus of Jaujar, who lived in virginity with his wife; and Isaac of Samannud, who brought the Barsanuphians to the Orthodox faith.[111] These figures are, of course, in addition to Patriarch Michael's steadfast companions in suffering, especially Bishop Musa of Awsim, himself a healer and a prophet.[112] This multiplicity of saints with varying charismatic gifts amounts to a kind of orchestra of holiness—of which Patriarch Michael was the conductor:

> [It was said that] the Christians were of one heart, living in agreement together. For the conduct of the fathers in that generation resembled the works of the spiritual angels; for one cured diseases, and another showed forth wonders, and another expounded the scriptures and taught and exhorted, and another exercised his body in works and labours; and all the laity were filled with admiration of them, and sought their

blessing. And the father, Abba Michael, for this cause was happy in his bishops and all his flock, and used to go round among them, and enquire into all their circumstances with care, and exhort them with his life-giving words. . . .[113]

To sum up, John the Deacon portrays the patriarchs whose reigns he chronicled as having a distinctive relationship to power. On the one hand, they were often caught up in capricious exercises of power by caliphs and governors. On the other hand, they inhabited a world in which the power of God could be demonstrated at any moment, by a holy picture that resisted abuse, by the rise of the Nile or the fall of a tyrant, by a miracle accomplished with the sign of the cross. Patriarchs such as Alexander II or Michael I are portrayed as patient sufferers in the face of the capricious power of rulers, in the tradition of the martyrs. At the same time they are ministers of divine power, by no means controlling it, but trusting in it and pointing to it, for the edification and encouragement of a Christian population beginning to experience the lure of conversion to Islam.

Three

Crisis of Cohesion[1]

Menas I (#47, 767–776)
John IV (#48, 777–799)
Mark II (#49, 799–819)
Jacob (#50, 819–830)
Simon II (#51, 830)
Yusab I (#52, 831–849)
Michael (Kha'il) II (#53, 849–851)
Cosmas II (#54, 851–858)
Shenoute I (#55, 859–880)

Satan Hinders, but God Prevails

[T]he blessed patriarch . . . bore witness that no patriarch sits upon this throne except those whom God chooses, but that Satan resists their advancement and hinders their doing good.[2]

After the contributions of George the Archdeacon and John the Deacon, the author of the *History of the Patriarchs'* next set of papal biographies was another monk named John, who flourished in the middle third of the ninth century, and whom I shall call "John the Writer" in order to distinguish him from his predecessor.[3] John the Writer began his ecclesial career as a disciple of a monk of the Monastery of St. John Kame[4] named Amunah, who not only taught John to write but, as John himself tells the story, prophesied that he would be the author of the next section of the history of the Church.[5] Later, John became a spiritual son of Patriarch Yusab I (#52, 831–849),[6] for whom he at least on occasion served as scribe[7] and whom he accompanied into prison.[8] He was also close to Patriarch Shenoute I (#55, 859–880).[9] Once again, therefore, we are dealing with an author who was close to, and sometimes a participant in, many of the events he narrates.

John the Writer has his own distinctive way of relating the history of the Church. While God is at work in the world for good, Satan is constantly seeking the means through which to disturb the Church's well-being. Descriptions of peace and progress in the Church are regularly followed, in John's account, by a statement that Satan, "the hater of the good," found a way—usually a human instrument—through which to attack the Church.[10] John's account is therefore full of ups and downs, of cycles of progress and persecution, building and destruction, calm and chaos. Through it all, the patriarch and those around him bear trials and tribulations with patience, since "the Lord Jesus Christ the Merciful One does not cause anyone to be afflicted beyond the power of his endurance."[11] In the end, "the gates of Hell shall not prevail" against God's Church;[12] rather, "it is God who prevails."[13] God's victory is made manifest in the divine vengeance that inevitably (if not always immediately) catches up with the Church's enemies; "[h]e abases the nations that obey him not."[14] John describes the fall of persecutors, including the torments to which they are put and the diseases with which they are afflicted, with fierce exultation—although his *Schadenfreude* (joy in another's misfortune) serves as a foil for the humility and patience of the saintly patriarch, who prays for and forgives his persecutors.[15]

It is important to note that, in some contrast to a certain strain of Middle Eastern Christian martyrdom or apocalyptic texts, John the Writer does *not* make any correlation between the work of Satan and the Islamic religion.[16] While some Muslim officials were tyrants, they oppressed everyone, Christians and Muslims alike, so that suffering was shared by all.[17] Thankfully, such tyrants were frequently replaced by rulers who, precisely as good Muslims, would "do good" to all, including the Christians.[18] And it is a special feature of John's history that many of the human "vessels" with which Satan attacked the Church were, more often than not, members of the orthodox Christian community, including monks, deacons, and even bishops. This is a theme to which we shall return.

Patriarchs and Political Authority in 'Abbasid Egypt

The period covered in the chronicle of John the Writer (767–880) roughly corresponds to that of 'Abbasid authority in Egypt, that is, from the death of the Umayyad caliph Marwan II in 750 to the appointment of Ahmad ibn Tulun as governor in 868. The 'Abbasid period in Egypt was turbulent, marked by a rapid turnover of governors and other chief officials,[19] some of whom were more, and others less, favorably disposed toward their Christian subjects. Regardless of the officials' attitudes toward the Copts, John the Writer defines the chief duty of the patriarch with respect to civil authority as one of obedience: "the carrying out of decrees issued by the governor of Egypt to the patriarch and bishops, that the affairs of the orthodox churches may be kept in good order."[20] This theme runs throughout John's chronicle. In its opening pages, Patriarch Menas I (#47, 767–776) is hauled up before the governor, who says to him, regarding a caliphal mandate granting authority in the Church to a conniving rival:

> "Do not oppose the command of the prince, but perform what he ordains." Menas replied: "I will do so with joy, that I may carry out the Law which bids me obey the king as I would obey God; for it says: He who resists and disputes authority, resists God, his Lord."[21]

The biblical reference is to Romans 13:1–2, the foremost New Testament proof-text for the necessity of subjection to civil authority.[22] Similar affirmations of the obedience and non-resistance of the patriarch and his community run throughout John's biographies. He quotes Patriarch Yusab, under arrest and just about to receive a blow to the head, as counseling his grieving people: "We do not resist the government."[23] Patriarch Shenoute assures a tyrant who had kept him waiting for three days and who was about to impose huge new tax demands on the Church: "Whatever your highness commands I will do."[24]

As this last example indicates, the principal area in which the patriarch was called to obedience continued to be financial. John the Deacon had already noted that, at the beginning of 'Abbasid rule, Patriarch Michael I (743–767) and his close advisor Bishop Musa of Awsim spent great amounts of time in Misr, negotiating tax relief for the Alexandrian churches' endowment lands.[25] In the eyes of some government authorities, the patriarch was little more than a cog in the machinery for the financial exploitation of the province of Egypt. This comes out clearly in the story of the election of Mark II (#49, 799–819): once the assembly of bishops and clergy in Alexandria had acclaimed Mark as pope, they wrote to Michael, bishop of Misr, whose delicate task it was to convince the governor to confirm this choice. Accompanied by a few bishops, Michael was granted an audience with the governor:

> [The governor] said to them: "What is your business?" Abba Michael replied: "We make it known to thy lordship that our father, the chief and father of our religion, whom we had, is dead." Then the governor asked: "What then do you desire?" They answered: "May God lengthen thy days! There are heavy

taxes upon the property of the Church, and therefore we desire
to appoint a successor to him, who may administer the affairs
of the Church and the people." Then the governor enquired:
"And what is his name?" They said that it was Mark. So he ordered
that Mark's name should be written in the *diwan*, and then gave
them permission to appoint him in the place of Abba John.[26]

According to this account, Mark had been presented to and accepted by
the governor . . . as a tax administrator.

As John the Writer portrays them, the patriarchs of the 'Abbasid period
had varying capacities for the administrative tasks set before them. It is not
surprising that some of the patriarchs who were most effective (at least, in
times of peace) were those who had previous administrative experience.
John IV (#48, 777–799) had been *oikonomos* ("steward" or even "Chief
Financial Officer") at the shrine of St. Menas in Mareotis, pilgrimage to which
had long been one of the Alexandrian Church's major sources of income.[27]
His spiritual son and successor Mark II had also had administrative responsibilities there.[28] Blessed by peaceful times and a governor who respected
him,[29] Patriarch John, with Mark's competent assistance, was able to rebuild
and embellish churches and the patriarchal residence, erect the new Church
of the Archangel Michael in Alexandria, and mount a major relief effort in a
time of famine.[30] As patriarch (799–819), Mark too, for a time, enjoyed
the good graces of the governor,[31] and continued in his spiritual father's
footsteps: "He loved good works and the building of churches."[32] Patriarch
Yusab I (#52, 831–849) had been raised by a Coptic *archon* in the upper
ranks of the civil service;[33] early in his patriarchate he stressed the development
of income-generating projects for the Church, including both pilgrimage
sites and productive enterprises ("vineyards and mills and oil-presses").[34] And
Patriarch Shenoute I (#55, 859–880) had been *oikonomos* of the Monastery
of St. Macarius before his election;[35] among his early acts as patriarch were
projects to improve the fresh-water supply in Alexandria and Mareotis.[36]
John the Writer is unafraid to admit that administration, especially
with regard to taxes, was not every patriarch's gift. According to John,
Patriarch Michael II (#53, 849–851) experienced great "sorrows and trials"
in connection with the tax demands he faced. He prayed for release from
his trials—and when he fell terminally ill on Easter Day 851, his prayer
was granted.[37] His successor Cosmas II (#54, 851–858) was, by contrast,
fortunate: he could rely on the financial expertise of two wealthy Coptic
notables, Maqarah ibn Yusuf and Ibrahim ibn Sawirus. They established
the patriarch in the Nile Delta town of Damirah, at a safe distance from

government officials in both Alexandria and Misr. There Cosmas could live and pray in quietness while Maqarah and Ibrahim "took care of the affairs of the Church" and dealt with "the affairs of the Sultan."[38]

Trials from Without

The Egyptian Church experienced a number of external blows during the 'Abbasid period. The authorities' tax policies ranged from difficult to downright cruel. Popular uprisings in Egypt, sometimes involving the Christian population, were common; a recent study counts thirteen of them between 767 and 832.[39] Chaos at the 'Abbasid center could spill over into the provinces, as during the civil war over the succession to Harun al-Rashid for much of the decade following his death in 809, or the rapid succession of caliphs after the murder of the caliph al-Mutawakkil (by his son, al-Mustansir) in 861. These blows resulted in the erosion of various aspects of the Egyptian Christian "infrastructure," induced major changes in the financing and even the location of the patriarchate, and made conversion to Islam an attractive option for many Egyptian Christians.

John the Writer devotes a considerable amount of space to the disturbances that had broken out in Egypt as early as the year 806, and which were exacerbated by the death of the caliph Harun al-Rashid in 809 and the outbreak of civil war between his sons al-Amin and al-Ma'mun. Military leaders who were relative newcomers to Egypt jockeyed for authority, mostly at the expense of the long-established Muslim families in the country. By 813 they had effectively split Egypt into northern (including Alexandria) and southern (including Misr) zones of influence.[40] The area around Alexandria was largely under the control of Arab tribesmen who originally hailed from Yemen, although the older Arab families who had inhabited Alexandria since the time of the conquest clung to their sense of superiority and entitlement. The power equation in Alexandria was made yet more difficult in 815, when the area around the city was invaded by Arab refugees fleeing autocratic rule in al-Andalus (Islamic Spain).[41] According to John the Writer, Patriarch Mark II watched the unfolding situation in his city with pastoral concern: noting that the Andalusians held Byzantine Christian captives who were regularly sold into slavery and frequently converted to Islam, he did his best to purchase their freedom (and to arrange, if they so desired, for instruction in the Coptic Orthodox faith).[42] Shortly afterward, however, chaos erupted in Alexandria as it became the scene of a fierce three-way struggle among the older Arab families, the Arab tribesmen, and the Andalusian refugees.[43] When in 816 the Andalusians went on a murderous rampage in the city, the Church of the Savior (the *Soter*) and many other buildings were destroyed by fire, and the patriarch with two disciples was obliged to flee. They eventually settled in the Delta town of Nabaruh, the hometown of a pious Coptic official who negotiated with the regional strongman for their safe sojourn there.[44]

At about the same time that blood and fire were defiling the city of the patriarch, Beduin were plundering Scetis (or "the Wadi Habib"), demolishing churches and cells and killing, scattering, or enslaving the monks.[45] The horror of this event is magnified in John's account by his reverence for Scetis, to which he regularly gives names such as the "Paradise of God," the "Garden of Eden," the "Holy of Holies," or the "Holy Jerusalem."[46]

If Patriarch Mark had been presented at the beginning of his biography as an efficient administrator and builder, at its end we are left with a portrait of a figure like Jeremiah, an exile who gives voice to his people's lament over the destruction wrought in the "holy temples" (of Alexandria) or the "Holy of Holies" (Scetis):[47]

> The gentiles have entered [the Lord's] inheritance,
>   and defiled our holy temples,
>   and made the great city of Alexandria like a prison,
>   through the fighting that has taken place therein between
>   the tribes.
> At last the slain found none to bury them;
>   and many of their corpses became food for the birds of the
>   air and the beasts of the earth.[48]

> My heart is disquieted within me,
>   and in my reins a fire is kindled.
> O Lord, let me know my end;
>   for my hope is vanished, and I have no harbour of safety
>   where I can be secure.
> For the joy of Egypt has ceased,
>   and Wadi Habib, the Holy of Holies, has become a ruin,
>   the dwelling of wild beasts.
> The homes of our blessed fathers, who passed their nights
>   in prayer,
>   have become the resort of the owl
>   and the dens of cruel foxes, namely this foul tribe.[49]

The patriarch's words are full of biblical echoes, especially of Israel's laments over Jerusalem as well as of her prophets' oracles against the nations.[50]

The patriarch himself had become an exile. This is a turning point in the story of the patriarchs of Alexandria. Their connection with their city, while not completely severed, would never be quite the same.

Patriarch Mark II was succeeded by Jacob (#50, 819–830), a monk of St. Macarius who had fled to Upper Egypt when Scetis was sacked, but who soon returned (in response to a vision of the Virgin Mary, John the Writer tells us) in order to head up the effort of rebuilding and regathering the monks.[51] Egypt was still in a chaotic state when Jacob became patriarch in 819: control of Alexandria continued to be contested, and the lamentable security situation interrupted pilgrimage to the shrine of St. Menas, normally one of the patriarchate's major sources of revenue.[52] Order was finally restored in 826 with the arrival of the caliph al-Ma'mun's general and governor-designate 'Abd Allah ibn Tahir, who quickly reconquered the province. While John the Writer characterizes 'Abd Allah as "a good and merciful man in his religion" who "loved justice and hated tyranny,"[53] he only remained in Egypt for seventeen months, and the governors who followed him promptly increased their tax demands.[54] John the Writer relates that Patriarch Jacob found these demands so difficult that he resorted to handing over gold Eucharistic vessels in partial payment of his debt—but that God intervened with a miracle: the vessels flowed with blood when a goldsmith attempted to break them up.[55]

Onerous tax policies and the cruelty with which they were implemented led to renewed rebellion, including a major uprising in 831 in which Muslims and Copts alike participated.[56] The caliph al-Ma'mun's forces under his Persian general al-Afshin were largely successful in putting down the revolt, but ran into difficulties in pacifying the Copts of the Bashmur district of the northern Delta, where the marshy terrain favored the defenders. According to John's chronicle, the new patriarch Yusab I (#52, 831–849), in the company of his Syrian counterpart Dionysius I (818–845), who had come to Egypt in the company of the caliph al-Ma'mun himself, tried to persuade the Bashmurites to give up their resistance to the authorities, but in vain.[57] Al-Afshin eventually put down the uprising with great violence, burning villages (and churches), executing men, and enslaving women and children.[58] The result of this revolt was the de-Christianization of an entire region; some historians have seen the failure of the "Coptic" or "Bashmuric" revolt of 831 as a point at which many Egyptian Christians decided to convert to Islam.[59]

Conversions were certainly reported during the reign of the caliph al-Mutawakkil (847–861), who, as part of his policy of promoting a traditionalist Sunni understanding of Islam, passed edicts in 850 and 853 calling for the destruction of "renovated" churches, the dismissal of non-Muslim civil servants, and a variety of measures designed to mark out non-Muslims and keep them in their (subservient) place.[60]

John the Writer reports his edicts as follows:

> [Al-Mutawakkil] brought down upon the churches in every place innumerable afflictions which were that he ordered all the churches to be demolished, and that none of the Orthodox Christians, Melkites, Nestorians, or Jews should wear white garments, but that they should wear dyed garments, so that they might be distinguished among the Muslims. He ordered that frightful pictures should be made on wooden boards and that they should be nailed over the doors of the Christians. He forced most of them to embrace al-Islam, and ordered that Christians should not serve in the employment of the Sultan at all, but only Muslims and those who had gone over to al-Islam.[61]

According to John, al-Mutawakkil's governor in Egypt, 'Anbasah ibn Ishaq,[62] not only implemented the above stipulations but forbade any public display of Christian religion (crosses, funeral processions, striking of the *naqus*[63] to summon the faithful to prayer), and outlawed the possession of wine, even for liturgical purposes.[64]

The legal traditions reflected in al-Mutawakkil's decrees would eventually crystallize as the "Covenant of 'Umar," allegedly an agreement made between the "rightly guided" caliph 'Umar ibn al-Khattab (634–644) and his new non-Muslim subjects in the early days of the Islamic conquests.[65] As false as their attribution to 'Umar may have been, such traditions, with their provisions for distinguishing (and humiliating) non-Muslims, had been seen in Egypt before (under the Umayyad caliph 'Umar II, 717–720), would flare up again under the Fatimid caliph al-Hakim (996–1021),[66] and would become a regular feature of Coptic life under the Mamluks.[67] While neither the *ghiyar* legislation (that is, those measures aimed at differentiating non-Muslims from Muslims) nor the demand for the dismissal of non-Muslim civil servants tended to stay in force for very long, they served as periodic prods to conversion. As John the Writer reports:

> Many people could not endure these conditions, and they did not trust in their God, but denied the Name of the Saviour in those days of adversity, and they forgot what is said in the Holy Gospel: "But he that endureth to the end, the

same shall be saved. And this gospel of the Kingdom shall
be preached."[68]

We note, though, that John does not only *report* unhappy events, he also
preaches to strengthen the resolve of Christians tempted to deny their faith.

In spite of al-Mutawakkil's discriminatory decrees, his reign represented
a period of political stability, allowing for relative peace during the reign of
Cosmas II (#54, 851–858) as well as a period of intensive pastoral work,
including a tour of Upper Egypt, by his active and saintly successor Shenoute
I (#55, 859–880). That stability came to an end with al-Mutawakkil's
assassination in 861. His son, murderer, and successor al-Mustansir
appointed a finance minister in Egypt[69] who immediately doubled taxes,
cancelled exemptions, and invented new forms of extortion;[70] Shenoute soon
found himself either in hiding[71] or desperately attempting with his bishops
to work out a payment plan.[72] Soon afterward, however, grievances against
the caliph and his officers led to rebellion throughout the caliphate; in Egypt
it was led by the tribe of the Banu Mudlij near Alexandria. As order broke
down, Upper Egyptian monasteries were destroyed by Beduin,[73] Scetis was
threatened,[74] and pilgrimage to the shrine of St. Menas was cut off—this
time, it seems, for good: "The church of the martyr Saint Menas at Maryut
which was the delight of all the Orthodox people of Egypt became a
desert."[75] It is indicative of the times that, once Ahmad ibn Tulun had
restored order (and opened a new chapter in the history of Egypt), Patriarch
Shenoute, who earlier had undertaken public works projects in Alexandria
and Mareotis, now built a *wall* around the Church of St. Macarius—creating
the fortress-like monastery with which we are familiar today.[76]

Trials from Within

If the Church suffered from external trials during the 'Abbasid period,
one of the most striking features of the account of John the Writer is the
regularity with which the Church suffered from internal strife. It may be that
this feature receives special emphasis because of the way John orders his plot:
the Church thrives for a time, then Satan enters into someone in order to
create trials for God's people, but eventually divine vengeance catches up
with that person. That vengeance is sometimes swift, as when one of the
administrative assistants of Patriarch Mark II, in a bid for power at a rival's
expense, swore falsely on an icon of the Virgin and Christ Child—and
his entire right side was immediately paralyzed.[77] It is sometimes widely
encompassing, as when a deacon who had spoken insolently to Patriarch
Jacob suddenly died—with all his household.[78] But there are also cases in

which the ambitious are bought off, as when Ishaq ibn Andunah, a wealthy rival of Yusab I for the office of patriarch despite being a married layman,[79] was made bishop of Awsim with authority over the diocese of Misr as well.[80] Upon Ishaq's death, his son Theodore aspired to succeed him as bishop of Awsim. He eventually got his way when the governor (who had been promised payment for his support) began to pull down one of the most celebrated churches of Misr, the Mu'allaqah or "Hanging" Church, in order to persuade the patriarch to proceed with the consecration.[81] John the Writer reports that divine retribution did fall—but on the governor, who later died in battle against the Byzantines, rather than on Bishop Theodore.[82]

A number of stories in John's chronicle are of this nature: individuals seeking the office of deacon, bishop, or even patriarch with the support of Muslim authorities (who have often been bribed). Two stories of this sort, both of which resulted in severe suffering for the patriarch, bracket John's narrative. His first biography, of Menas I (#47, 767–776), is almost entirely taken up with the story of the renegade monk Peter, who won the confidence first of the patriarch of Antioch, and then of the 'Abbasid caliph al-Mansur (754–775), and who attempted to have himself imposed as patriarch of Alexandria. Menas and many of his bishops resisted steadfastly—but spent a year doing backbreaking, degrading work in a shipyard before Peter's overweening arrogance triggered his downfall.[83] John's final story has to do with the monk Theodore of the Monastery of St. John Kame, who, frustrated in his ambition to be ordained deacon, falsely claimed that Patriarch Shenoute was converting Muslims to Christianity. Shenoute, already crippled with gout, was imprisoned for a time with a number of members of his entourage.[84]

Perhaps the patriarch of this era who faced the greatest internal challenges was Yusab I (#52, 831–849). His dealings with his rival Ishaq ibn Andunah (the married lay notable or *archon* who was a candidate for patriarch) and his son Theodore (who became a bishop as a result of a Muslim governor's violent pressure) have already been mentioned. Shortly after the pacification of the rebellion of 831, Yusab was obliged to suspend two bishops, Isaac of Tinnis and Theodore of Misr, who had alienated their people to the point that the people threatened apostasy or even murder.[85] They then denounced the patriarch to General al-Afshin as being the person behind the Bashmurite Christians' participation in the rebellion.[86] Their denunciation led to an assassination attempt against the patriarch, and then his arrest and maltreatment, before he was finally vindicated before the general.[87] Perhaps even more disturbing was a plot among a number of the bishops, with the support of the chief Muslim legal authority, the *qadi*, to depose Yusab and replace him with Yannah, bishop of Misr.[88] This time around, Yusab was saved by careful documentation: diplomas recognizing his position from both the caliph al-Ma'mun and his brother, the super-governor of Egypt (and future caliph) al-Mu'tasim.[89] John the Writer portrays his spiritual father Yusab as a holy man, but cannot disguise the fact that the Church in Yusab's days was riven by ambition, dissatisfaction with the patriarch, and an unseemly readiness to resort to alliances with those outside the Church.

A Crisis of Cohesion?
A Battered Church

Was the Egyptian Church, to put the matter bluntly, falling apart? External blows during the 'Abbasid period had badly degraded the Egyptian Church's sacred geography. Pilgrimage to the shrine of St. Menas had effectively come to an end. The patriarchs had been driven out of Alexandria into the Delta, where they took refuge in out-of-the-way places. Monasteries had been attacked, and were trying to ensure their survival by building fortress-like walls. Internally, John the Writer gives us a melancholy picture of party spirit and ambition that regularly took a sinister and destructive turn.

Ignorance and Heresy

John's melancholy picture is by no means relieved by the state of Christian teaching in the Coptic Church in the period he chronicles. When Syrian Orthodox Patriarch Dionysius I (818–845) visited Egypt in the company of the caliph al-Ma'mun in 832, it was not his first visit to Egypt; some years earlier (826) he had come in the company of al-Ma'mun's general 'Abd Allah ibn Tahir. According to Dionysius's own account, the Coptic patriarch Jacob and his bishops received him with joy and said:

> "We have not seen a [Syrian] patriarch in Egypt since Mar Severus!" Then we reminded him of the coming of Athanasius Gammolo, and the union that he made with Anastasius after the schism of Peter and Damian.[90] We realized that, not caring about book-learning, conventions had fallen into disuse among them. Jacob was rich in good works but was not skilled in speaking and administration.[91]

The charge (by a theological ally) that the leadership of the ninth-century Egyptian church did not care about book-learning may simply reflect the prejudices of a highly cultured foreign visitor. One could assemble evidence to the contrary from the *History of the Patriarchs*: Mark II, himself the author of "twenty-one books of Mystagogia,"[92] saw to the Christian education of the Byzantine captives he had ransomed.[93] Yusab I was trained in Greek.[94] Shenoute I "was very solicitous for the books of the Church."[95] And yet, Shenoute spent many of his early days as patriarch combating odd heresies and heretics: 'Quartodecimans' in Mareotis;[96] bishops in al-Balyana teaching that "the Nature of the Divinity died";[97] a teacher who reviled Cyril of Alexandria in Upper Egypt;[98] and teachers elsewhere who claimed that the Resurrection took place on 11 April rather than on 25 March.[99] John the Writer is candid about one cause of the spread of false teaching among the people: "the scantiness of the knowledge of their shepherds (the bishops) was manifest in those days."[100] It is probably not too much to speak of a crisis in Christian education in the mid-ninth century.

One recent writer, reflecting on the strange appearance of 'Quartodecimans' in Mareotis, suggests that it is "the sign of a tear in the religious fabric, of a breakup, of a crisis of cohesion among the Christians." He finds in the appearance of this and other ancient heresies "a symptom of religious deculturation."[101] Such a process of deculturation could only pave the way for increased Islamization.[102]

Conversion

'Abbasid ideology stressed both the equality of Muslims regardless of ethnic background and the desirability of non-Muslims' conversion to Islam. This marked a break with the instincts of the Umayyad Arab elite, in general happy to allow Christians and Jews to remain in their religion as long as they paid the poll tax or *jizyah*.[103] From the time that the 'Abbasids succeeded in asserting their authority, they encouraged conversion by exempting converts from the *jizyah*, as well as by other means. The Mu'tazilite theologians who dominated official 'Abbasid discourse under the caliph al-Ma'mun and his immediate successors produced a large volume of 'refutation of the Christians' literature that may have served both "evangelistic" and catechetical purposes.[104] While the caliph al-Mutawakkil suppressed the Mu'tazilite dialecticians in favor of a more text-based, traditionist discourse, he continued to patronize writers of anti-*dhimmi* literature,[105] and John the Writer bears witness that the caliph's dismissal of non-Muslims from the civil service induced many to convert.[106]

For John, the phenomenon of Christians converting to Islam is a reality, but one against which he can preach. In his account of the false monk Peter, who tormented Patriarch Menas I, John relates that Peter converted to Islam at the hand of the caliph al-Mansur, who rewarded him with "many gifts . . . garments and money and horses and female slaves."[107] When al-Mansur died in 775, however, Peter (or Abu l-Khayr, as he had come to be known) encountered nothing but contempt and shame from his family and acquaintances, who spoke to him as follows:

> "Ah thou that art become a son of Satan, and hast strayed from the way of life, where hast thou left the fear of God and of Hell, and the voice of our Creator pronouncing the terrible sentence: 'Whosoever shall deny me before men, him will I deny before the Father who is in heaven?' Thou hast rejected this true voice, and therefore thou shalt hear instead of it: 'Take him away to the fire which is not quenched and the worm which sleeps not.' This shall be the reward of thy apostasy."[108]

The verbal violence of this statement may well indicate the degree to which conversion to Islam was, for John the Writer in the mid-ninth century, a painful reality. While evidence outside the literary sources for conversion to Islam in ninth-century Egypt is limited, what evidence does exist is striking —for example, funerary stelae from Aswan for persons with startling names such as Muhammad ibn Yuhannis ("Muhammad son of John") or Abu l-Harith Bilal ibn Andriya ("Abu l-Harith Bilal son of Andrew"), presumably sons of Christian converts to Islam.[109] Medieval Islamic biographical dictionaries yield similar examples of prominent Muslim individuals with Christian ancestors, as is clear from the Christian names of their forebears; the limited evidence for Egypt indicates a heightened conversion rate in the ninth century lasting into the tenth.[110] Christians and Muslims (including converts to Islam) may well have been living together peacefully in common communities by the time John the Writer produced his chronicle. Indeed, some evidence of intermarriage exists: we possess an Arabic contract from Edfu for the sale of a house, dating to AD 854, between Yuna bint Halis (Johanna daughter of Elisha?) and her husband Yazid ibn Qasim, signed by three Christian witnesses (one of whom signed his name in Coptic).[111] John's description of the shame that Peter's kin heaped upon him for converting may have been more an expression of what John thought proper than a reflection of actual conditions, in which conversion to Islam and intermarriage were becoming accepted realities.[112]

The religious conversion of a population is, of course, an extraordinarily complex process, progressing at different rates in different places, and proceeding in any given locality in a series of fits and starts, with a number of plateaus along the way. Later, we shall see that the twelfth century, and again the fourteenth, offered conditions and witnessed events that made conversion to Islam an attractive possibility, or at least a rational choice, for many of Egypt's remaining Christians. Still, there seems to be no reason to dispute the scholarly consensus that the ninth century was a crucial period in the process of conversion to Islam in Egypt, even if we have no way of measuring the exact proportions of Egyptian Christians and Muslims at the end of that century—or at any other time.[113]

Hanging On

The preceding section has painted a rather bleak picture of the Egyptian Church in the ninth century. Is the gloom unrelieved? Are there elements in the picture provided by John the Writer (and other sources) that point to adaptability and possibilities of renewal in the Church?

One such element, possibly, is the important role played by the *arakhinah* or Coptic lay notables in some of John's biographies.[114] Although this role could be disruptive, at other times the *arakhinah* came to the rescue in difficult situations. Thus it was the *archon* Maqarah ibn Shath who settled Patriarch Mark II in the Delta town of Nabaruh after he had been obliged to flee Alexandria in 816.[115] As noted earlier, the *arakhinah* Maqarah ibn Yusuf and Ibrahim ibn Sawirus spirited Patriarch Cosmas II (851–858) away from the clutches of the local governor *(wali)* in Alexandria to Damirah in the Delta, leaving him to pray there while they effectively ran the Church.[116] Ibrahim continued in an active role after his colleague's death, and at the height of oppressive financial extortions (in 861–862) undertook an embassy to the caliphs al-Mu'tazz and al-Musta'in, from whom he obtained a decree restoring much church property.[117] The contributions of these *arakhinah* foreshadow the leading role that Coptic laity would take in the affairs of the Church at various times of difficulty and opportunity, in which the history of the patriarchs tends to give way to the history of the lay notables.

Another element of renewal in the life of the Egyptian Church has to do with its connections with Christians beyond the lands ruled by the governor. John the Writer makes the patriarch's responsibilities for these relations explicit when he states that the patriarch's duties are threefold:

> the care for the synodical letter to the patriarch of Antioch;
> secondly our relations with the Abyssinians and the Nubians;
> and thirdly the carrying out of decrees issued by the governor
> of Egypt to the patriarchs and bishops. . . .[118]

We have treated the third responsibility, that of obedience to the Muslim authorities, at some length. Relations with the Abyssinians and Nubians only come into John's chronicle at one point, when Patriarch Yusab I counsels the Nubians to fulfill their treaty obligations to the 'Abbasids, meets the Nubian prince George on his way to and from Baghdad, and consecrates a bishop for the Abyssinians.[119] What may be surprising is the stress John places on the synodical letters between the patriarchs of Alexandria and Antioch, that is, the statements of faith addressed by each new patriarch to his counterpart, and the responses to them. John documents these exchanges diligently,[120]and at least three of them have been preserved.[121]

This "Syrian connection" was important to the life of the Coptic Church.[122] Periodic formal exchanges of letters provided opportunities for each community to reaffirm its loyalty to—and to reflect upon—the faith of Athanasius, Cyril, Dioscorus, Severus, and Theodosius. Of particular importance to the life of the Coptic Church was the presence of Syrian monks, who, by the early ninth century, had established themselves at the Monastery of the Theotokos of Bishoi,[123] which came to be known as Dayr al-Suryan or the Syrian Monastery. Recent restoration work at the monastery has led to the discovery of ninth-century Syriac inscriptions on the wall of the old church.[124] One of them names the Antiochian patriarch Cyriacus (793–817). Another, which presumably dates to the period immediately after the sack of Scetis in 816/817, refers to the rebuilding efforts of the monks Mattai and Ya'qub and names the patriarchs Jacob of Alexandria (819–830) and Dionysius I of Antioch (818–845). Mattai and Ya'qub are also known as two of the monks responsible for assembling the core of an extraordinary library at the Syrian Monastery.[125]At the same time that Dionysius was complaining about the Copts' disinterest in book-learning, monks from his own community were assembling a remarkable theological resource center in the heart of the Egyptian "Paradise of God" that was Scetis, one that continues to be of great significance today.[126]

Embattled Saints

John the Writer presents the patriarchs of the difficult 'Abbasid period as embattled saints. As portrayed, they are distinctive in their saintliness: Mark II is a practical man who builds churches and writes books;[127] Jacob is a holy man who sees saints in visions, prophesies, has remarkable capacities of both healing and cursing, and was "intercessor for the land of Egypt";[128] the prayers of Yusab I are likewise heard, whether for healing or for vengeance;[129] Shenoute I is not only an attractive pastor and teacher but also a model of monastic humility, weeping with ease and regularly praying for the forgiveness of his enemies.[130] All the patriarchs of this period suffered trials and afflictions patiently. The Arabic redaction that has preserved their story regularly uses the language of *jihad*, "struggle," to describe their endurance of adversity: they were *mujahidin* who earned the crown of life/victory through their patience.[131]

Just so, the patriarchs of this period stood in continuity with the great "fighters" of old such as Athanasius, Dioscorus, Severus, and Theodosius. They themselves claimed this continuity, in the anti-Arian, anti-Chalcedonian, and anti-Julianist affirmations of the synodical letters that they regularly exchanged with their Antiochian counterparts. At the point that the actual residence of the patriarch in Alexandria began to become an occasional reality rather than something taken for granted, John the Writer intensifies his references to these great "fighters," all of whom, of course, endured exile. Mark II, driven from Alexandria by mayhem in the streets, found refuge in a town in the Egyptian countryside—like Severus of Antioch.[132] An aged monk had a vision of Dioscorus and Severus holding the Gospel book at the consecration of Mark's successor Jacob; on his deathbed, Jacob was heard to greet the same two fathers, whose *jihad* his own resembled.[133] Much was changing during the 'Abbasid period. Foes assaulted the Church from within and without, and the patriarchal residence in Alexandria was in the process of being abandoned. For the successors of the militant patriarchs and exiles Athanasius, Dioscorus, Severus, and Theodosius, however, this was nothing new. Satan might rage, but God would surely prevail.

Four

Saints and Sinners

Michael (Kha'il) III (#56, 880–907)
Gabriel I (#57, 909–920)
Cosmas III (#58, 920–932)
Macarius I (#59, 932–952)
Theophanius (#60, 952–956)
Menas II (#61, 956–974)
Abraham (Afraham ibn Zur'ah) (#62, 975–978)
Philotheus (#63, 979–1003)
Zacharias (#64, 1004–1032)
Shenoute II (#65, 1032–1046)

Bishop Michael's Account: Warts and All

The author of the next set of patriarchal biographies collected in the *History of the Patriarchs* was Michael of Damru (Mikha'il al-Damrawi), bishop of Tinnis, who finished his contribution, written in Coptic, in AD 1051.[1] He was especially well acquainted with Patriarch Shenoute II (#65, 1032–1046), whom he had served as scribe and who had ordained him priest. It is something of a shock to the reader accustomed to earlier biographers' praise of the patriarchs they served to find that Michael did not think very highly of Shenoute, and was unafraid to portray him to his readers as an ambitious[2] and rather vindictive[3] man who "loved money" and "the glory of this world,"[4] who regularly went back on his agreements,[5] and who remained "desirous of the world" even upon his deathbed.[6] Still, Michael's unflattering portrayal is bracketed by language more typical of the *Lives* of great saints. Michael reports that, before Shenoute's election as patriarch, he was granted a dream in which Peter the Apostle and John the Evangelist delivered him keys—clearly a sign of his divine election to be patriarch.[7] And at the conclusion of the biography, Michael prays that "God grant to us acceptance of the blessing of his prayers"—ranging Shenoute with the saintly intercessors in Paradise.[8]

43

In his conviction that God is in control of human affairs and that it is God who chooses the patriarch, Bishop Michael differs little from his predecessors in the project of patriarchal biography.[9] What does distinguish Michael's accounts, however, is his unembarrassed readiness to portray the patriarchs with sometimes brutal honesty, warts and all. If the patriarchal biographers John the Deacon and John the Writer had described the patriarchs as saints, Michael describes a mix of saints and sinners confronting difficult challenges (and temptations) with uneven measures of gravity and grace. It is an account that makes for lively reading.

Before the Fatimids

The first six biographies in Bishop Michael's account are quite brief, although they cover a tumultuous century (880–974) in Egyptian history, including the rule of the Tulunids (868–905), the shaky reassertion of 'Abbasid authority (905–935), and the Ikhshidid-Kafurid regime (935–969).[10] In particular, Egyptian history throughout the tenth century was marked by the rise of an Isma'ili Shi'i rival to the 'Abbasid Sunni caliph as proper leader of the Islamic world. From his base in what is now Tunisia, the Isma'ili ("Fatimid") ruler al-Mahdi declared himself caliph as well as imam in 910, and his armies unsuccessfully invaded Egypt—seen as the best base from which to challenge the rival 'Abbasid caliphs in Iraq or even as a way station on the way to Baghdad—in 914–915 and 919–921; another attempt was made by al-Mahdi's son al-Qa'im in 935–936. The Fatimids would finally succeed in conquering Egypt, with surprisingly little bloodshed, in 969.[11]

This political background is sometimes noted by Bishop Michael in passing. The great Ahmad ibn Tulun (near-sovereign ruler of Egypt, 868–884) plays a role in the biography of Patriarch Michael III (#56, 880–907), as does the infighting *within* the Church that was highlighted in the previous chapter. According to Bishop Michael, a deposed and vengeful bishop led Ibn Tulun to believe that the patriarch had vast wealth. Ibn Tulun, in need of financing for his military campaigns in Syria, imprisoned Patriarch Michael for a year, during which time the Coptic *arakhinah* carried out the behind-the-scenes negotiations that led to the patriarch's release in return for twenty thousand dinars to be paid in two installments.[12] This story is important because it explains the background to the distasteful fundraising measures that the patriarchate was compelled to adopt (and to which we shall return). About the patriarch, we learn that he faced Ibn Tulun with the composure and courage of a martyr;[13] that he built a private latrine for himself in prison (at a cost, Bishop Michael makes a point of informing us, of three hundred dinars);[14] and that, once recovered from his prison experience, he participated in fundraising activities to pay the debt to Ibn Tulun.[15] Other than this, Bishop Michael has little to say about the patriarch's twenty-eight years in office. This may reflect relatively prosperous and uneventful times for the Church under Ibn Tulun and his son Khumarawayh (884–896), who, as independent local rulers rather than servants of Baghdad, pursued policies that were economically advantageous to the inhabitants of Egypt and were generally on good terms with Christians.[16] It may also be indicative of a situation in which much of the decision-making power in the Church lay not with the patriarch but elsewhere—with wealthy and well-connected lay notables, or with a few particularly powerful bishops.[17]

If we know little about Patriarch Michael III, we know even less about his immediate successors. Gabriel I (#57, 909–920) was a saintly monk who after his consecration as patriarch remained in Scetis, where for two years he cleaned latrines at night in order to defeat the demon of lust.[18] All we know of Cosmas III (#58, 920–932) is that he consecrated one Peter as metropolitan of Abyssinia, and later excommunicated Peter's usurper.[19] Of Macarius I (#59, 932–952), all we are told is that his aged mother publicly rebuked the exultant new patriarch: "Would that they had brought thee to me borne dead on a bier than that thou shouldst come in to me with this empty glory!"[20] The next twenty years of Macarius' patriarchate are passed over in silence.[21] His successor, Theophanius (#60, 952–956), was an elderly man who apparently suffered from dementia, which manifested itself at first in ill-temper and later in blasphemous rages. He is reported to have been murdered (suffocated with a pillow or poisoned) while being taken, under restraint, to Misr for treatment.[22]

We learn a little more about Menas II (#61, 956–974). He had married, but he and his wife decided to preserve their virginity and pursue the ascetic life. There was some consternation among the bishops when they discovered that the holy monk they had elevated to the patriarchate in fact had a wife, but eventually they were reassured by her testimony to his holiness.[23] It was during Menas' patriarchate that severe and protracted famine (963–969) led to the depopulation and consolidation of some bishoprics; Menas himself moved to the village of Mahallat Danyal, where he was supported throughout the famine by a wealthy woman, and where he built a church to St. Mark.[24] Despite Menas's building activity, one senses that the patriarchate in his time was a much more modest institution than it had been in earlier Islamic times. We recall that Patriarch John IV (#49, 777–799) had been able to mount a major relief campaign during an earlier time of famine.[25] In his days the patriarch, who still resided in Alexandria, had significant resources that could be mobilized in time of need; as for Menas II, he was dependent on the charity of a pious woman in an obscure Delta town.

Simony:
"The Word of God Became as a Merchandise"

The plight of Menas II illustrates a deep conundrum faced by the patriarchate of his day. It could no longer look for income either to revenue from international pilgrimage to the shrine of St. Menas or to the variety of commercial enterprises that it had once pursued in Alexandria. At the same time, it faced continuing financial obligations: the costs of the patriarchal institution itself; those of the churches and clergy in Alexandria; taxes, in particular on land owned by the patriarchate; and the occasional arbitrary exactions of rulers. Bishop Michael informs us that the patriarchate received some income in the form of remittances from the bishops, who collected *diyariyat*, "alms for the monasteries," from the faithful. These "alms" had become a kind of church tax; under Patriarch Gabriel I it was set at one gold *keration* per adult worshiper. Beyond this, there was another money-making possibility: that of collecting specified sums from those who wished to be ordained bishop, priest, or deacon. In Coptic and Copto-Arabic sources this practice is sometimes signified by the Greek word *cheirotonia*—literally and ordinarily the "laying on of hands" (as in ordination), but also used figuratively to refer to *payment for* ordination. In the west, the practice was known as 'simony', with a reference to the biblical story of Simon Magus (Acts 8:9–24), who coveted the apostles' authority to bestow the Holy Spirit through the laying on of hands, and offered them money for it.

While simony in the Coptic Church did not originate in the period that Bishop Michael chronicles—earlier, the saintly patriarch Shenoute I (#55, 859–880) is specifically reported to have forbidden it, implying its existence[26]—according to Bishop Michael it took root when the Church under Patriarch Michael III was obliged to find a way to raise the twenty thousand dinars pledged to Ahmad ibn Tulun. That patriarch (and those around him) had recourse to a number of money-making expedients, including the regulation of the *diyariyat* and fees to be paid by the monks, the sale of objects in the monasteries at Scetis, and a fund-raising tour.[27] Two other fund-raising measures were especially significant: one was the sale of buildings in Alexandria, to which the Alexandrians would only agree in return for a pledge of one thousand dinars per year for the expenses of their churches. Not only did the patriarchate's sale of property in Alexandria—probably including the patriarchal residence—underline the growing distance between the patriarchate and the city that was officially its home,[28] Patriarch

Michael's short-term financial gain became his successors' long-term liability. Already Michael's successor Gabriel I found himself in the position of having to resort to simony in order to pay the Alexandrians.[29] Later, a quarrel with the Alexandrian clergy over the annual payment appears to have sparked Patriarch Theophanius' slide into raging dementia.[30]

Patriarch Michael's other major fund-raising method was simony pure and simple: the demand of a large sum of money from anyone desiring to be consecrated to one of the ten vacant bishoprics in his time.[31] This "saintly patriarch" is represented as honestly distressed by the desperate financial measures to which he was compelled;[32] the same was undoubtedly true of his successor Gabriel, who collected fees for ordination to the priesthood:

> The circumstances made it necessary for him to journey through the see and to violate the canons, and the word of God became as a merchandise which is sold for dinars to him who asks to be ordained priest.[33]

For later hierarchs, however, simony became part of life, as we shall soon see. But first we pause for an interlude of remarkable saintliness.

Contrapuntal Saintliness

Egypt in the year 969 was in turmoil both economically (because of the years of famine mentioned earlier) and politically (because of the death of the strongman Kafur in 968 without a clear successor). The Fatimid armies that had unsuccessfully invaded Egypt three times previously now moved quickly to take and secure the country. Shortly afterward, the triumphant Fatimid general Jawhar laid out a new capital a little to the north of the existing city of Fustat-Misr, which came to be called *al-Qahirah*, Cairo. Building there commenced immediately. In 972 Friday prayers were inaugurated in the new Azhar Mosque within the city, and in 973 the Fatimad imam and caliph al-Mu'izz li-Din Allah moved his court to the city's newly built grand palaces. Cairo quickly became a "ritual city" marked by elaborate ceremonial and public displays of text in stone and textile that enacted and proclaimed the authority and numinous power of the Fatimid caliphs.[34] It was the spiritual and political heart of an empire that laid claim on the entire Islamic world for two centuries.

It is the widely accepted judgment of historians that the Copts fared well during the Fatimid period, "probably the best in their history under Arab rule," or even "the golden age for the *Dhimmis* in the history of Egypt."[35]

Coptic civil servants rose to positions of great wealth and authority.[36] The caliphs made outings to pleasantly situated churches and monasteries[37] and made grants of land to them.[38] New churches were built and dilapidated ones restored.[39] And as for the patriarchate, it was gradually "reeled in" toward the center of power after its "exile" in obscure Delta towns; we may note that Patriarchs Abraham and Zacharias were the first to be buried in Cairo-Misr.

As to the question of *why* the Fatimids were generally well disposed toward the Christians, historians have offered a number of observations, many of them having to do with the pragmatism of rulers who, themselves (as Isma'ili Shi'a) a religious minority among Egypt's Sunni Muslims and Christians, in a detached manner pursued policies that made for the efficient administration of an economically and socially complex society.[40] Coptic tradition, however, offers another explanation: it was an evidentiary miracle performed already in the days of the imam-caliph al-Mu'izz that left the Fatimid leadership marveling at the power of the Christian religion. The story, known to every Coptic child, is that of the moving of the Muqattam mountain outside of Cairo. This miraculous event has left its mark on the liturgical calendar in the form of three additional days of fasting before Christmas;[41] is recited in the churches every 6 Kiyahk (2 December);[42] and in recent times is commemorated in a much-visited complex of churches in the Muqattam hills themselves.[43]

At least until modern times, the most highly celebrated figure associated with the Muqattam miracle was Patriarch Abraham (Abra'am or Afraham)[44] ibn Zur'ah (#62, 975–978). Despite his short reign, Bishop Michael has given us a fairly substantial biography of this patriarch,[45] which served as the basis for a number of other accounts.[46] I propose to examine the way in which Abraham is portrayed in Bishop Michael's eleventh-century account, after which some remarks about the development of the tradition may be in order.

In the last chapter we pointed out the importance of Syrian connections and of the activities of pious lay notables to the continuing health of the Coptic Church. Abraham represents both factors: he was a Syrian merchant well loved for his almsgiving and highly respected both at the Fatimid court and by the Coptic notables of Cairo.[47] Once elected patriarch, he became a reformer who aimed at putting a halt to the Church's assimilation to the patterns of "the world." In particular, this meant bringing an end to simony (and the stranglehold of financial obligations and opportunities on the interior ordering of the Church's life) and concubinage (a glaring sign of the Coptic notables' adoption of the lifestyle of high-ranking Muslim officials). Abraham was empowered in his campaign against simony by his own personal fortune, which he spent freely (and, in the end, entirely) in the service of the Church and of the poor. The campaign against concubinage ran into opposition, as one can well imagine. In one incident reported by Bishop Michael, Abraham excommunicated an *archon* who refused even to open his door to the patiently knocking patriarch. When after two hours the patriarch gave up and departed, shaking the dust of the notable's doorstep from his feet, that doorstep was immediately split in two, and the notable himself died shortly thereafter.[48] Like many holy men before him, Abraham had turned out to be an effective curser.[49] Later, however, another *archon* who was reluctant to give up his concubines did *not* expire upon excommunication, but (according to a rumor reported by Bishop Michael) retaliated: he slipped the patriarch poison in his drink and thus brought about Abraham's death, less than three years into his patriarchate.[50]

If stories like these do not present the Coptic notables in a very favorable light, Bishop Michael does give his readers to know that most of them heeded the patriarch's call to put away their concubines.[51] Furthermore, one Coptic layman comes in for special commendation. Abu l-Yumn Quzman ibn Mina was a pious and celibate civil servant who was already serving as *wazir*[52] when the Fatimids arrived in Egypt, and whom they kept on as a high administrative official.[53] Upon being assigned as the caliph's viceroy in Syria, he entrusted his personal fortune of ninety thousand dinars to Patriarch Abraham for safekeeping, with the instructions that, in the event he did not return, it should be used in the service of the Church, the poor, and captives.[54] Quzman had not underestimated the dangers he faced, and in fact had a series of adventures during which it was reported in Cairo that he had behaved treacherously toward al-Mu'izz. When the enraged caliph responded by arresting Quzman's family members and seizing their possessions, the patriarch decided to make use of the money that had been entrusted to him. One can imagine some awkward moments when Quzman eventually returned to Cairo-Misr, cleared his name, discharged his obligations, was honored by the caliph . . . and then approached Patriarch Abraham to reclaim his fortune! When the patriarch explained what he had done, however, Quzman blessed him for using his money well, rather than risking its confiscation by the caliph.[55]

The well-known story of the Muqattam miracle begins with jealousy at court, where Quzman had a rival in Ya'qub ibn Killis, a Jew who had converted to Islam, and like Quzman was a holdover from the previous administration.[56] Ya'qub resented the access that the patriarch had to the caliph and thought that a religious debate might provide a way to put the patriarch to shame.[57] The caliph welcomed the idea of a debate, but did not insist that the patriarch *himself* engage in it, permitting him to choose a proxy. Abraham called in one of the best-known figures in the literary history of the Copts, the government scribe-become-monk and then bishop of al-Ashmunayn, Sawirus ibn al-Muqaffaʻ.[58] An experienced controversialist and prolific theologian–apologist in the Arabic language, Sawirus's reputation as the first major Coptic theologian to write in Arabic has been so great that all manner of texts have been falsely attributed to him in the manuscript tradition.[59] In the debate (according to Bishop Michael's report, at least), Sawirus made quick work of Ibn Killis's protégé Musa.[60]

According to Bishop Michael, this defeat in debate simply increased the enmity of Ibn Killis toward the patriarch. When he discovered the word of the Gospel, "If you have faith as a grain of mustard seed, you will say to this mountain, 'Move from here to there,' and it will move" (Matthew 17:20),[61] he maliciously suggested to the caliph that he demand a demonstration in order to test whether the Christian faith was merely a fraud. Al-Muʻizz agreed, and delivered an ultimatum to the patriarch: move the mountain, or the Christian community will be put to the sword.[62]

The patriarch sought and received a three-day delay, during which he mobilized his resources:

> [H]e caused to be brought to him the priests and archons of Misr and all the Orthodox people, and weeping he made known to them the matter. There were in Misr a number of monks of Wadi Habib, and [Abraham] imposed upon them all a penance that none of them should go to his dwelling-place for three days, but that they should assemble to continue in prayer in the church night and day.[63]

A recension of the story written after convents of nuns had been established in Cairo-Misr adds:

> That father sent to all the convents of pious virgin nuns in Cairo-Misr, informed them of the matter, and commanded them to fast day and night for three successive days; and to devote themselves constantly, night and day, to prayer, petition and beseeching God (may he be exalted!) and Our Lady, the pride of our race. And they did as he commanded them.[64]

All were engaged in a common effort of intercession, at the center of which was the patriarch himself, who for three days engaged in uninterrupted prayer and the severest fasting at the Muʻallaqah Church.[65] On the morning of the appointed trial, Abraham fainted from his exertions—and the Virgin Mary appeared to him with reassurance and instructions: he was to go out into the street and seize a one-eyed man carrying a jar of water, "for he it is at whose hands this miracle shall be manifested."[66] Abraham found the man, a tanner who had once plucked out his eye after looking at a woman with lust (in literal application of Matthew 18:9);[67] he turned out to be a "hidden saint"—Bishop Michael does not even report his name—who served the poor and worked by day while praying by night, without seeking any recognition for himself.[68]

Following the pious tanner's instructions, patriarch, clergy, and people went out in solemn procession to the mountain (the tanner anonymously following the patriarch), along with the caliph and his retinue. After a long period of crying out *"Kyrie eleison,"* the patriarch commanded silence and led all the Christian people in three prostrations—in which the mountain participated, lifting up from the ground and returning to its place as the host of Christians rose and fell! Great fear seized the caliph, who, after the third elevation of the mountain, cried out, "Enough, O patriarch, I have recognized, indeed, the correctness of thy faith."[69] From this time on the caliph honored the patriarch, and allowed the restoration of the Church of St. Mercurius (which had become a warehouse for sugarcane) and a number of other churches.[70]

The story of the moving of the Muqattam mountain would later be elaborated as a great evidentiary miracle for the truth of the Christian faith in competition with its Jewish and Islamic rivals,[71] leading to a religious discussion in which that truth was again plainly demonstrated,[72] culminating in the conversion and baptism of the caliph himself![73] Nothing of this development is unprecedented or surprising,[74] but the elaborations do run the risk of obscuring the story as Bishop Michael first told it. A striking feature in Michael's portrait of Abraham is the way the patriarch stands at the center of a diverse community with a variety of gifts that can be mobilized for the defense of the faith: Abraham's own financial resources were supplemented by those of the pious *archon*, Quzman ibn Mina; for help in interreligious controversy he called on the arabophone theologian Sawirus ibn al-Muqaffaʿ; when a miracle was needed an anonymous tanner provided the requisite calm faith in the power of God; and, in time of crisis, *all* the people—clergy, monks, laity—gathered around the patriarch to fast, pray, and beg the Lord for mercy. In an earlier chapter we suggested that Patriarch Michael I (#46, 743–767) had been portrayed as the "conductor" of a kind of "orchestra of holiness";[75] two centuries later, we have another prominent example of such sainthood in Patriarch Abraham. While Michael's "orchestra" consisted mostly of bishops and monks, however, the saints surrounding Abraham—himself once a merchant—include a high-ranking civil servant, a bishop who started his career as a government scribe, and a humble tanner. However many distasteful stories Bishop Michael has to tell about worldly clergymen (and we are about to turn to one), he would have his readers know that God does protect and renew the Church, and regularly raises up saints from every corner of it.

Unexpected Saintliness

That God raises up saints in unexpected places continues to be a theme in Bishop Michael's biography of Patriarch Abraham's successor Philotheus (#63, 979–1003), most of which is given over to the story of al-Wadih (Paul) ibn Raja', a young Muslim who converted to Christianity and eventually became a monk, priest, and (with his friend Sawirus ibn al-Muqaffaʿ) apologist.[76] Bishop Michael passes over other events in Philotheus's quarter-century reign rather quickly;[77] he emphasizes that the new patriarch reinstated the practice of simony and moved the patriarchate to the town of Damru in the Delta, both in spite of objections from Coptic notables.[78] In Damru he installed a puppet bishop[79] and lived in considerable luxury, devoting much time to the pleasures of the bath and the table.[80] When he died (perhaps as the result of a stroke), he was found to have amassed a sizable fortune, which was then divided among family members.[81] A damning judgment on him came from the saint al-Wadih, whose family had resorted to extreme measures to turn him back from his decision to become a Christian:

> All that happened to me in the way of torture and what befell me in the way of degradation did not trouble me, with the exception of three things: the copulation of my brother with my concubine in my presence; the drowning of my son from her in my presence while I was looking at him; but even more serious than either of them was when the patriarch looked on at me while his disciples were demanding from me the dinars for his ordaining me priest, and yet kept silent, and did not forbid them and did not send them away.[82]

Philotheus's successor as patriarch was Zacharias (#64, 1004–1032), to the present day commemorated as a saint of the Church on 13 Hatur (9 November).[83] Zacharias hardly seemed destined for either the patriarchate or sainthood: he was an inconspicuous ("poor, wretched and pure")[84] steward of the churches in Alexandria who came to the notice of the bishops gathered to choose the new patriarch[85] when he slipped and fell with a jar of vinegar that he was fetching for their meal—and the jar landed without breaking or spilling! This "miracle"—so Bishop Michael—indicated to the bishops that they had found their candidate. Zacharias was an attractive candidate to the bishops precisely because he would be weak and pliable, in contrast to the Alexandrian *archon* Ibrahim ibn Bishr who was seeking the patriarchate with the support of the Fatimid authorities.[86] And so it turned out: Zacharias was an amiable patriarch who was completely dominated by those around him, including his nephew Anba Kha'il, bishop of Sakha, who operated the patriarchate as a for-profit enterprise.

> The . . . patriarch was very modest, as a gentle lamb, and he had not done anything of what we have mentioned [sale of bishoprics] of his own accord. . . . He was as one dumb. His relatives and his disciples dominated him and they were directing him in everything.[87]

Bishop Michael clearly deplores the return to simoniacal practices, and is scathing in his denunciation of the bishops:

> [T]hey were become as *walis* who lorded over the priests. They invented pretexts for collecting money by every means, and they trafficked in the Church of God on account of the love of silver and gold, and they sold the gift of God for money. . . .[88]

Furthermore,

> In their days . . . instruction also ceased . . . The heads of the Church used previously to look for a person in whom was learning and knowledge that they might make him a priest. . . . Matters were now reversed, and the intelligent scholar was of no account, especially if he were a poor man, but the ignorant and he who was without intelligence was honoured and revered by them, especially if he were rich, that they might advance him to the exalted rank of the ranks of the priests.[89]

According to Bishop Michael, these sins of the shepherds were the ultimate cause of God's wrath falling on the Church.[90] While the Church had enjoyed peaceful and prosperous times under the Fatimid caliph al-Mu'izz, his successor al-'Aziz (975–996), and the early years of al-'Aziz's son al-Hakim bi-Amr Allah (996–1020), about the time Zacharias became patriarch the enigmatic al-Hakim began to adopt a number of discriminatory and repressive measures against Christians (and other non-Shiites).[91] Christian civil servants fell into disfavor.[92] The sale of wine was prohibited and fermentable grapes, raisins, and honey destroyed.[93] Measures specifying distinctive dress for *dhimmi*s and prohibiting public displays of their faith were once again enacted and year after year elaborated.[94] Churches were closed or demolished.[95] According to Bishop Michael, it was in November 1010 that Patriarch Zacharias was summoned to Cairo, imprisoned, and even thrown to starved lions—who did not harm him at all![96] By late 1012 the persecution had moved into high gear with demolitions of churches and the forced conversion of Christian civil servants. As a Melkite Christian reported:

> The Christians were fear-stricken and terrified, and false rumours and calumnies spread among them. Many of the leading secretaries, administrators and other Christians became Muslims, and many ordinary people followed them.[97]

Others feigned conversion:

> Most of the Egyptian Christians divested themselves of their distinctive dress and the cross and the girdle and the wooden stirrups, and they imitated the Muslims, and no one exposed them, and he who saw them thought that they had embraced Al-Islam.[98]

In the midst of the persecution and the wave of conversions, permanent or feigned, Bishop Michael tells stories of great heroism: about Coptic civil servants who died rather than give up their faith;[99] or the saintly *archon* Buqayrah al-Rashidi, who upon his own release from prison devoted himself to the care of prisoners and those made destitute by the persecution;[100] or about his own father, a builder, who was granted a vision of Paradise to help him to endure abuse patiently.[101] At the center of all of this, the "dismally weak" and "hapless"[102] Patriarch Zacharias became, for his biographer, a confessor of the faith. While in prison, Zacharias responded to invitations to renounce his faith by saying, "My reliance is in God Who has power, and He will help me." When beaten, he responded with the typical language of the martyrs: "As for the body, ye have power over it to destroy it as ye will, but as for the soul, it is in the hand of the Lord."[103] Like the prophet Daniel, he had refused to compromise his faith, and had come through the lions' den unscathed.[104]

Patriarch Zacharias was released after three months and made his way to Scetis, which providentially had been spared al-Hakim's wrath so as to become a refuge for many, including most of the bishops, as well as one of the few places in the Egyptian sacred geography where the liturgy was celebrated without interruption. Indeed, Bishop Michael reports that at the height of the persecution the monasteries were the *only* places where the divine liturgy was openly celebrated, although some of the faithful arranged for secret celebrations by night in homes and ruined churches.[105]

As terrifying as the persecution had been, by the year 1020 the worst had passed. Some of the converts received the caliph's permission to return to their Christian faith.[106] Bishop Michael reports that the monk Poemen, who had rebuilt the Shahran Monastery south of Misr and was a confidant of al-Hakim who enjoyed spending time there, arranged a meeting between the caliph and the patriarch and bishops.

> When al-Hakim came to him, as was his custom, [Poemen] brought forth the patriarch to him. [Zacharias] saluted him with the salutation of kings and he blessed him and prayed for him. Al-Hakim said to Poemen the monk: "Who is this?" [Poemen] said: "It is our father, the patriarch, whom I sent to bring, as thou didst command." [Al-Hakim] beckoned to him with his finger, and he saluted him. There was with [Zacharias] a number of bishops. [Al-Hakim] said: "Who are these?" The monk Poemen said to him: "These are his vicars in the lands, namely, the bishops." Al-Hakim looked at [Zacharias] attentively and he marveled at him, because he was humble in appearance but was awe-inspiring in himself. He was small of stature, thin bearded and ugly by nature. [Al-Hakim] saw the bishops who were with him, elders of handsome aspect, splendid in appearance and of complete stature. He said to them: "Is this the chief of you all?" They said to him: "Yea, O our master. . . ."[107]

In Bishop Michael's description of the meeting, we once again hear echoes of the encounter between 'Amr and Benjamin: with a Copt (then the duke Shenoute, now the monk Poemen) acting as go-between, the Coptic patriarch is called out of hiding and meets and prays for the Muslim ruler, who marvels at the patriarch's appearance.[108] In Zacharias's case, however, there is a curious twist: al-Hakim marvels at the patriarch's authority *despite* his ugly features, thin beard, and unimposing stature, in comparison with his magnificent bishops! Still, the reader expects good to come out of this encounter between caliph and patriarch, and is not surprised to hear Bishop Michael report that discriminatory measures against the Christians were soon lifted.[109]

After al-Hakim mysteriously disappeared while on one of his nocturnal rambles in the Muqattam hills (February 1021), the Christians enjoyed a period of peace and rebuilding under al-Hakim's young son al-Zahir (1021–1035), which continued into the reign of al-Mustansir (1036–1094). In 1032, Patriarch Zacharias died, no longer the insignificant steward who had been chosen patriarch because of his weakness, but a confessor who had come through a great persecution, surviving prison and the lions' den to oversee a time of peace and rebuilding; the faithful visited his grave, seeking blessings.[110] The *History of the Patriarchs* reinforces its portrayal of Zacharias as a saint in two ways.[111] In the first place, his biography rather surprisingly contains a long and to some extent parallel passage about his Syrian Orthodox contemporary, John VII bar 'Abdun (1004–1033), who courageously confessed the "orthodox" faith before the Byzantine emperor and his patriarch and who patiently endured exile near Constantinople.[112] In the second place, the biography of Patriarch Zacharias includes a brief collection of his *miracles*. As miracles go, they are more curious than impressive; one consists in healing a deacon who had been stricken with leprosy (as a consequence of a sexual transgression) by having him stand, fasting, in a barrel of brine for forty days![113] But no matter. The *Life-Miracles* form is a standard feature of medieval Coptic hagiography,[114] and the text's use of it asserts Zacharias's sainthood in no uncertain terms.

Saints and Sinners

Zacharias's successor as patriarch was a learned monk of the Monastery of St. Macarius named Shenoute (Shenoute II, #65, 1032–1046), the ambitious and rather vindictive patriarch mentioned at the beginning of this chapter. Once elected, Shenoute promptly went back on his pledge to the Alexandrians to avoid simony and sold a bishopric for six hundred dinars.[115] The deacon Buqayrah al-Rashidi, a saintly notable of Cairo-Misr who had been a pillar of the faith during the persecution of al-Hakim,[116] did his best to dissuade the new patriarch from his simoniacal inclinations, but in the end without success. Buqayrah not only saw the written agreement that he had made with the patriarch publicly torn to pieces, but also received a beating from the patriarch's disciples.[117] Bishop Michael's judgment on Shenoute's reign is stark: there was "no salvation" in it,[118] and through his simony he had achieved an "evil name which God and the people abhor."[119] And yet, the biographer mitigates his judgment somewhat by reminding his readers of some harsh financial realities: the patriarch-elect would normally owe three thousand dinars to the Treasury,[120] one hundred to the *wali* of Alexandria, and five hundred per year to the Alexandrians, as well as expenses and land taxes;[121] the bishops' remissions from the *diyariyat* would not necessarily cover expenditures. And so, Michael says, "necessity caused them [the patriarchs] to do what they did in this matter, on account of what was demanded of them in the way of money and of what they undertook in the way of burdens."[122]

Shenoute died, "still desirous of the world,"[123] just a few years before Bishop Michael wrote his biographies. While Michael painted a bleak picture of certain patriarchs, in the end his contribution to the *History of the Patriarchs* is not pessimistic in tone: although the Coptic Orthodox patriarchate faced serious internal difficulties, God continued to raise up saints within it, around it, or even in spite of it. Michael's four long biographies deal with a remarkable saint (Abraham), a lover of luxury about whom his biographer could say little good (Philotheus), an apparent weakling who had sainthood thrust upon him by crisis (Zacharias), and a worldly patriarch the blessing of whose prayers, all the same, his biographer covets (Shenoute). As varied as these stories are, interspersed among them are many examples of lived holiness, ranging from a young Muslim convert (al-Wadih ibn Raja') to a Syrian Orthodox patriarch (John VII of Antioch), and from a senior civil servant (Buqayrah al-Rashidi) to a humble builder (Bishop Michael's father). Bishop Michael may have called a spade a spade, but he was confident that the garden was still the Lord's.

Five

Transitions

Christodoulos (#66, 1046–1077)
Cyril II (#67, 1078–1092)
Michael IV (#68, 1092–1102)
Macarius II (#69, 1102–1128)
Gabriel II (ibn Turayk) (#70, 1131–1145)
Michael V (#71, 1145–1146)
John V (#72, 1147–1166)
Mark III (ibn Zur'ah) (#73, 1166–1189)
John VI (#74, 1189–1216)

Language Shift, Lay Concerns, and Ecclesiastical History
Arabic as a Christian Language?

One of the more curious texts of the Copto-Arabic heritage is an apocalypse whose anonymous author puts his words into the mouth of a seventh-century Coptic saint, Samuel of the Monastery of Qalamun.[1] According to the story, Samuel complains about what the future holds for the Coptic Church:

> [The Christians] do something else, that if I were to tell you of it your hearts would be greatly pained: they are abandoning the beautiful Coptic language, in which the Holy Spirit has spoken many times through the mouths of their spiritual fathers, and they are teaching their children from infancy to speak the language of the Arabs, and to take pride in it! Even the priests and monks—they as well!—dare to speak in Arabic and to take pride in it, and that within the sanctuary! Woe upon woe!!

> O my beloved children, what shall I say in these times, when readers in the Church do not understand what they are reading,

or what they are saying, because they have forgotten their language? These truly are miserable people, deserving of being wept over, because they have forgotten their language and speak the language of the *hajarah*.[2]

But woe to every Christian who teaches his son the language of the *hajarah* from his infancy, and causes him to forget the language of his fathers! . . .

[Later, an elderly monk says to Samuel:] "Understand what I tell you, Samuel, my son. At the time when the Christians shall have the audacity to speak the language of the *hajarah* inside the sanctuary . . . woe to the Christians at that time! Woe multiplied seven-fold!"[3]

The text—composed in Coptic but preserved, ironically enough, only in Arabic translation[4]—bears eloquent witness both to the phenomenon of the Arabization of the Coptic community, as well as to the alarm that this phenomenon occasioned in conservative monastic circles. As eloquent as the text is, so far it has frustrated the best efforts of scholars to determine its date (although recent studies tend toward the tenth or eleventh centuries).[5] In any event, the text is a single localized witness to a complex process of linguistic transition, which undoubtedly affected the Egyptian Christian population at varying rates according to social and geographical location; in all probability, Arabization proceeded most quickly among the class of Coptic lay notables in Alexandria and Misr-Cairo.

The *Apocalypse of Samuel* is but one example among many of originally Coptic texts that have only been preserved in Arabic translation. Indeed, the first four chapters of this book have followed originally Coptic-language sources that today are known *only* through their translation into Arabic and incorporation into the compilation known as the *History of the Patriarchs*. But unlike the *Apocalypse of Samuel*, for the *History of the Patriarchs* we know to whom we are indebted for the translation and preservation of these sources: a well-to-do Alexandrian lay notable and deacon named Mawhub ibn Mansur ibn Mufarrij.[6] In the 1080s he led a project[7] to gather Coptic-language sources for the lives of the first sixty-five patriarchs of the Coptic Orthodox Church from monastery libraries and translate them into Arabic—thereby creating what has been called "Part One" of the *History of the Patriarchs*.[8] Mawhub, however, did not stop with the last *Life* for which he had a Coptic source, that of Patriarch Shenoute II (#65, 1032–1046).

Instead, soon after completing his great work of compilation and translation he composed—now directly in Arabic—biographies of two contemporary patriarchs, Christodoulos (#66, 1046–1077) and Cyril II (#67, 1078–1092).[9] Later, three other authors, laymen like Mawhub (although one became patriarch), provided the growing collection with biographies of seven more patriarchs, through John VI (#74, 1189–1216).[10] Together, the nine Arabic-language *Lives* by Mawhub and his continuators comprise what may be considered "Part Two" of the *History of the Patriarchs*.[11] It is this "Part Two" that determines the scope of the present chapter.

As will become evident in the course of this (and subsequent) chapters, the transition from a Part One compiled out of Coptic sources written by monks and bishops to a Part Two written in Arabic by lay notables reflects significant shifts in the life and culture of the Coptic Orthodox Church. Of special significance is the linguistic shift: despite cries of woe in the *Apocalypse of Samuel*, the process of Arabization was proceeding apace among literate Copts. Indeed, the compilation of a patriarchal history in Arabic appears to be part of a larger enterprise in the late eleventh century that began to provide the Copts with a working library of Arabic-language ecclesiastical resources, in canon law and theology as well as church history.[12] Both patriarchs Christodoulos and Cyril II issued sets of Arabic-language canons, shortly after 1046 and in 1086, respectively.[13] An Arabic-language theological florilegium entitled *The Confession of the Fathers* was compiled around 1078; it gathered together key patristic and medieval theological texts, including many in exposition and defense of the Coptic one-nature Christology.[14] While the precise course of the linguistic shift by which a once largely Coptic-speaking community became an Arabic-speaking one is still a matter for debate, these eleventh-century literary monuments indicate that far-reaching changes in the culture of the Coptic Orthodox community were in the making.

Mawhub: A Historian between Two Worlds

Mawhub ibn Mansur ibn Mufarrij was undoubtedly formed as an ecclesiastical historian in part by the *Lives* he had translated from Coptic into Arabic. In his biographies of the patriarchs Christodoulos and Cyril II, we encounter interpretive patterns characteristic of earlier patriarchal biographers like John the Deacon (see Chapter Two) and John the Writer (see Chapter Three). For Mawhub, as for these earlier historians, trials and tribulations may be explained as divine chastisement. At the same time, one must understand that Satan is ever on the loose, stirring up trouble for the Christian community from the outside as well as from within. But while Satan may rage, the power of God flares out in unexpected places, and God's retribution regularly catches up with evildoers.

Mawhub had plenty of material to which to apply these tools for the interpretation of history. The period about which he wrote, 1046–1092, lies entirely within the reign of the fifth Fatimid caliph of Egypt, al-Mustansir (1036–1094)—who, for the greatest part of his exceptionally long reign, enjoyed little real power and was often little more than a figurehead and even prisoner of a series of *wazirs* and military commanders.[15] One powerful *wazir*, al-Yazuri (held office 1050–1058), is remembered in Mawhub's account as a persecutor who in 1057 closed churches, arrested the patriarch, tortured three bishops to death, and extorted funds—but divine retribution quickly overtook him, as al-Yazuri was soon thereafter banished and executed.[16] Other officials who had contributed to the persecution of the Church likewise came to unpleasant ends. Take, for example, the *qadi* al-Sinraqi, who had egged al-Yazuri to action against the Christians with his complaints that Christodoulos's patriarchal residence of Damru in the Delta had become a "second Constantinople."[17] Mawhub reports that a "wonder was shewn forth" in him: the persecuting *qadi* developed an infection in his lower body and was consumed by worms, which could not be drawn out of him even when his wounds were dressed with raw meat! "This (was) a reward in the present world, and he experienced great difficulty until he died an evil death."[18]

If the trials of the late 1050s could be interpreted according to the pattern of diabolical trouble-making followed by divine retribution, the following decade brought suffering that could only be interpreted as a "time of great chastisement" for the Church.[19] The Great Tribulation *(al-shiddah al-'uzma)* of 1066–1073 came about when civil war between military factions severely disrupted normal agricultural life: to the misery of arbitrary violence, destruction, and looting was added that of inflation and famine, exacerbated by outbreaks of disease.[20] The appearance of a pair of comets (according to the text; Halley's comet is known to have appeared in 1066) and an earthquake (in 1068) heightened the sense of apocalyptic breakdown.[21] At one point, Patriarch Christodoulos—then in residence in Damru—was seized, tortured (suspended by the testicles, we are told), and held for ransom by Lawatah Berbers who were then terrorizing the Delta.[22] Desperately seeking a way out of anarchy and his own powerlessness, the caliph al-Mustansir invited the governor of 'Akka, the Armenian general Badr al-Jamali, to invade Egypt. Badr, to whom a contemporary apocalyptic text refers as "the Terror,"[23] moved in swiftly with his own troops in 1074 and with brutal decisiveness asserted his authority (as *amir al-juyush*, commander-in-chief, and governor, leaving the caliph as a figurehead) and restored order—for which Mawhub offered a prayer of thanksgiving.[24] With Badr in power (1074–1094), the remaining years of Christodoulos's patriarchate, as well as the patriarchate of Cyril II, were relatively peaceful. Indeed, under Badr there was an influx of Armenians into Egypt, including Armenian Christians, who shared the Christological confession of the Copts.[25] For a time, medieval Copts had the rare experience of receiving and providing hospitality to coreligionists (including the Armenian patriarch) who were well connected with the supreme authority in the land.[26]

As well as employing traditional models (Satanic irruptions/divine retribution; divine chastisement) for the interpretation of this period, Mawhub inherited a number of traditional motifs for depicting the patriarchs whose biographies he composed. They were, in the first place, divinely chosen. Holy monks foresaw the elevation of both Christodoulos and Cyril to the patriarchate.[27] Mawhub himself heard Patriarch Christodoulos relate that, just before the arrival of the party that came to take him to his consecration, he dreamt that Saint Peter and Saint Mark came to him and offered him a bunch of keys.[28]

In the second place, the patriarchs were saints. Mawhub's case for the sainthood of Patriarch Christodoulos seems a bit forced, tempered by his knowledge of a not-entirely-successful patriarchate. He reports, for example, that a large number of bishops moved to depose Christodoulos (for reasons that are not made clear) early in his patriarchate, although a prominent *archon* took the lead in smoothing matters over.[29] Christodoulos's financial dealings avoided simony, it appears, by not much more than a technicality: claiming 50 percent of the income of each diocese for the patriarchate, he demanded an immediate "loan on the half of the See" upon a bishop's consecration.[30] His pleas for financial support during the troubled years of his patriarchate brought a gentle rebuke from the patriarch of Antioch: "What wealth do we possess . . . beyond the riches of the Lord Christ, our God?"[31] But whatever doubts Mawhub may have had about Christodoulos's financial or other dealings, early in his biography he exploits the *Life-Miracles* hagiographical genre to assure the reader of the patriarch's sanctity: "miracles . . . were manifested through him."[32] Mawhub goes on to list three "miracles": Christodoulos excommunicated a man who promptly became paralyzed and died; he refused to lift the excommunication of the nephew of a high-ranking Copt, despite the pleas of the notables of Misr; and he had the caliph's personal physician, a Syrian-background Christian, physically thrown out of his presence in the midst of a liturgical dispute (and got away with it).[33] If readers are inclined to wonder whether these "miracles" are indications of ill-temper rather than sanctity, Mawhub quickly reassures them that Christodoulos "did *many* wondrous deeds in Cairo (Misr), the description of which would be lengthy."[34]

As for Cyril II, Mawhub assures the reader that he was a saintly monk, even if he was perceived by many contemporaries as a man of little learning who could easily be controlled. Indeed, a number of bishops (especially from the Delta) vied to wrest that control for themselves, away from the members of Cyril's inner circle (including his scribe, Bishop Afraham of Dibqu', who was particularly detested by the opposition party).[35] In contrast to the perception that Cyril was ill-educated, Mawhub reports that, once he became patriarch, Cyril set himself assiduously to the study of scripture and its Coptic-language commentaries, and could answer questions and explain the scripture in a way superior to that of the bishops and priests.[36] For Mawhub, the winds of church politics may have blown strong during Cyril's patriarchate, but at the storm's calm center there was a saintly student of scripture.

In the third place, Mawhub does not neglect to share with the reader the drama of the encounter between patriarch and ruler, in scenes reminiscent of previous such meetings, especially the paradigmatic encounter between Patriarch Benjamin (#38, 623–662) and the Arab conqueror of Egypt, 'Amr ibn al-'As.[37] Shortly after the Armenian general Badr al-Jamali had assumed power in 1074, he had Patriarch Christodoulos arrested because of a complaint that had been lodged against him. After a hearing in which the patriarch's name was cleared (and the author of the false report sentenced to death), the two men took each other's measure. "A long conversation took place between [the general] and the father, the patriarch, Abba Christodoulos at this council-meeting in which the father, the patriarch, displayed virtue, understanding and leadership, so that his worth was magnified in the eyes of those present"—including Badr al-Jamali, who did him honor.[38] As for Patriarch Cyril II, Badr was himself responsible in the year 1086 for calling a council, held in his own garden, to deal with the controversies swirling around Cyril. Mawhub, rather remarkably, casts the Muslim Badr in a prophetic role: he "addressed a severe speech which God pronounced through him" to the bishops. But as for the patriarch, Badr "showed kindness . . . , and he honoured him, and he revered him and he extolled his rank and his case before them, and he ordered him to depart to his church."[39]

Finally, Mawhub continues a pattern that we have encountered in previous chapters: that patriarchs are portrayed not only in the light of their own holiness, but also in the light of *the saints of their day*.[40] Indeed, he carries this pattern to an extreme. If Mawhub could only find three rather unconvincing miracles for Patriarch Christodoulos, he records a series of ten miracles attributed to the holy monk Bisus of the Monastery of St. John Kame, who had the gift of clairvoyance, healed a leper and a blind man, traveled long distances instantaneously, and displayed superhuman strength in defense of his monastery.[41] Mawhub catalogues the miracles of other holy men scattered through the land, and records instances of icons that emitted light, tears, sweat, or blood[42]—or that worked vengeance on oppressors.[43] Of special interest for all later historians of the Coptic Orthodox Church are Mawhub's catalogues that "map" the Egyptian sacred geography: in addition to his list of living saints and their monasteries or hermitages, he provides a roster of bishops and their sees,[44] a detailed catalog of relics and their shrines,[45] and a list of sites associated with the Holy Family's Flight into Egypt.[46]

For all the traditional elements in Mawhub's portrayal of patriarchs Christodoulos and Cyril II, there is something quite new about the way he writes history (apart from the mere fact of doing so in Arabic). While the patriarchs provide an occasion for Mawhub to write, they are not his sole interest. This may be due, in part, to the fact that the patriarchs about whom he wrote were not normally at the center of events. Christodoulos preferred to stay at the patriarchal residence in Damru, in the Delta, and Cyril II would have preferred to stay there, except that after 1084 the new military governor Badr al-Jamali required his presence in the vicinity of Cairo.[47]

Mawhub devotes considerable space, as we have seen, to cataloging miracles and shrines; he also devotes long passages to his own family and other lay notables in the Church, or to events in the secular world.[48] Perhaps we can say that Mawhub lived simultaneously in two worlds: a world of practical affairs, in which lay leaders of the community did their best to navigate political vicissitudes against a background of sweeping historical movements such as the irruption of the Seljuk Turks into the Middle East; and a world of wonders, in which holy monks practiced bilocation and icons might weep, bleed, or sweat. These worlds could impinge upon one other in curious ways. As Brigitte Voile observed, when Mawhub was confronted with the holy man Bisus's mysterious ability to travel significant distances in almost no time at all, he brought all his practical worldly wisdom to the interrogation of the holy man and those who witnessed his near-simultaneous presence in monasteries separated by a three-hour journey.[49] At other times, however, the two worlds are curiously distinct. At the moment of the community's greatest need, icons bled and sweated and saints appeared to those who sought their intercession—but to no practical effect.[50] One Copt had a vision of St. Mercurius, who showed him a vast pit filled with the horses and weapons of the equestrian saints—which could not be used. The divine chastisement had to run its course; in the meantime, the Copts' beloved equestrian saints were prohibited from making intercession for the people.[51]

Ibn al-Qulzumi: A Critic of Patriarchs

The *History of the Patriarchs* as compiled by Mawhub proved useful in the Coptic Orthodox community, in which it was not only copied, but regularly "updated" by later writers. Mawhub's first continuator was an *archon* of Cairo named Yuhanna ibn Sa'id, known as Ibn al-Qulzumi, who was knowledgeable in Coptic theology, an accomplished Arabic stylist, and very much a citizen of the practical world of secular and ecclesial politics. His primary ecclesiastical loyalty was to Bishop Sanhut of Misr (Old Cairo), a fact that decisively colored his portrayal of the two patriarchs about whom he wrote, Michael IV (#68, 1092–1102) and Macarius II (#69, 1102–1128).[52] With the move of the patriarchate to Misr (Old Cairo) under Patriarch Cyril II, and to the Mu'allaqah Church in particular, the presence of a Bishop of Misr at the Abu Sarjah Church just a few yards away could well be experienced as awkward: precisely what authority did the patriarch possess in his own backyard? Patriarch Michael wanted the matter settled decisively: he actively worked to depose Bishop Sanhut and to make Abu Sarjah a patriarchal church.[53] In a remarkable reversal of a familiar narrative pattern in the *History of the Patriarchs*, Ibn al-Qulzumi presents the pope in the role of persecutor (like Cyrus al-Muqawqas just before the Arab conquest), and reports that Bishop Sanhut repeatedly had to flee to the south (like Patriarch Benjamin in Cyrus's time),[54] on one occasion to the Monastery of St. Samuel of Qalamun,[55] on another to the Monastery of St. Severus at Asyut.[56] During the saintly bishop's last exile, the patriarch fell ill; Ibn al-Qulzumi reports that his last words were, "I have caught the plague." Anba Sanhut was able to return to his see, amid general rejoicing.[57]

When Bishop Sanhut went to his rest and the time came to consecrate a successor, Michael's successor, Patriarch Macarius II, stalled as long as he could, taking months to respond to requests, and then, in letters written in exquisitely courteous Arabic prose (Ibn al-Qulzumi preserves the correspondence), devising reasons for further inaction.[58] Eventually a new bishop of Misr was consecrated, but it is clear that Ibn al-Qulzumi had not come to think highly of Macarius II. Indeed, much of Ibn al-Qulzumi's pair of patriarchal *Lives* is not devoted to the patriarchs and affairs of the Church at all, but rather to secular history, including the succession to both Badr al-Jamali (by his son al-Afdal) and the Fatimid caliph al-Mustansir in 1094, and the appearance of western Crusaders in the region at the end of the decade.

At this point in the story of Coptic Orthodox history-writing, which is now exclusively in Arabic and dominated by the concerns of lay notables, the popes appear to be at risk of falling out of the narrative almost completely. However, that is about to change, with the accession of a lay notable well-schooled in Arabic—a member of the historians' own class—to the patriarchate. To him we now turn.

Gabriel II ibn Turayk: An Attempt at Reform
Introduction: New Sources[59]

Of all the patriarchs treated in Part Two of the *History of the Patriarchs*, it is Macarius's successor, Gabriel II ibn Turayk (#70, 1131–1145), who commands the greatest interest from—note, now, the *plural*—his chroniclers. The *History of the Patriarchs* continues to be an important source: Gabriel's biography and those of his two immediate successors were written by a later pope (but, like Gabriel, a layman before becoming pope), Mark III ibn Zur'ah (#73, 1166–1189).[60] In addition to Mark's work, we possess a very interesting biography in another patriarchal history, the *History of the Fathers, the Patriarchs* attributed to Yusab, bishop of Fuwwah in the mid-thirteenth century.[61] The work is in fact a seventeenth-century compilation, so that while it is convenient to refer to "Yusab," the attribution should not be taken literally.[62] This anonymity by no means diminishes the importance of the work; in fact, "Yusab's" biography of Patriarch Gabriel II is rich in detail, independent of Mark's biography, and may well come from one of Gabriel's contemporaries.[63] Yet another work that includes twelfth-century material is the *History of the Churches and Monasteries of Egypt*, attributed sometimes to Abu l-Makarim Sa'dallah ibn Jirjis ibn Mas'ud and sometimes to one Abu Salih al-Armani. It is a layered work that saw its first stages of compilation in the 1160s, and that preserves a number of notices concerning Gabriel and other popes treated in this chapter.[64]

Before he became patriarch, Gabriel II had been the layman Abu l-'Ala' Sa'id ibn Turayk, a civil servant in the Fatimid administration and deacon at the Church of Abu Sayfayn (St. Mercurius) in Old Cairo.[65] Made patriarch at age 47, for fourteen years he strove to renew and reform many aspects of the life of the Coptic Orthodox Church. In particular, he forbade all forms of simony, and is remembered for having consecrated fifty-three bishops without receiving any money. He issued decisive canons on this as on many other matters, so that his is a significant name in the history of Coptic canon law.[66]

Gabriel's patriarchate largely coincides with the caliphate of al-Hafiz, the seventh of the Fatimid caliphs of Egypt (1132–1146).[67] Like many of the Fatimid caliphs, he was favorably inclined toward Christians, and for a brief period actually had a Christian *wazir*, the Armenian general Bahram (in office 1135–1137). Thus the Copts were usually able to obtain just treatment from the Fatimid administration in Gabriel's days. Exceptions occurred in the year 1134, during the revolt of the caliph's son al-Hasan, who had Gabriel arrested, imprisoned, and released only upon payment of one thousand dinars.[68] A few years later, the Christian *wazir* Bahram's pro-Armenian and pro-Christian activities led to a reaction and revolt that brought a certain Ridwan ibn Walkhashi to the vizierate for a time, during which churches were plundered, the *jizyah* raised, and discriminatory measures against *dhimmi*s enacted.[69] Other challenges in Gabriel's days included famine and disease in the last five years of his patriarchate, during which time Gabriel took measures to stabilize the grain supply, especially for the preparation of Eucharistic loaves.[70]

We find a number of traditional elements in the way that Patriarch Gabriel is portrayed by his biographers. As a child, we are told, he "played church" with himself in the role of patriarch,[71] and his elevation to the patriarchate was foreseen by a Syrian holy man.[72] Mark ibn Zur'ah reports that "God performed at the hands of this patriarch wonders and miracles and good works,"[73] and immediately follows that comment with three stories about remarkable happenings in which Patriarch Gabriel had a role.[74] One of these stories concerns a vision that Gabriel saw during a serious illness a year before his death, in which "a company of priests and monks, and with them Gospels and crosses and censers" came to greet Gabriel—and promised to return in a year.[75]

If, however, there are many elements in Gabriel's biographies that are traditional, there is much in them that is specific to Gabriel and to Gabriel's times—and that provides a vivid picture of the challenges facing the Coptic community, and a reforming patriarch's attempts to address them. It may be worth, then, devoting a few pages to specific, arresting, and sometimes even startling elements that we find in Gabriel's biographies.

Strange Religiosity, Ready Conversion

It is especially in the *History of the Fathers, the Patriarchs* attributed to Yusab that we find several stories that point to instances of religiosity of a strange and somewhat disturbing sort in Gabriel's days. For example, a monk of St. Macarius claimed that he could prophesy the future, and even offered his services to the *wazir* Bahram, who, however, "found him to be diseased in his intellect and sent him away."[76] Yusab goes on to report on groups that celebrated the Sacrifice of Michael—that is, animal sacrifices on the Feast of the Archangel Michael. They asked Patriarch Gabriel for his opinion on the matter, and were not pleased when he responded that "when the Lord Christ came, he abolished the sacrifices of idols, and established the sacrifices of almsgiving to God."[77] Later, while reporting on some of Gabriel's canons (including the rule that widowed priests not be allowed to keep servant girls), Yusab mentions Gabriel's prohibition of all forms of sorcery:

> He wrote another decree, in which he censured those who made use of astrology, charms, astrolabes, sorcery or spellbinding, [threatening them] with definitive excommunication.[78]

Taken one by one, none of these reports is particularly strange. Apocalypticism is a red thread that runs through the history of Egyptian Christianity.[79] The characteristic Egyptian Christian veneration of angels could sometimes lead to odd observances, as we know from tenth- and eleventh-century witnesses to the cult of the Angel of Death in the far south of the country.[80] And with recent investigations into the various ritual practices that can be labeled "magical,"[81] we must not be surprised to find references to them in a witness to twelfth-century Egyptian religion. Still, Yusab leaves the impression that there was some malady within the Egyptian Christian community that had, as one of its symptoms, a search hither and yon—and *not* primarily in the liturgy, the scripture, or the theological tradition—for ways of securing one's place in the spiritual world.

Another sign that all may not have been well in the Church in Gabriel's day was the ease with which members of the community left the community and converted to Islam. There were, of course, financial incentives to conversion. Yusab reports that at a certain point, probably during the vizierate of Ridwan ibn Walkhashi (who raised the rates for the *jizyah*), Christians were in dire straits because of the taxes being assessed on them: "some of them departed and became monks, and some of them converted to Islam."[82] But some of the stories from Gabriel's time indicate that conversion had become almost a casual weapon in ecclesiastical disputes. Mark ibn Zur'ah tells the story of the monk Buqayrah, who offered the patriarch money in return for his consecration as Bishop of Akhmim. When Gabriel refused, in strict accordance with his no-simony policy, Buqayrah tried to bring pressure on Gabriel by enlisting the aid—for a consideration—of the son of the caliph. Gabriel successfully resisted this pressure also, but then we read:

Afterward the patriarch learned that [Buqayrah] had great
wealth, and he feared that if he barred him from the episcopate
that *he would abandon his religion* and that his wealth would
be lost. And so he consecrated him for another bishopric,
other than the one he had requested. By that he intended that
his soul be won—and his wealth not lost.[83]

Buqayrah delivered the money he had promised to the patriarch, who
refused to look at it, but directed that it be spent on building a keep for
Dayr al-Sham', a monastery that Gabriel had restored after it had fallen
into decay.[84]

The Buqayrah episode might strike a present-day reader as a rather
shocking victory of expediency over principle, a blot on the patriarch's
otherwise immaculate record of fifty-three simony-free episcopal conse-
crations. For Gabriel's biographer, however, the episode is an example of
astute leadership: a disappointed Buqayrah, even though a monk and aspirant
to episcopal office in the Coptic Orthodox Church, could very well have
converted to Islam—and the patriarch, by making startling and perhaps even
humiliating concessions, prevented it, to the benefit of Buqayrah's soul *and*
the financial stability of the Coptic community.

Another anecdote from Gabriel's patriarchate is told in each of the three
major histories of the period.[85] It goes something as follows:[86] a leading
Coptic civil servant by the name of Abu l-Yumn Yahya ibn al-'Ubaydi[87]
withdrew from his post and devoted himself to the care of the church at Dayr
al-Tin, to the south of Old Cairo, between Lake Habash and the Nile. The
monastery with its lush gardens occupied a beautiful and agriculturally
productive site. But church authorities began to receive disturbing reports
from the monastery. According to Yusab, Abu l-Yumn had appointed *himself*
priest in the church, even though he was totally unqualified for the position.
It was also reported that Abu l-Yumn hired Muslim bakers to prepare the
Eucharistic loaves.[88] And all the sources agree that Patriarch Gabriel received
reports of other suspicious but unspecified deeds or conspiracies. Gabriel
summoned Abu l-Yumn and rebuked him; but after some period of struggle
Abu l-Yumn converted to Islam, leading to a battle over the monastery's
property, in which Abu l-Yumn established a mosque.[89]

In his version of the story, Yusab relates Abu l-Yumn's eventual fate: in
the end, he ran afoul of a prominent *faqih* and was arrested, viciously beaten,
and ejected from the monastery property and thrown out into the cemetery,
no more to disturb the peace of the Christian community.[90] For Yusab, the
story shows how Satan stirs up trouble within the Church, but that God

triumphs in the end and brings retribution to his foes. By contrast, Mark ibn Zur'ah tells the story of Abu l-Yumn as that of one of Patriarch Gabriel's failures. The patriarch had been too severe with Abu l-Yumn, too quick to believe the evil reports about him.

> This matter was grievous to the father, the patriarch. He deeply regretted what had happened, and was never again severe with anyone, out of fear that another might act in the same fashion.[91]

Modern interpreters have followed the lead of Mark ibn Zur'ah and have interpreted the incident as providing a glimpse into Gabriel's character: he was of an "impetuous temperament, but humble."[92] But is there more that can be drawn from this incident? What may be said about a Church in which discipline is not just difficult but risky because of the very real possibility that a disaffected monk or lay leader might convert to Islam (and take church property with them)? Do the stories about conversion to Islam in Gabriel's day, like the stories about manifestations of strange religiosity related earlier, point to some underlying weakness or need within the Church of the time?

Linguistic In/competence

A striking feature in Gabriel's biographies is the number of times one encounters comments about linguistic competence. The patriarch is praised for his facility in Arabic: according to Yusab, "the patriarch could write in Arabic, and had a good flowing hand and beautiful pronunciation."[93] This statement is borne out by manuscript studies: we possess two Arabic manuscripts, one a work of apologetics and one on the preparation of the *myron* (the oil of chrismation), which were copied from originals in Gabriel's handwriting.[94] In addition, Mark ibn Zur'ah assures us that Gabriel was doubly competent, "a good copyist of Coptic and Arabic, copying for himself many books and volumes which he had bought of the Old and the New Testaments, of what was suitable for the Holy Church and the Christian (al-Masihi) religion."[95]

Not everyone in the Church of Gabriel's day shared this double competence. Yusab informs us that Gabriel's personal secretary, Bishop Butrus of Sarsina, knew only Coptic; presumably the former government secretary Gabriel was more in need of clerical assistance in that language than in Arabic. Yusab also gives us a rather amusing detail about Abu l-Yumn, the civil servant who administered the church at Dayr al-Tin. According to

Yusab, Abu l-Yumn originally brought in priests to take the services at the church, but then:

> [H]is soul became jealous, and *he* became priest over the church. He didn't know Coptic, so he strove, to the best of his ability, to memorize the liturgy by rote repetition.[96]

Gabriel, according to Yusab, would have allowed Abu l-Yumn to perform the liturgy in this uncomprehending fashion, as long as he reformed other aspects of his activities.[97]

Having priests reciting the liturgy in uncomprehended Coptic, even if a real possibility in Gabriel's day, was by no means an ideal state of affairs. Therefore we find Gabriel addressing the issue in Canon Ten of the set of thirty-two canons promulgated early in his patriarchate, in which he exhorts priests to prepare their own children for the priesthood:

> Teach your children the books of the Church. . . . It is necessary that you also begin to teach the priesthood to your children at the outset of each day, before the Arabic [instruction].[98]

Patriarch Gabriel here takes it for granted that, even for the children of priests, Arabic will be the primary language of instruction. His hope, however, was to raise up a generation of priests who would be competent in the Coptic ecclesiastical books as well.

The problem of the incomprehension of the Coptic liturgy was not limited to government civil servants such as Abu l-Yumn, as we see from Canon Three of the same set of thirty-two canons. It reads as follows:

> It is incumbent upon each of you, O bishops, that he instruct the Christian people whom he shepherds, and that he admonish them to memorize the Doxology, the Prayer that our Lord Christ taught to his disciples, and the Holy Creed in the tongue that the people know and understand, so that in this way they may pray during the prayer, and not be yammering in a language they don't know. And whoever is able to do more than that shall receive his desire.[99]

This extraordinarily important text bears witness to a situation in which great numbers of Arabic-speaking Egyptian Christians were going to church without understanding any part of the liturgy, still exclusively in the Coptic language. But if this was so, it may provide one key to under-standing the malady within the Coptic Church to which we have already alluded, the symptoms of which included outbreaks of strange religiosity, and also of the threat (or actuality) of conversion to Islam being exploited for advantage in church political disputes. Gabriel found himself charged to shepherd an under-catechized Church, full of people who were naturally religious but who lacked the basic Christian formation necessary to sort out traditional church teaching from heresy, or Christian sense from nonsense. Perhaps many of them, almost by a process of osmosis, were becoming social-ized into the specifically religious language of the mosque. A very well-known preface from a work entitled *Kitab al-Idah (The Book of the Elucidation),* usually but probably incorrectly attributed to Sawirus ibn al-Muqaffaʻ, sums up this possibility eloquently. There, the root of Christian confusion about the core doctrines of Trinity, Incarnation, and redemption is identified as the believers' "mingling with the *hunafa*" (Christian code for the Muslims) and "the disappearance of their language, through which they know the truth of their religion."[100] The writer goes on:

> It has come to be the case that they do not hear any mention of "the Trinity" among themselves except rarely; nor do they hear any mention of "the Son of God" except in a metaphorical sense. Instead, most of what they hear is that God is "unique" *(fard)*, "everlasting" *(samad)*,[101] and the rest of the language that the *hunafa'* use. The believers have become accustomed to this, and have been brought up with it, so that the mention of "the Son of God" has come to be difficult for them; they do not know any interpretation or meaning for it.[102]

Gabriel's reforming activity may best be seen against the background of a serious deficit in fundamental Christian education within the Coptic Orthodox Church, brought about, at least in part, by the community's loss in competence in the Coptic language and its slowness to respond, either with renewed catechesis in Coptic or with new resources in Arabic.[103] Gabriel, we have seen, was concerned about competence in *both* languages. For him, the Church requires a clergy that is fluent in its own heritage, carried by the Coptic language. But the people must be taught and must know how to pray—in a language they know and understand. .

To what extent did Gabriel encourage Arabic-language catechesis in the Church? The Syriac *Chronicle* of the Syrian Orthodox patriarch Michael the Great (1126–1199) provides a precious notice:

[Gabriel] was competent in doctrine, and also very capable in writing the Arabic language. Seeing that all the people of Egypt were speaking the Arabic language and using Arabic script, since Arab domination had long held sway in all that country, he took care to translate the books of the Old and New Testament, other books, and the priestly rituals *into the Arabic language*, so that the hearers—that is, all the people— could understand the holy books.[104]

If this report is correct, we see that Gabriel's work in teaching the faith in Arabic was not limited to the Doxology, the Lord's Prayer, and the Creed. Rather, Gabriel undertook, or at least inspired, a major endeavor to translate the fundamental books of the faith into Arabic.

Opposition to Reform

Another striking feature of the biographies of Gabriel is that, as an activist reformer, he ran into controversy and opposition at every turn. He began his patriarchate with a quarrel with the monks of St. Macarius over an addition to the text of the final confession before the communion, "I believe and confess that this is the Body of our Lord and Savior Jesus Christ, which he took from the God-bearer, the blessed Virgin Mary, *and it became one with his divinity*." Finally, a compromise was reached by adding the words "without confusion and without mingling"—although this formula was *not* immediately accepted in Upper Egypt.[105] And this is the typical pattern of stories about Gabriel's reforms. He would make a decision or issue a decree . . . and someone regularly refused to accept it.

Shortly after becoming patriarch, for example, Gabriel forbade the burial of the dead in churches, but:

> it came to his attention that a group of people had *transgressed and disobeyed his command* in that matter, since they had buried the *qummus* Bessus in the Church of Harat al-Rum in Cairo....[106]

Another unpopular reform had to do with priests and their drinking habits:

> When he took on the headship [of the community], he commanded that the priests should not drink a great deal of wine, and he defined for them the amount they should drink. *They did not obey*, but continued according to their custom.[107]

And again:

> They had another habit, which was that the priests ordained
> by the patriarch used to lord it over priests ordained by the
> bishops. Gabriel did not leave them to behave in this way, but
> rebuked this behavior and insisted that they work together in
> every place. They all accepted his command, *except* for the
> clergy of Alexandria and of the wilderness of St. Macarius.[108]

Earlier we mentioned that a group of people asked Gabriel about the Sacrifice of Michael, and were unhappy when he criticized it as a pre-Christian practice. According to Yusab, they responded to the patriarch with impertinence[109] and "departed from him, determined that they would not be changed in their customs."[110]

One of Gabriel's bigger showdowns with the community was over concubinage, which throughout the medieval period appears to have been practiced by those members of the Coptic bureaucratic class whose lives were most assimilated to those of their Muslim peers. According to Yusab, at the beginning of the Lenten fast one year Gabriel issued a decree forbidding the taking of concubines—but some refused to obey him and had the patriarch's decree trampled underfoot.[111]

Some Copts went so far as to question the patriarch's authority to issue canons. After Yusab presents Gabriel's prohibitions of widowed priests taking servant girls into their homes, and of any form of sorcery, he records that some people asked, "How is it that he writes these things in his own handwriting?"[112] This appears to be a question about Gabriel's authority to *issue* canons. Perhaps it is in the light of this question that we should interpret Gabriel's *Nomocanon*, an Arabic-language compilation of the Church's canonical tradition from carefully documented sources.[113] Such a collection may have served as a reference work for Gabriel—but also a justification for Gabriel's own canonical activity, showing it to be not an arbitrary claim to power, but rather an exercise of authority firmly grounded in the canonical traditions of the universal Church.

Having ascended to the patriarchal throne at a time of catechetical crisis within the Coptic Orthodox Church, due largely to the Church's delayed response to the seismic shifts in linguistic competence that were taking place within it, he energetically sought to bring the Church new discipline and vigor through renewed attention to the life of worship and to Christian education in both Coptic and Arabic. At the same time, it is clear that in the course of his reforming patriarchate he ruffled many feathers; we frequently hear that people ignored his canons and even questioned his competence to issue them. Gabriel ibn Turayk may be remembered today as a great reformer of the Coptic Orthodox Church, but it is not at all clear how effective he was in his own day.

After the Reform Attempt
How to Choose a Patriarch

Given the strength of the opposition to the vigorous and learned Patriarch Gabriel ibn Turayk, it is perhaps not entirely surprising that the man chosen to be his successor was elderly and illiterate, unable to sign his own name, let alone read the liturgy (which he feebly attempted to memorize). Patriarch Michael V (#71, 1145–1146) had been the saintly monk Mikha'il "of the Great Cell"[114] at the Monastery of St. Macarius, and although his short patriarchate included but three months of relatively good health in Misr, his biographer Mark ibn Zur'ah recalls that "the days of his patriarchate were exceedingly good"[115] and that "no one left his religion in his days."[116] Perhaps there was a general sense of relief in the community that the days of Gabriel's reforming zeal had passed, and that practices that Gabriel had forbidden— for example, the celebration of the Feast of the Martyr, a spring festival in which a relic of the martyr John of Sanhut was immersed in the Nile as prayers were said for the river's increase—could now be quietly restored.[117]

If literacy was *not* a qualification for the patriarchate, controversies over the selection of both Patriarch Michael and his successor occasioned reflection and public statements about what *were* the proper qualifications. Another monk of St. Macarius, a learned father named Yu'annis ibn Kadran, was ambitious to be made patriarch, and after the death of Patriarch Gabriel he very nearly succeeded in his quest, with the aid of a forged testimonial of lay notables' support and promises of money to bishops and the *wazir*.[118] Clerical and lay leaders in the Church (just barely) managed to block Yu'annis's bid, and instead adopted a method for choosing a patriarch that has remained an ideal in the Coptic Orthodox Church ever since: a sacred lottery, in which papers bearing the names of each of three worthy candidates would be placed in a box or on the altar along with a paper bearing the name of Christ. After a lengthy period of prayer, a small child would choose one paper.[119] Mikha'il's name was chosen in this way at the Mu'allaqah Church in Old Cairo,[120] and the pious monk, upon hearing his name read out in the church, conformed to the Coptic ideal of a worthy patriarch by dropping his monastic crutch and taking to his heels in flight.[121]

Mikha'il was eventually found, of course, and consecrated patriarch. But when he died just fifteen months later, Yu'annis ibn Kadran renewed his campaign for the patriarchate by enlisting the support of Muslim officials, who convened a council of leaders in the Church. Chronicler Mark ibn Zur'ah records a speech in which those leaders made their position on the qualifications of the patriarch plain:

> [W]hen they have the assurance that the man whom they desire to consecrate . . . fulfils the prescriptions of their law in the way of sanctity and religion and learning and good-conduct and chastity and charity . . . , they take him by force, without his choice, and they bind him with an iron fetter, lest he escape from them into the inner desert, and they have no power over him; for few are the people of this qualification. . . . And it is not lawful for them to consecrate . . . him who desires [the office], nor him who solicits [it] through the Sultan.[122]

The council in Cairo was followed by another in Alexandria, where the modest monk Yu'annis ibn Abi l-Fath of the Monastery of St. John the Little, rather than the ambitious Yu'annis ibn Kadran, was acclaimed by the assembly and consecrated Patriarch John V (#72, 1147–1166).[123]

Lay Concerns, Lay Leadership

Reading on in the *History of the Patriarchs*,[124] readers may be struck by the fact that they learn little about the actual activities of Patriarch John V or his successors, Mark III ibn Zur'ah (#73, 1166–1189) and John VI (#74, 1189–1216). This is not to say that the entries about these patriarchs are particularly brief; on the contrary, Mark ibn Zur'ah (who wrote the biography of John V)[125] and his continuator, sometimes identified as a layman from al-Mahallah named Ma'ani ibn Abi l-Makarim (who wrote the biographies of Mark III and John VI),[126] devote most of their space to secular history. They had much about which to write: the growing weakness of the Fatimid dynasty; the drama of the 1160s (in which troops of the *amir* Nur al-Din of Damascus under his general Shirkuh, the Latin troops of Amalric I of Jerusalem, and troops loyal to the Fatimid *wazir* Shawar fought a series of destructive campaigns up and down the length of the country); the end of the Fatimid state in 1171; and the establishment of the new Ayyubid state under Salah al-Din al-Ayyubi and his successors, and their dealings with the Crusaders. Not only do the biographies covering the half century from 1166 to 1216 focus on secular affairs; their authors, themselves laymen (in Mark ibn Zur'ah's case, before becoming patriarch), are attentive to the consequences of events for members of their own social class. One particularly telling passage comes at the end of the biography of Patriarch Mark III ibn Zur'ah in the *History of the Patriarchs*. There, the chronicler had just described the sufferings of the Christian community at the very beginning of the new, militantly Sunni regime of Salah al-Din al-Ayyubi: discriminatory rules were enforced, mobs destroyed some churches, and a number of Christian scribes converted to Islam.[127] However:

> [Patriarch Mark] was contending for his people and his flock until God set right for them the heart of their Sultan through the blessing of his prayers. And [the Sultan] caused them to draw nigh, and he favoured them, and he employed them in his *diwan* in the finances of his State and he was gracious toward them.... And every Christian attached himself to the scribes of an *amir* of the *amirs* of [Salah al-Din's] State and of his family and his relatives. And every one of [the *amirs*] respected the wife of his scribe, and there was for every one of them elegance and wealth and dignity and an influential word and power. And through their patience and the prayers of their patriarch and their return to God and their obedience to their head, God turned their lowliness into power....[128]

The passage goes on to say that Christian scribes immediately made use of their wealth and influence to repair or rebuild destroyed churches, and "affairs returned to what was better than before."[129]

We note in this passage (as in the whole of the biography from which it is taken) that the principal role of the patriarch is clear: he prays. Once the Coptic lay secretarial class had proven itself indispensable to the smooth running of the Ayyubid state, however, it was *this* class that would take leadership in the community in practical matters such as relating to the Muslim authorities, bestowing patronage, and restoring and rebuilding churches. These roles are confirmed by what we read in the *History of the Churches and Monasteries*, in which a number of entries bear witness that both Mark III and John VI were kept busy consecrating churches that had either been abandoned (e.g., by the Armenian Christians who had departed Egypt after the fall of the *wazir* Bahram) or damaged (e.g., in the fire of Fustat-Misr in November 1168, deliberately set by Shawar in order to deny the city to the advancing Crusaders).[130] Again and again, however, rebuilding projects were *sponsored* by lay notables; the patriarch's role was to say the appropriate prayers.[131]

Tired Theology?

We have already taken note of some of the odd teachings and practices that Gabriel II ibn Turayk encountered during the course of his reforming patriarchate. A number of events in the life of the church in the half century following Gabriel's death reinforce the impression that the theological culture of the twelfth-century Coptic Orthodox Church was in need of revitalization.

One case in point is a controversy that broke out toward the end of the patriarchate of John V (#72, 1147–1166).[132] A group of monks gathered around a certain Abba Solomon had added a word to the prayer of confession in the presence of the consecrated Eucharistic bread: "I believe and confess until the last breath that this is the *life-giving* flesh [of Christ]."[133] The patriarch moved from disapproval of the addition as innovation, to acceptance (since for him the flesh of Christ obviously was "life-giving"), to promulgation of the change throughout the Church. However, the liturgically conservative monks of the Monastery of St. Macarius vehemently opposed any innovation and complained to the *wazir* al-Salih ibn Ruzzik (d. 1161)—a "lover of money" (according to one of the accounts) who sensed opportunities for himself in the Christians' divisions.[134] The council that he called nearly erupted in a brawl, and was brought to an abrupt end when the *wazir* ordered that the patriarch be imprisoned and the episcopal sees of the Delta fined. The patriarch was eventually released—and, according to the *History of the Patriarchs*, his curse of the *wazir* upon his arrest proved effective, since al-Salih was murdered shortly afterward.[135] While the Christian chroniclers of these troubles ascribe them to the way that Satan "finds a way for the perdition of souls through his blows,"[136] there is still something very unedifying about a theological dispute that developed in such a way as to allow an unsympathetic *wazir* to hold the community to ransom.

The greatest theological controversy of the second half of the twelfth century was stirred up by one Marqus ibn al-Qunbar.[137] Marqus was a blind Copt who became a monk and priest sometime before the year 1166, and who then embarked upon a career of public preaching and exegesis of scripture, in the course of which he gathered a large following of people who regarded him as their spiritual master.[138] He was a charismatic figure who laid out for his followers a clear path to salvation, which can be summed up in three interconnected convictions: all Christians must with great regularity confess their sins aloud to a priest and perform penance; they must—also with great regularity—receive the Holy Communion (but, of course, only after confession); for this to work, *every* Christian must have a spiritual guide and father–confessor.[139] Part of Marqus's appeal may have been the fact that he did all of his teaching in Arabic at a time when, despite Patriarch Gabriel's reforms, much of the Church's teaching and liturgy was still, for many, locked away in the Coptic language.

Marqus's teaching was controversial because the practice of making confession aloud to a priest had recently been abandoned in the Coptic Orthodox Church, probably for legitimate pastoral reasons: some unworthy priests had been taking personal advantage of their people's confessions. But if Marqus may have had a legitimate point in calling for the restoration of an ancient practice, the discussion unfolded in such a way as to lead to sharp antagonism. Patriarch Mark III Ibn Zur'ah (1166–1189) held a synod against Marqus and forbade him from speaking—quite ineffectively, it turned out, and eventually Marqus and his followers went over to the Melkite (Chalcedonian) Church. After a time, however, Marqus and his followers became disillusioned and attempted to return to the Coptic Church, but were refused. By this time Marqus had antagonized both the Coptic and the Melkite hierarchies, and he spent the last twenty years of his life (ca. 1186–1206) confined to the Melkite monastery of al-Qusayr, south of Cairo.

Reading Marqus's writings today (some of which have recently been re-discovered), we find he was a rather careless theologian who was readily led astray by a good analogy.[140] For example, he could speak about God the Holy Trinity by analogy with the first human family, Adam, Eve, and their son: the three shared one nature, but were distinguished from one another by the relationships of fatherhood, procession (that is, Eve's procession from Adam's side), and sonship. So far so good,[141] but then Marqus was carried away into saying that as Abel was begotten of Adam and Eve, so the divine Son was begotten of the Father *and the Holy Spirit*—which in effect makes the Holy Spirit into God the Father's female consort.[142]

Marqus's greatest theological antagonist was Mikha'il, Coptic Orthodox metropolitan of Damietta, a canon lawyer who scoured Marqus's writings for errors, such as the one just mentioned.[143] Perhaps in reaction to the conversion of Marqus to the Melkite Church, Mikha'il also composed a work entitled *Usages that Distinguish the Copts*, in which he attempted to justify practices in which the Copts differed from the Melkites.[144] In contrast to Marqus's insistence on the necessity of auricular confession of sins to a spiritual master, Mikha'il defended the practice of confession to God alone. Other Coptic particularities that Mikha'il defended included the practice of circumcision, the marriage of first cousins, and making the sign of the cross with one finger from left to right, as opposed to the Melkites's two-fingered right-to-left crossing. Did not the Lord Jesus speak of casting out demons by "the *finger* of God" (Luke 11:20)—rather than by the *fingers* of God? And does not the single finger properly express one's belief in one God and one Son of God and one nature of Christ (as opposed to the Chalcedonian's splitting of Christ into two natures)? As for making the sign of the cross from left to right, it reflects the believer's hope of joining the sheep at Christ's right hand rather than the goats at his left (Matthew 25:31–33).[145] The distinction between Coptic Orthodox practice and Melkite practice is made perfectly clear.

The confrontation of Marqus ibn al-Qunbar and Mikha'il al-Dumyati does not appear to be a particularly high point in the history of Coptic theology. Marqus was an idiosyncratic and sometimes theologically careless teacher who had one very important idea for the reform of the Church of his day; Mikha'il was a loyal Coptic Orthodox bishop who saw much of what was careless about Marqus's teaching, but who also doggedly defended current practice against Marqus's best idea for reform.[146] Perhaps their encounter represents the last gasps of tired theology at the end of a gloomy century for the Copts,[147] one marked by a sustained crisis in Christian formation—despite the best reforming attempts of Patriarch Gabriel II ibn Turayk.

What is remarkable, then, is how the story goes on from here. The new prominence of Coptic lay notables in the administration of the Ayyubid state created a new capacity for patronage and service to the Coptic community. Simultaneously, a new generation of creative scholars was emerging, for whom speaking "the language of the *hajarah* inside the sanctuary" of Coptic Orthodox theology was not an occasion for woe, but rather an opportunity to sing a new Christian song. Patronage and talent met, preparing the way for a new blooming of churchly literature—in Arabic.[148]

Six

Chaos and Glory

Nineteen-year vacancy (1216–1235)
Cyril III ibn Laqlaq (#75, 1235–1243)
Seven-year vacancy (1243–1250)

A Strange Period

When Patriarch John VI died at the beginning of 1216, he left behind a community that had much for which to be grateful. Coptic notables occupied positions of considerable authority and influence in government *diwan*s, especially that of the army.[1] Under the Ayyubid sultan al-Malik al-'Adil (1200–1218), Egypt had come to enjoy generally peaceful and prosperous times, while his son al-Malik al-Kamil, who was the effective ruler of Egypt, had already in John's days shown himself to be a just ruler who would not allow the Copts to be scapegoated or victimized.[2]

Furthermore, although perhaps imperceptible as yet, the Coptic Church stood on the brink of a period of profound cultural flowering, so much so that modern scholars of Copto-Arabic literature speak of a thirteenth-century "renaissance" or "Golden Age,"[3] while art-historical studies have shown that the cultural flowering was by no means limited to the written word.[4] A number of factors would contribute to this flowering, including generally peaceful and prosperous times; the possibility within the Ayyubid empire of sharing ideas, texts, and artistic styles between Egypt and other regions, Syria in particular; and the existence of a class of Coptic notables with the capacity to lavish patronage on artists and scholars. It should be noted that this class of notables would itself provide a number of scholars in the course of the "renaissance." An early case in point is provided by Sim'an ibn Kalil ibn Maqarah, who had served in the army *diwan* under none other than Salah al-Din al-Ayyubi (1271–1293). Sometime during the reign of Salah al-Din's younger brother al-Malik al-'Adil, however, Sim'an withdrew

83

from public life and became a hermit at the Monastery of St. John the Little in the Wadi l-Natrun, where he wrote the much-beloved book *Rawdat al-farid wa-salwat al-wahid* ("The Garden of the Hermit and the Consolation of the Solitary"), an explanation of Christian faith and practice in rhymed Arabic prose.[5] Throughout Egypt, monks and lay scholars were either beginning to write (in Arabic, let it be noted), or were receiving the formation and reading the books (not only the Bible and patristic works, but also Arabic Christian texts from Iraq and Syria) that would enable intensive literary activity in the middle decades of the century.

The great irony of Coptic Church history in the early thirteenth century is that, at the same time that an extraordinary cultural flowering was taking shape, near-chaos reigned at the Church's institutional level. As we shall see, after John's death nineteen years passed before a new patriarch was consecrated, during which time many bishops and priests died and were not replaced. The vacancy finally was ended when Cyril III ibn Laqlaq (#75, 1235–1243) became patriarch—but this ushered in a tumultuous eight-year patriarchate after which the Church seemed to be in no hurry to find a replacement. After Cyril's death, in fact, another seven years (1243–1250) passed with no patriarch. The present chapter will attempt to tell the story of this strange period—and the connection of Pope Cyril III with both the chaos and the glory of it.

Chroniclers

One reason that this relatively short period in the history of the Coptic Church deserves its own chapter is that it had its own chroniclers. When we examine the *History of the Patriarchs*, we find that it can be divided into three main parts: the first, which was translated into Arabic in the late eleventh century from Coptic sources (*Lives* 1–65); the second, composed in Arabic by Mawhub ibn Mansur ibn Mufarrij and his principal continuators (*Lives* 66–74, covering the period of the previous chapter); and the third, almost a kind of appendix consisting (mostly) of very brief notices about popes from the thirteenth to the twentieth centuries (*Lives* 75–113).[6] However, in a single fifteenth-century manuscript of the *History of the Patriarchs* conserved in Paris,[7] we find an independent chronicle of the years 1216–1243 by a Coptic notable named Yuhanna ibn Wahb ibn Yuhanna ibn Yahya ibn Bulus, who was a friend and supporter of the monk Da'ud al-Fayyumi who eventually became Pope Cyril III (#75, 1235–1243).[8] Furthermore, the work usually known as the *History of the Patriarchs* by Yusab, bishop of Fuwwah, while properly speaking a seventeenth-century compilation of materials,[9] does appear to have preserved some reminiscences by Yusab, who was consecrated bishop of Fuwwah by Pope Cyril and who played a prominent role in Coptic church politics at least through the patriarchal election of 1250, when he helped broker the agreement that brought Pope Athanasius III (#76, 1250–1261) to the patriarchal throne.[10] As a result, then, we (at least appear to) possess eyewitness accounts by well-placed, if by no means neutral, observers of the events surrounding Cyril's patriarchate.

The Person at the Center of the Story[11]

The chronicler Yuhanna ibn Wahb claims that it was *he* who chose 'Cyril' as the name by which his friend Da'ud ibn Yuhanna ibn Laqlaq al-Fayyumi (David son of John, known as "Ibn Laqlaq,"[12] from al-Fayyum) should be known as patriarch.[13] Da'ud was already a controversial figure when, at the death of Patriarch John VI, he became a leading candidate as his successor. Although our knowledge of his earlier life and career is rather fragmentary, we do know that he was a scholarly monk at one of the monasteries of the Fayyum, where he counted as one of his *confrères* the monk Bulus al-Bushi (Paul of al-Bush), later (from 1240) bishop of Misr. Da'ud incurred the wrath of Patriarch John and a considerable number of local clergy, with the result that at an unknown date the Muslim notables of Madinat al-Fayyum, the regional capital, had him imprisoned. However, one of the greatest Coptic notables of the day, Nash' al-Khilafah Abu l-Futuh ibn al-Miqaz,[14] head of the *diwan* responsible for the finances of the Sultan al-'Adil's troops, was one of Da'ud's admirers. He had Da'ud freed from prison, and afterward installed him in his own house in Cairo.[15]

Both the wrath and the admiration that Da'ud aroused appear to have had their roots in his defense of the ancient practice of confessing one's sins regularly and aloud to a spiritual master or priest.[16] As Patriarch John (and many other Copts of the day) understood the matter, that was the position of the trouble-maker—and Melkite turncoat—Marqus ibn al-Qunbar (introduced in the previous chapter). For Marqus's opponents, it mattered little what biblical and patristic arguments a scholarly monk like Da'ud might be able to compile in defense of the historic practice of confession;[17] the matter had become a mere shibboleth serving to distinguish between authentic Coptic and heretical Melkite practice. Other Copts, however, including the powerful *archon* Nash' al-Khilafah, were convinced of the propriety and pastoral necessity of auricular confession. It appears that al-Nash'[18] was happy to have a personal father–confessor such as Da'ud on call, regardless of Patriarch John's disapproval; a person in his position of authority may well have believed that the matter of his eternal salvation required some special care and attention.

For a number of Copts, therefore, a whiff of Melkite heresy hung about the monk Da'ud. In addition, it appears that friends as well as foes were sometimes put off by Da'ud's open ambition to be made patriarch, unseemly in a tradition in which candidates for the patriarchate were traditionally expected to show reluctance to the point of being dragged to their consecration weeping and in chains.[19] Yuhanna ibn Wahb—who, we must remember, supported Da'ud's bid for the patriarchate—wrote about his friend as follows:

> I knew him to be a brilliant scholar, a good priest and a trans-
> lator of languages. I only disliked the way he rushed into an
> outward display of seeking [the patriarchate], and his lack of
> avoiding the matter in his speech. I used to counsel him
> about that—but he did not accept the counsel. I would say
> to him: "It is appropriate in this matter that the wise person
> make a show of *not* wanting it, and, if anyone should speak
> about it in front of him, that he disdain the speech, get
> up, and go away from that place! (This [making a show of
> reluctance] is [necessary] only if he isn't a righteous person.
> If righteous, this [reluctance] is both his inner attitude and
> outward behavior.) For this matter [of the patriarchate] is
> a venture into matters of terrible weight, an investment of
> authority over a great flock on whose account one will
> be judged! One should bear this matter only when one is
> invested with it." But he did not go back on his course, nor
> did he put his trust in God to give him [the patriarchate],
> but rather in his own effort and endeavor.[20]

1216–1217: Attempts at Making a Pope[21]

As the Coptic community took stock of itself after the death of Patriarch John, it could see a number of possible candidates for patriarch. Still, there were just two major parties that crystallized. The first was made up of the supporters of Da'ud al-Fayyumi, led by the great *archon* Nash' al-Khilafah, who had the ear of the sultan al-Malik al-'Adil. The other party that hurried to organize consisted of the opponents of Da'ud al-Fayyumi, led by al-Hakim Abu Shakir ibn Abi Sulayman, the personal physician of the sultan's son (and viceroy in Egypt) al-Malik al-Kamil. In the maneuvering that took place during the year 1216, each party gathered its supporters among the bishops as well as the priests and *arakhinah* of Cairo and Misr, and collected signatures on documents in support of or in opposition to the consecration of Da'ud. At least in the early stages of the contest, neither party gained a decisive advantage; each succeeded in blocking the moves of the other, sometimes by playing al-ʿAdil and al-Malik off one another.

Attempts at compromise were made. One of the most significant was a proposal to choose the patriarch by ecclesiastical lottery. According to Yuhanna ibn Wahb, the *archon* al-Hakim Abu Shakir described the process to the sultan as follows:

> "Sire, we choose three good, pious and learned men upon whom there is agreement, and write their names on three slips of paper, one name on each, and on another slip of paper we write the name of the Lord Christ. All this is left upon the altar, and we pray for three days with many petitions and continuous supplications. At the end of the third day, we bring a child, not yet of age, and leave him to pick up one of the pieces of paper in the presence of all the people, and they read it. If we find on it the name of one of the three chosen [candidates], we advance him to be patriarch over us. And if the piece of paper upon which is written the name of the Lord Christ appears, we know that he was not satisfied with any of those [three], and we nullify [their candidacy] and go back and choose three others. And we continue in this way until one of the names appears, and him we advance [to the patriarchate]."[22]

Al-Hakim (who opposed Daʾud) and Yuhanna ibn Wahb (who supported him) were willing to compromise on an ecclesiastical ballot that would include Daʾud's name on one of the four slips of paper, but Daʾud himself and many of his supporters would have nothing of it. They sensed that success would be theirs, as long as they played their cards well. (Perhaps Yuhanna's statement that Daʾud did not "trust in God to give him [the patriarchate]" is a rueful comment on the failure of this attempt at compromise.) As the pro-Daʾud and anti-Daʾud factions sparred, the names of other candidates were raised. One was that of the monk and theologian Bulus al-Bushi, but he quickly thought it best to withdraw from contention.[23] Another candidate was a hermit from Abyar in the western Delta; according to one source, it was al-Malik al-Kamil who suggested that he be made patriarch, after he had been healed of a heart ailment by the hermit's prayers. The matter advanced so far that the hermit was brought all the way to Cairo when, as the result of an intervention by al-Nashʾ, he was whisked away to his hermitage, to the great joy of the people of Abyar.[24]

About a year after the death of Patriarch John, al-Hakim Abu Shakir also died. Sensing an opportunity, al-Nash' (along with Yuhanna ibn Wahb, who relates the story)[25] moved quickly to set up a nominating process over which the sultan al-Malik al-'Adil would preside. At first all went well for them: a proposal for an ecclesiastical lottery without Da'ud's name gave way to a lottery including his name, after the sultan himself vetoed the candidacy of al-Sani'a Ghalib ibn al-Sukkari, a financial administrator whom the sultan did not want to lose to the Church. But once the representatives of the anti-Da'ud faction had given their consent to Da'ud as *a* candidate, a process of eliminating other names from consideration (including those of an elderly priest and the hermit of Abyar) left Da'ud as *sole* candidate— and Da'ud's critics in little position to argue. Everything seemed to be set for Da'ud's consecration as patriarch on Palm Sunday 1217, but in the meantime Da'ud's opponents appealed to al-Malik al-Kamil, who intervened with his father. At the very last minute proceedings were called off and the bishops sent away to their sees.[26] Seeing their hopes dashed after coming so tantalizingly close to their fulfillment, al-Nash' fell silent and Da'ud retired to the Monastery of St. Philotheus (known as the Monastery of the Nestorians) outside of Fustat-Misr.[27]

The Monk Da'ud Becomes Pope Cyril, Successor of Saint Mark

We do not hear much of Da'ud for the following eighteen years. A note in a manuscript written at the monastery (and now preserved in Paris) confirms that he was at the Monastery of St. Philotheus in 1227 and engaged in a scholarly endeavor: he helped check the manuscript's copy of an apology by the great tenth-century Syrian Orthodox philosopher and apologist Yahya ibn 'Adi against the original.[28] It is perhaps natural to think of this period as the time he researched and wrote his *Book of Confession*, also known as *The Book of the Master and the Disciple*—in which endeavor he was helped by his old *confrère*, the biblical and patristic scholar Bulus al-Bushi, and by al-As'ad ibn al-'Assal, a man who later would become famous for a critical Arabic translation of the Gospels.[29]

By the year 1235, the absence of a patriarch—who alone could consecrate bishops—had led to a critical situation in the church, in which all but four or five of the bishops had died since 1216. The shortage of bishops had led, in turn, to a shortage of priests.[30] There was, then, little effective opposition when a monk named 'Imad took up Da'ud's cause with a plan to guarantee the payment of three thousand dinars in return for the support of al-Malik al-Kamil (1218–1238), sultan since his father's death in 1218, for Da'ud's consecration. 'Imad also found an intermediary who had al-Kamil's ear, the diplomat and policy advisor Fakhr al-Din ibn al-Shaykh.[31] Al-Kamil's approval—of Da'ud's consecration as patriarch *and* the promise of three thousand dinars—was soon secured. Da'ud's supporters gathered quietly, and on 17 June 1235, Da'ud was consecrated Pope Cyril III by a pair of bishops at the Church of the Savior in Alexandria. On the next day he departed for Cairo by way of the Monastery of St. Macarius—but not before visiting the house where the head of St. Mark the Evangelist was kept, where he placed the sacred relic in his lap and wrapped it in a piece of rich new fabric.[32]

The symbolic possibilities of the occasion, in which Da'ud (David) became Cyril, successor to St. Mark, were not lost upon the lay theologian al-Safi ibn al-'Assal, who wrote an encomium for the day[33] that ended with the following invocation:

> O Mark, God has chosen for your throne one who will follow
> in your footsteps as leader and pastor!
> O Cyril, God has raised up for the orthodox faith one who
> will bless you in name, striving, and endeavor!
> O David, God has by your exaltedness taken away the lowli-
> ness from this community, as of old He removed it from
> the righteous people of Israel![34]

Earlier in the encomium, al-Safi mentioned another biblical figure who may have been especially pertinent to the monk who had waited nineteen years to be consecrated patriarch: he praised the new patriarch for being "Job-like in patience."[35]

Cyril's Patriarchate

The new patriarch got off to a good start. He visited the monasteries of the Wadi l-Natrun and ordained priests and deacons. After a festive entry into Misr (Old Cairo), he visited churches (that of St. Mercurius in Misr, that of Harat al-Rum in Cairo) and sought out and honored one of his critics, the monk Butrus at the Church of Abu Sarjah, who before becoming a monk was known as al-Sana' Abu l-Majd and had been a secretary in the army *diwan*.[36] As well as paying attention to his flock close at hand, Cyril gave attention to more distant Copts, as may be seen in elegant pastoral letters that he wrote to the Copts in Alexandria and in Damascus.[37] For the benefit of the Copts in Syria, he consecrated a Coptic metropolitan of Jerusalem—but if the intent was pastoral, the execution was politically clumsy: Cyril had not consulted with the Syrian Orthodox Patriarch of Antioch, who protested sharply at what he saw as encroachment on his territory.[38] Tempers were raw for a time, but the matter was smoothed over with a diplomatic exchange of letters and a careful delineation of the new metropolitan's authority.[39]

From the very beginning of his patriarchate, however, Cyril had a problem: he needed money, as he had nothing with which to pay the three thousand dinars promised to the sultan. The Egyptian clergy shortage offered an obvious solution: Cyril would restore the ranks of the Church's bishops, priests, and deacons, so depleted by the nineteen-year vacancy in the patriarchate, and an appropriate fee would be charged for each consecration or ordination. Contemporary sources provide a fee schedule: normally one hundred to two hundred dinars for the consecration of a bishop (although a handful paid just fifty); up to five dinars for a priest; and up to three for a deacon—although Cyril sometimes charged ten to people who had been antagonistic to him. In less than a year, Cyril consecrated forty bishops— and none without payment except for his old acquaintance al-'Amid ibn al-Duhayri, who became metropolitan of Damietta.[40]

This large-scale return of simony to the heart of patriarchal activity antagonized many in the Church, including many who probably needed very little reason to be aggrieved with Cyril. The monk Butrus started to avoid him; perhaps surprisingly, so did his former patron and champion, Nash' al-Khilafah Abu l-Futuh.[41] In Holy Week of 1236, a gathering with twenty bishops at the Monastery of St. Macarius in order to consecrate the holy *myron*, that is, the oil used for chrismation after baptism,[42] nearly ended in disaster when the patriarch ordered an inventory of the monastery's sacred vessels.[43] The monks, convinced that the patriarch was preparing to confiscate anything of value in order to pay his debt to the sultan, rampaged through the Sanctuary of Benjamin in the middle of the liturgy of consecrating the *myron*, smashing lamps and spilling oil and water all over the floor. They were about to set off to make a formal complaint to the sultan when the future bishop Yusab (then a senior monk named Yusuf at the Monastery of St. John the Little) deftly negotiated a reconciliation between (as they are presented in Yusab's own, first-person account) the hot-headed monks on the one hand, and an arrogant and politically tone-deaf patriarch on the other.[44]

Later that year, Cyril received a delegation of *arakhinah* at the patriarchal seat, the Mu'allaqah Church. The dialogue that ensued was recorded by Yuhanna ibn Wahb:

> They said to him, "How long will you do these things that have
> made us a disgrace among the nations and peoples?"

He said to them, "What things?"

"Your accepting simony for the priesthood!"

"We're discharging our debt to the sultan!"

"And who required you to settle money on the sultan?"

"It was *you* who settled money on the king!"

"You were not appointed to enter into this, nor was the patriarchate forced on you, but you bribed your way to it and
engaged it for yourself, chasing after it for what today is a
period of twenty years! You have ruined our church!"

"I have *not* ruined your church, but have built it up! There was
hardly a bishop left in it, and today there are fifty, and
priests beyond number!"[45]

Yuhanna ibn Wahb goes on to report that it came out at the meeting that
the patriarch still owed three hundred dinars to the sultan. The notables
pressed some reform measures on the patriarch, who promised to write them
in a decree . . . but did nothing. According to Yuhanna, "The council broke
up with nothing to show for it."[46]

Cyril appears to have had a talent for alienating people, including his
supporters. Two defections from Cyril's "team" were especially damaging.
One was by the monk 'Imad who had played the key role in Cyril's election
in 1235. It appears that Cyril failed to reward him for this role in a way that
'Imad thought suitable (a bishopric, perhaps?), and by 1237–1238 he had
become a bitter opponent who worked obsessively for Cyril's downfall.
Another damaging defection was that of al-As'ad Abu l-Karam, who had been
Cyril's secretary and had kept his accounts in the early days of the patriarchate
—and who, after his break with Cyril, went public with evidence that the
patriarch's income through simony and other revenue sources during the period
for which he had records amounted to 9,200 dinars, far in excess of the three
thousand dinars promised to the sultan.[47] The natural conclusion, which
Cyril's friendly chronicler Yuhanna does little to counter, was that Cyril's debt
to the sultan had become little more than an excuse for money-gathering.

Cyril's standing among the Copts of Misr-Cairo fell yet more in 1238,
when the inhabitants of the cities were put to forced labor in order to
construct a stretch of the new Ayyubid wall. While the Jewish community
organized so as to tend to the needs of workers and provide substitutes for
those unable to perform hard labor, Christians suffered—and the patriarch
was conspicuous by his absence.[48] In the period that followed, the monk
'Imad agitated to have Cyril deposed (and managed at one point to have him
arrested and publicly humiliated).[49] Others—in particular the monk Butrus

(al-Sana' Abu l-Majd) and Yusab, bishop of Fuwwah—began to develop an agenda of reform, including an end to simony and stipulations that legitimate church revenues be used for their intended purposes.[50] These efforts culminated in a synod held at the church at Harat Zuwaylah, at the western edge of the Fatimid city of Cairo. Fourteen bishops were in attendance; al-Safi ibn al-'Assal, who had prepared a new collection of ecclesiastical canon law for their approval, served as secretary. On 3 September 1238, the synod issued a set of canons reflecting the reform agenda, and al-Safi's compilation of canon law was adopted.[51]

The crisis should have been over, but there is no evidence that Cyril made any effort to implement the reform program; even if he had, the monk 'Imad may well have continued his obsessive quest to have Cyril deposed. Muslim officials of the sultans al-'Adil II (1238–1240) and al-Salih (1240–1249) became aware that the Christian community had become infected with *fitnah*—that is, "dissension" threatening social harmony. The result was a series of hearings between April and September 1240 in which Christians aired their dispute in the presence of Muslim notables and judges, including a representative of the sultan.[52] The September hearing was particularly significant: held at the Citadel before the *wazir* Mu'in al-Din ibn al-Shaykh (the younger brother of Fakhr al-Din ibn al-Shaykh who had helped to bring Cyril to power), the gathered Christians (for whom Bishop Yusab of Fuwwah served as secretary) not only ratified the reform program but appointed two bishops to supervise the patriarch in all his decisions. One of them was Bulus al-Bushi, who was consecrated Bishop of Misr. In addition, al-Safi ibn al-'Assal was commissioned to produce a definitive collection of recent canonical work.[53] The result, *al-Majmu' al-Safawi* ("al-Safi's Compilation") has played a huge role in the Coptic and Ethiopian Orthodox Churches, and even today is in print in Cairo in an inexpensive paperback volume.[54]

Humiliated and overwhelmed by events beyond his control,[55] including a series of aggressions and legal actions against the Mu'allaqah Church,[56] Cyril soon retired to the al-Sham' Monastery in Giza, where he died on 10 March 1243.[57] Under orders (and threat of torture) from the governor of Giza to retrieve any wealth that Cyril left behind, Cyril's nephew discovered a hiding place under a tile in the floor in which there were over a thousand gold dinars, and silver coins worth another thousand dinars.[58] A variety of ecclesiastical vessels such as chalices and patens were also found in the patriarch's possession.[59] In addition, Yuhanna ibn Wahb reports as follows:

> It is said that they found sixteen capes,[60] wine-colored and
> otherwise, and forty costly wraps. As for his outer-garments

and turbans and trousers and [ecclesiastical vestments such as] the *epitrachelion*,[61] the *omophorion*[62] and the liturgical head-covering,[63] there was a lot (but I did not ascertain their number). One of the company mentioned to me that the number of pairs of trousers was forty (but the responsibility for the statement is his). He was found to have possessed, it was said, sixteen boxes of sweets (but they had turned rancid and some had rotted), six pots of old dates, and other things like that.[64]

When we reflect that Yuhanna's earliest readers were members of a church where the monastic ideals of poverty and humility had always been strong, it is hard to imagine a more eloquent statement of the hollowness of Cyril's patriarchate than this catalogue of (rich) vestments and (spoiled) sweets.[65]

A Failed "Great Man"?
Or a Scholar among Scholars?

In Cyril's defense, it may be suggested that he was merely a product of his time. "Great men" in Ayyubid Egypt were expected to practice "glorified forms of self-presentation"[66]—and Cyril, with his love of fine vestments, appears to have conformed to expectations.[67] The Ayyubid rulers of Egypt were always concerned about consolidating their power in Syria—and Cyril appointed a Coptic metropolitan of Jerusalem, who soon was asserting himself in areas traditionally under the authority of the Syrian Orthodox patriarch of Antioch.[68] On a small scale, Cyril's financial administration mirrors that of al-Malik al-Kamil himself; if Cyril wanted lists of the ecclesiastical vessels belonging to the Monastery of St. Macarius, we may think of the detailed cadastral surveys ordered by al-Malik al-Kamil, such as al-Nabulusi's survey of al-Fayyum with its exact determination of the amount of hay and the number of chickens to be collected from each locality.[69] And if Cyril left behind coins worth two thousand dinars, when al-Malik al-Kamil died in 1238 he left behind a treasure worth a full year's budget![70]

Still, Cyril did not quite manage to play the part of a "great man." We have no record of his showing extravagant hospitality, and certainly not of any skill in binding people to himself with lasting ties of love and service.[71] If Cyril was a worldly man, he was not worldly enough to be effective in an arena in which the expectations, ambitions, and pride of allies and servants needed astute tending. Yuhanna ibn Wahb probably intended a compliment when he wrote of Cyril, "He didn't let things bother him,"[72] but this character trait, which Yuhanna takes as evidence of "strength, patience and long-suffering of soul,"[73] may also have reflected a lack of engagement and attention to the art of people management. In the secular politics of medieval Egypt, such inattention could be deadly; in ecclesiastical politics, it could doom a career to failure.

Cyril's eulogy, written by al-Safi ibn al-'Assal, has been preserved.[74] A striking feature of this eulogy is the number of times words of the root 'LM are used: *'ilm* (science), *'alim* (scholar), *mu'allim* (teacher), *ta'alim* (teachings), and so on. Al-Safi wanted people to remember Cyril as

> your pastor, who sought your souls' salvation;
> your teacher of sciences, in your intellects and in the world
>   of perception.[75]

Al-Safi later prays—playing on the text of the Twenty-Third Psalm—that God will appoint a suitable successor

> . . . who will shepherd us, so that we lack nothing in the
>   pastures of fertile sciences [*fi muruj al-'ulum al-khasibah*],
> and give us to drink from the water of his pure and fragrant
>   teachings [*min miyah ta'alimihi al-tahirah al-tayyibah*].[76]

Whatever else may be said about Cyril, he led the Coptic Orthodox Church in a time of great fertility in the ecclesiastical sciences. As one reads his history, one encounters names that are landmarks in the history of Copto-Arabic literature. Among those who became bishops under Cyril, we find Yuhanna, bishop of Samannud, who wrote the first scientific grammar of the Coptic language;[77] Yusab, bishop of Fuwwah, the historian;[78] and Bulus al-Bushi, one of the greatest preachers of Coptic history and a theologian who is attracting attention today because of his deep patristic knowledge.[79] The "Awlad al-'Assal," four brothers of whom one was a wealthy civil servant and the other three writers and theologians, serve for many Copts and scholars as a symbol of the thirteenth-century "renaissance" of Coptic Orthodox literature.[80] Two of them, al-As'ad and al-Safi, make appearances in Cyril's story; al-Safi in particular was deeply involved in the affairs of the patriarchate, and did some of his most fruitful work (in canon law, in apologetics, and in transmitting the Arabic Christian literature of Syria and Iraq to Egypt) during and immediately after Cyril's patriarchate.[81] Cyril's critic, the monk Butrus al-Sana', was the father of al-Nushu'[82] Abu Shakir ibn al-Rahib, who in the generation after Cyril composed encyclopedic works of history, theology, and the study of the Coptic language.[83]

Earlier historians of the Coptic patriarchs did not judge particular patriarchs solely on their own merits, but also on the basis of "the saints of his day."[84] This suggests that the most generous way to assess the legacy of Cyril III is to judge him as a scholar and author, surrounded in "pastures of fertile sciences" by the *scholars* of his day. If Cyril is to be held responsible for much of the Church's administrative chaos in his day, he should also be allowed some glimmers of the glory of the "golden age" of the sciences of the Coptic Orthodox Church.

Seven

Marginalized Patriarchs

Athanasius III (#76, 1250–1261)
Gabriel III (#77, 1268–1271)
John VII (#78, 1262–1268, 1271–1293)
Theodosius II (#79, 1294–1300)
John VIII (#80, 1300–1320)
John IX (#81, 1320–1327)
Benjamin II (#82, 1327–1339)
Peter V (#83, 1340–1348)
Mark IV (#84, 1348–1363)
John X (#85, 1363–1369)
Gabriel IV (#86, 1370–1378)

Internal Rivalry, External Interference

After its experience with Pope Cyril III ibn Laqlaq (#75, 1235–1243), the Coptic community was in no hurry to elect a new patriarch. "We no longer desire a patriarch," some said. "What happened with that one [Cyril] whom we chose over another . . . is enough for us!"[1] In the year 1250, however, the Egyptian Melkite Church elected a new patriarch, and leading Copts realized that they would be placed at a disadvantage over against the governing authorities if they could not produce a patriarch of their own.

The election of a new patriarch quickly became bogged down in the rivalry between the lay notables of Misr (Old Cairo) and those of al-Qahirah (Cairo). The Misr faction was led by al-Sana' Abu l-Majd. This veteran of the church political struggles of Cyril's time had ties to the sultan: his nephew (who had converted to Islam) served as *wazir* to the new Mamluk ruler al-Mu'izz 'Izz al-Din Aybak (1250–1257).[2] This faction held its own patriarchal election, in the absence of the bishops, by sacred lot. The name that was chosen was that of a monk of the Monastery of St. Antony named Bulus, known as Ibn Kalil. The Cairo faction, led by the wealthy civil servant (and patron of his brothers' theological projects) al-Amjad ibn al-'Assal, had its own candidate: the monk Ghubriyal, also for a time a monk of the

97

Monastery of St. Antony.[3] Ghubriyal was a learned scribe and manuscript copyist who for several years had served al-Amjad as scribe, assistant in his brothers' scholarly projects,[4] and tutor to his son.[5] A tense standoff between more or less evenly matched parties ensued. Ghubriyal's supporters approached the governing authorities with the readiness to spend one thousand dinars in bribes; Bulus's supporters, noting that "the gate of expenditure had been opened,"[6] upped the offer to three thousand. Violence was beginning to mar the contest when a decisive intervention was made by a group of bishops led by another veteran of church-political disputes, Bishop Yusab of Fuwwah.[7] He regarded Ghubriyal, like Cyril III before him, as too "ambitious for the patriarchate,"[8] and led the bishops in brokering a deal that resulted in the monk Bulus ibn Kalil becoming patriarch under the name Athanasius III.[9]

The contest between the lay notables of Misr and those of Cairo was renewed upon Athanasius's death eleven years later. Once again the election was closely contested, and once again the monk Ghubriyal was the candidate of the al-ʿAssal brothers and the notables of Cairo. This time Ghubriyal was chosen by sacred lot, fairly and squarely—but before he could be consecrated patriarch he was "set aside" (as his brief notice in the *History of the Patriarchs* tells us), and his rival, Yuʾannis ibn Saʿid al-Sukkari, became Patriarch John VII.[10]

If this seems confusing, what happened next is even more so. John served as patriarch from 1262 to 1268, but then, according to the *History of the Patriarchs*, he in his turn was "set aside" and Ghubriyal recalled; consecrated as Patriarch Gabriel III in 1268, he served for a little more than two years until he in his turn was "removed" from the patriarchate and John "brought back" at the beginning of 1271.[11] One puzzle that this unique set of events has set for Coptic historians is: Which of these two patriarchs is to be considered the seventy-seventh, and which the seventy-eighth? (Most Coptic historians list Gabriel first, since it was his name that was selected in the sacred lottery of 1261, even though he was not consecrated until 1268.) But the more important question is: Can we explain what happened?

Fortunately, at a point where both the *History of the Patriarchs* and the patriarchal history attributed to Yusab give us little information, we find a detailed passage about patriarchs Gabriel III and John VII in *al-Nahj al-sadid wa-l-durr al-farid fima baʿd Tarikh Ibn al-ʿAmid* ("The correct way and singular pearl, concerning what comes after the *History* of Ibn al-ʿAmid"), a chronicle of the years 1260–1341 by the Coptic historian al-Mufaddal ibn Abi l-Fadaʾil.[12] According to al-Mufaddal, after a child had drawn Gabriel's name at a solemn liturgy in December 1261, his rival John appealed to the civil authorities now responsible to the great Mamluk sultan al-Malik al-Zahir Baybars (1260–1277).[13] The sultan's *wazir*, one Baha' al-Din ibn Hanna, was happy to accept a bribe of five thousand dinars; with his support, John was made patriarch and Gabriel sent away to the Monastery of St. Antony.[14] However, trouble lay ahead. In June or July of the year 1265, the same Baha' al-Din was instrumental in imposing the stupendous fine of fifty thousand dinars on the Coptic community.[15] Patriarch John was unable to produce the money, and so in 1268 Baha' al-Din had John deposed and Gabriel recalled—to give *Gabriel* a chance at raising the necessary funds. But Gabriel was no more successful a fundraiser than John had been, and so the decision was taken in 1271 to depose Gabriel (who died a few years later)[16] and recall John (who served as patriarch until 1293).

If the sequence of events as related by al-Mufaddal is at all close to the truth, we are dealing with the most blatant intervention by the governing authorities in Church affairs since the time of Cyrus al-Muqawqas, before the Arab conquest.[17] Certainly, nothing that follows in the annals of Coptic Church history provides any real parallel to the episode of "musical patriarchs" in the decade between 1261 and 1271. And yet, the story is to a certain extent emblematic of the circumscribed role and exposed position of the Coptic Orthodox patriarchs throughout the Mamluk period in Egypt (1250–1517): especially in times of political instability or military crisis, the governing authorities might see the Coptic Orthodox patriarchate merely as a point of financial transfer from the Coptic community to those in power. The patriarchs, for their part, were hard pressed to fulfill the role that was thrust upon them, sometimes with threats (or actual exercise) of violence.

Before we leave Patriarch Gabriel III, it is worth noting that he was regarded as a saint—by the Ethiopian Church, where he is remembered in the Synaxarion[18] as well as in an Ethiopic collection of Marian miracles.[19] The latter relates a story from Gabriel's days of exile in the monasteries of the Eastern Desert. Having been denied the patriarchate, Gabriel had gone to the Monastery of St. Paul,[20] where he devoted himself to prayer and to writing a great book, the *Mashafa Hawi*, meaning (the text explains) "The Compilation of Every Good Word."[21] Upon finishing the book, he endowed it to the Monastery of St. Antony for reading in the monastery church, then loaded the large volume onto a donkey and sent it off with a monk. The monk, however, fell among Beduin thieves who took the book, the donkey, and even the monk's clothing. Upon receiving this news, Gabriel prostrated himself before the image of the Virgin Mary in the monastery church, and swore not to eat, drink, or depart until she had acted to save the book. At the end of three full days and nights, the Virgin spoke to him:

"Do not be sad, O Gabriel, minister of my beloved Son.
Tomorrow you shall see my miracle because I will destroy those
who took the book, and it shall arrive in the place to which
you sent it. And you shall return to your old office because
of your faith in me. Only do not be hasty in the episcopal
dignity before you have thoroughly examined it. The Lord has
forgiven you."[22]

The thieves were struck down in the desert, and angels guided the
donkey, with the book and the monk's clothes, to the Monastery of
St. Antony. Soon afterward, Gabriel received the summons to return to
Cairo as patriarch. He hesitated, but again the Virgin spoke to him: "Do
not refuse to go with your people, because this is the command of my
beloved Son, that you return to your [patriarchal] throne."[23]

The story is remarkable because it seems to be aware of the charge against
Gabriel that he was "ambitious for the patriarchate" (or "hasty in the
episcopal dignity"), and shows how he was healed of that ambition. When
the call did come for him to take up the patriarchal dignity, Gabriel required
a word of encouragement from the Blessed Virgin herself before accepting
it. It may be that the story represents a tradition passed along by Ethiopian
monks at the Monastery of St. Antony.[24] When they thought of Gabriel,
they thought of the exile of 1262–1268: not merely an ambitious cleric or
competent scholar and copyist, but rather and especially a penitent and
saintly monk who spent his days in prayer, who conversed with the Virgin,
and who in the end was vindicated and recalled to the patriarchate.

Scattered Portrayals, Incidental Mentions

The description of the career and person of Patriarch Gabriel III just offered
has been pieced together from a variety of sources, of which the *History of
the Patriarchs* is by no means the most important. If it is correct to say that
the Coptic Orthodox patriarchs of the Mamluk period very often played
a sharply delimited role (of financial transfer point), it may be that this is
mirrored in the brevity of their "biographies" in what we might call "Part
Three" of the *History of the Patriarchs*.[25] These "biographies" consist of very
brief entries that—with an exception to which we shall return in Chapter
Eight—can very nearly be reduced to entries in a table: name, place of origin,
monastery, date of consecration, date of death, place of burial, length of
patriarchate, additional comments. For example, the biography of patriarch
Mark IV (#84, 1348–1363) reads as follows:

This father Mark the patriarch was from the inhabitants of the district of Qalyub. He was chosen for the patriarchate, and advanced [to that rank] on 8 Abib, AM 1065. He remained patriarch for fourteen years and three months. He went to his rest on 6 Amshir, AM 1079. His days were peaceful.[26]

"His days were peaceful" is a curious comment, considering that Mark's days as patriarch began as Egypt was reeling from bubonic plague, which had arrived in Alexandria in 1347 and had spread throughout the country by the end of 1348.[27] "His days" also included the communal disturbances of 1354, regarded by some historians as a turning point in the history of the Islamization of Egypt.[28] In that year, anti-Christian rioting broke out, churches and monasteries were destroyed, and Christian civil servants were either dismissed or compelled not only to convert to Islam, but also to behave in a manner that demonstrated their willing integration into Islamic society. The statement in the *History of the Patriarchs* that Mark's "days were peaceful" obscures rather than illuminates.

Catastrophic events were by no means limited to the patriarchate of Mark IV. The Mamluk period in Egypt (1250–1517)—the setting of this and the following two chapters—was punctuated by crises of various kinds.[29] First of all, there were external military threats: from the Latin Crusader principalities, until the conquest of Acre in 1291; from the Mongols, who, while soundly defeated by the Mamluks at the epochal battle of 'Ayn Jalut in 1260, remained a threat to the Mamluks until peace was definitively established in 1328; from Timur-Lenk, who swept into Syria in 1399, but in 1402 decided to turn his attention to the Ottomans rather than to Egypt; and, a century later, from the Portuguese, whose ships in the Indian Ocean demolished Cairo's central and lucrative position in the international spice trade, and from the Ottomans, who defeated a Mamluk army in 1516 and occupied Cairo the following year. Then there were invisible enemies: the bubonic plague that carried away about a third of the Egyptian population in 1347–1349 was followed by periodic outbreaks of pneumonic plague, for a total of about twenty major epidemics between 1347 and 1517.[30] To this one can add natural disasters: earthquakes such as that of 1303, which toppled the famous lighthouse of Alexandria and left Cairo looking like a war zone;[31] or insufficient Nile flooding (as occurred in 1295, 1374, and 1403), leading to crop failure, inflation, and famine.[32]

Given the frequency of crises during the Mamluk period, one might not be surprised that these were difficult years for the Copts; times of trial often lead to the scapegoating of minority communities (as occurred in time of plague in western Europe, where Jews were targeted). Indeed, the "early

Mamluk period" (1250–1382) is remembered as a grievous one for the Coptic Christian community.[33] On at least four occasions (1293, 1301, 1321, and 1354) the authorities decreed that senior non-Muslim civil servants either convert to Islam or be removed from office, and took measures to enforce the *ghiyar* or sumptuary laws of the so-called "Covenant of 'Umar,"[34] including (perhaps most noticeably) the requirement that Christian men wear a blue turban.[35] In 1301 some churches were destroyed, the rest were closed, and the spring Feast of the Martyr (at which the martyr's finger, kept as a relic in a church in Shubra, was cast into the Nile)[36] was suppressed. In 1321 major anti-Christian rioting led to the destruction of sixty churches throughout Egypt. The tribulations of 1354, mentioned already, included the destruction of the Church of the Martyr in Shubra; its famous relic was solemnly burned.[37] During this period many Copts converted to Islam: it was becoming clear to them that it was in the Muslim community that opportunities of social and career advancement lay, both for themselves and for their children.[38] Some of these conversions may have been purely formal at first, but eventually entire families were lost to the Coptic community.

While it may be helpful in a general way to speak about scapegoating mechanisms, this does not provide an adequate explanation of the anti-*dhimmi* measures and disturbances of the early Mamluk period. Unlike Europe, outbreaks of plague in Egypt do not appear to have resulted directly in anti-minority violence.[39] Indeed, the record of anti-*dhimmi* agitation does not appear to correlate in any simple way with the record of warfare, plague, earthquake, or famine. One factor that has been suggested is the intensification of a rigidly Sunni religious ethos during the period.[40] The conquests of the (pagan) Mongols, who had sacked Baghdad in 1258, left Egypt as the remaining bastion of the Islamic world and the Mamluks as the leaders of the Muslim community's *jihad* against outside aggression— including that coming from Latin Crusaders or from Armenian and Georgian Christians who had cast their lot with the Mongols. The ongoing process of restoring Sunni ascendancy in Egypt (after the long years of Isma'ili Shi'ism under the Fatimids) continued apace under the Mamluks, as may be seen in the scores of magnificent teaching-mosques *(madrasahs)* that still dominate Cairo's medieval streets. Non-Egyptian visitors and refugees from the Mongol advance brought a worldview that had not been tempered by Egypt's history of religious diversity;[41] scholars such as Ibn Taymiyya agitated and wrote enormous treatises against all that he saw as un-Islamic, including Christians playing influential roles in Egyptian society.[42] In addition, Copts in the financial bureaucracy often prospered, and a few converted Copts exercised—at least until their almost inevitable downfall—great authority and amassed huge fortunes. Converted or not, they became targets of anti-Coptic resentment. Crowded living conditions and mixed economic opportunity in Cairo gave rise to a situation in which a mob could quickly be gathered and incited to violence; the ruling authorities, if not always themselves intolerant of their Coptic subjects, sometimes made concessions to popular anti-*dhimmi* sentiment in order to preserve some degree of order.[43]

In the midst of all this, the Coptic patriarchs are, for the most part, invisible: they make incidental appearances in the Islamic sources (usually without being named), and, as we have seen, earn entries in the Christian chronicles that, for the most part, can be reduced to an index card. Take Patriarch John VIII (#80, 1300–1320), who suffered the disturbances of 1301 and their aftermath: his "biography" in the *History of the Patriarchs* contains just three notes beyond the standard data points:

> In his days there was the wearing of blue turbans and related occurrences. A great earthquake happened on Thursday, mid-Misra, AM 1019. . . . This father attended the funeral of St. Barsawma the Naked on 5 Nasi, AM 1021, and prayed over him.[44]

We note that nothing is said about anything that Patriarch John *did* during the crisis of "the wearing of blue turbans and related occurrences." In fact, we hear more about this crisis in the *Life* and *Miracles* of Barsawma/Barsum the Naked, the great lay ascetic and holy man who is remembered daily in the litany of the saints of the Coptic psalmody.[45] It is *he* who receives credit in the Christian sources for intervening with the Mamluk sultan al-Nasir Muhammad (1293–1341 with interruptions) and persuading him to allow the churches to reopen.[46] From the roof of the Shahran Monastery[47] to the south of Old Cairo, Barsum preached, healed, mediated disputes, and received Muslim visitors—all the while refusing to change his white turban for blue.[48] The Coptic patriarch is mostly noticeable by his *absence* from Barsum's story—until his death, when he leads the mourners.[49]

The figure of Barsum, the lay saint, was a dominant one in the Coptic Orthodox Church during his life and for several decades following his death. John VIII, who led the mourning at Barsum's death, was known as Ibn al-Qiddis, "the son of the saint"—perhaps the "spiritual son" of St. Barsum. John was buried at Dayr Shahran, as also was Patriarch Benjamin II (#82, 1327–1339), whose elevation to the patriarchate Barsum had foreseen. The following two patriarchs, Peter V (#83, 1340–1348) and Mark IV (#84, 1348–1363) had both been monks at Dayr Shahran.[50] Clearly, Barsum (and, by extension, his adopted monastery) had become a major center of holiness in the Church—to which several patriarchs were related.

The pattern of near-invisibility continues beyond John VIII. His successor John IX (#81, 1320–1327) was patriarch during the disturbances of 1321, as is mentioned in his brief entry in the *History of the Patriarchs*:

> In his days many afflictions came upon the Christians: some were killed and some burned; they nailed some and paraded them on camels; they forced them to wear blue turbans. Then [God] in his mercy gave relief to his people.[51]

Once again, however, nothing is said of anything that the patriarch actually did in response to the disturbances. John IX makes an appearance here (though only as "the patriarch" and not by name) in the chronicle of the Muslim historian al-Maqrizi—but only in order to leave a group of Coptic monks, who had undertaken arson attacks against mosques in response to the burning of churches, to the justice of the sultan.[52]

The *History of the Patriarchs* does attribute agency to John's successor, Patriarch Benjamin II (#82, 1327–1339). He lived during a period of relative peace and stability, and was able to fund the rebuilding of the Monastery of St. Bishoi in Scetis.[53] But he too faced trials:

> In his days, Sharaf al-Din al-Nash'[54] ibn al-Taj took office, and many afflictions came upon [the patriarch]. They humiliated the women and their children, the monks, nuns, and bishops. Al-Nash' died under chastisement, through the blessing of this father's prayer and his supplications; and vengeance from God came upon all the evildoers.[55]

Al-Nash' was a 'Muslim Copt' who rose to the office of *nazir al-khass* (supervisor of the sultan's privy purse) and, exercising extraordinary powers of taxation/extortion, achieved both general loathing and the accumulation of a great fortune before being arrested and dying under torture (though not before revealing the hiding places of his wealth).[56] It is interesting that the *History of the Patriarchs* should attribute the downfall of al-Nash' to the patriarch's prayers. According to al-Maqrizi, Patriarch Benjamin died *before* al-Nash'; in fact, when Benjamin died, al-Nash' descended upon the patriarchal church and confiscated the gold and silver in it.[57] Presumably the patriarch's prayers were effective even, or especially, after his death.

The Patriarch at the Center of the Story

There does exist a literary genre that places the patriarchs at the center of the story, in contrast to the brief and routine characterizations of the patriarchs of the early Mamluk period that we find in the *History of the Patriarchs*, or their marginal or almost incidental appearance elsewhere. Examples of this genre carry titles such as the *Book of the Chrism* (or *of the Holy Myron*), and detail the preparation of the aromatic oil used in the chrismation of the newly baptized, as well as a variety of other ceremonies in the Coptic Church.[58]

Each *Book of the Chrism* is, in a sense, a liturgical cookbook: it gives a detailed description of the sequence of cooking sessions or "coctions" that, over the course of several days, would allow the perfect blending of balsam ("balm of Gilead") from trees in the garden of the Virgin at Matariyyah (watered, it was believed, by the well in which the Virgin had washed the child Jesus' clothes during the Flight into Egypt),[59] with twenty or thirty other aromatic ingredients and fine olive oil.[60] These coctions were accompanied with prayers and the recitation of psalms, and the resulting *myron* or chrism (along with a simpler oil called the *kallielaion*—the "oil of gladness" or "oil of the catechumens"[61]) was consecrated in a solemn liturgy.[62] But these books do more than provide a recipe and liturgical details; they also provide documentation of the particular occasions on which the *myron* was prepared. And thus, even if our knowledge of the eleven patriarchs from Athanasius III to Gabriel IV (covering the years 1250–1378) is very limited, we *do* know that on no fewer than nine occasions during this period, the patriarch gathered the bishops of both Upper and Lower Egypt during Holy Week for the solemn and elaborate preparation of the *myron*, usually at the monastery of St. Macarius (but twice in Old Cairo).[63] Normally, the preparation of the *myron* would be complete by the end of Wednesday of Holy Week; on Thursday, it would be borne into the church in solemn procession. For example, on Maundy Thursday of the year 1305 at the Monastery of St. Macarius, Patriarch John VIII and the eighteen assembled bishops donned black robes

> and they went up to the cell of the *myron*. They took with them twelve priest-monks, each holding a censer, and twelve deacons carrying crosses and candles, and the patriarch and the bishops carried the *myron* and the *kallielaion*. . . . They went down from the cell and came to the Sanctuary of Mark, while the deacons chanted hymns ahead of them.[64]

As the liturgy progressed, the vessels of *myron* and *kallielaion* were carried in procession around the church and brought to the Sanctuary of Benjamin, where special altars had been prepared for them. And there, in the course of the Maundy Thursday liturgy, special rites of consecration for both of the holy substances were performed, in which patriarch, bishops, and people all had their assigned roles.[65]

The patriarchs of the early Mamluk period may not have possessed much in the way of worldly authority, and their energies may have been largely taken up with financial worries that had been imposed upon them from the outside. In the *Book of the Chrism* from which I have just quoted, however, one may forget the limitations and burdens that had been imposed upon a patriarch such as John VIII, or his near invisibility not only in historical chronicles but even in the *Life* of the great saint of his era. In this text, we find the patriarch at a monastery with the strongest claim to represent the center of the Egyptian sacred geography, moving between sanctuaries named for his great predecessors St. Mark and St. Benjamin. Priest–monks swing their censers before him, while deacons carry crosses and candles and sing hymns. At the altar he is surrounded by his bishops, who take their turns in speaking their assigned lines. Meanwhile, the people stand attentively, ready to play their role in the drama of the Maundy Thursday liturgy. For the early Mamluk rulers, the patriarch may have been a marginal figure, not much more than a functionary to be periodically exploited. In the *Book of the Chrism*, however, we see the successor of St. Mark presiding over a kind of miracle of provision of holy substance: not mere oil, but oil "invested with the Holy Spirit"; not mere bread, but "the Body of Christ."[66] He is at the center of things, surrounded by bishops, attended by clergy and monks, and venerated by the people, who receive blessing from his hand.

Eight

A Burst of Holiness

Matthew I (#87, 1378–1408)

The Patriarch as Saint and Holy Man

There is one exception in the *History of the Patriarchs* to the pattern of short, uninformative paragraphs for the patriarchs of the Mamluk period: the entry for Patriarch Matthew I (#87, 1378–1408),[1] which itself is an excerpt from an extensive *Life of Matthew*, composed soon after his death.[2] The whole of the *Life* has been preserved (and published): the biography that we find in the *History of the Patriarchs* was originally bracketed with material that made the whole a liturgical reading suitable for the commemoration of a great saint on the day of his death.[3]

Matthew was born in about 1336 to poor parents in a village outside al-Ashmunayn.[4] The *Life* describes him in terms full of echoes from the stories of the great saints of the Egyptian church: as a child he "played church," taking the role of the patriarch ordaining priests (like Patriarch Gabriel II or St. Athanasius);[5] later, he worked as a shepherd (like St. Shenoute, for example).[6] Later, as a desert ascetic, he battled the demons (like St. Antony) and befriended wild animals, who turned to him when food was scarce (which may remind us of St. Paul the Hermit's faithful lions).[7]

Matthew began his ascetic practices as a very young man. He attempted to resist the advances of a woman who was attracted to the beauty of his eyebrows by the simple expedient of shaving them off and giving them to her. (When that failed to quench the woman's ardor, Matthew ripped his bishop's liturgical garments to shreds so as to be sent away.) He was ordained priest at the tender age of eighteen, joined the Monastery of St. Antony, sojourned in Jerusalem until his spiritual gifts began to attract unwelcome attention, and then returned to St. Antony. Eventually he moved on and lived outside of Dayr al-Muharraq in Upper Egypt, where he practiced the greatest austerity.[8]

In 1378 Matthew was chosen patriarch, though only—according to his *Life*—after trying to evade the call to high office. We read that Matthew tried to escape those who had come to take him away to Cairo by stowing away aboard a sailboat—but God prevented the wind from blowing, and a child betrayed the monk's hiding place in the hold. Later, Matthew went so far as to cut off the tip of his tongue with scissors, but God miraculously restored his power of speech.[9]

Once installed as patriarch, Matthew became known for his piety and almsgiving: he visited monasteries and convents and provided for their needs, sought out the poor, and distributed all that he possessed, among Muslims as well as Christians.[10] The *Life* gives the impression that Matthew was heading up a huge project of food aid, and this impression is confirmed by the precious testimony of the French nobleman Ogier d'Anglure who visited Cairo in 1395. He noted that the patriarch was "a very good and charitable person, not only as it is reputed, but as he demonstrates in a definite manner by feeding a thousand or more poor people every day."[11] Such an operation required substantial financial backing, so Patriarch Matthew used his considerable powers of example and exhortation to move—or shame—wealthy Copts into charitable giving. Adding a fierce note, the *Life* reports on one wealthy Copt who refused the patriarch's request for him to help the poor: immediately after the patriarch's departure, a Muslim official confiscated the man's goods; moreover, we read that the man died an evil death and went to Hell, "for thus is the miserable fate which descends upon the rich who are without charity."[12]

The *Life of Matthew* emphasizes the patriarch's humility: he worked alongside laborers, unashamed to make mud for bricks or to run behind donkeys.[13] He tended sick people who had been abandoned by everyone else (perhaps during an outbreak of pneumonic plague?), washing them of their filth and either nursing them back to health or permitting them, Mother Teresa-like, to die in peace and dignity. Once he descended into a well in order to fetch the putrefying body of a murder victim, which he carefully prepared for burial. His healings were often of a simple sort: we are told of Matthew massaging palsied limbs into life, or using folk remedies to extract poison from a snakebite.[14]

But if the *Life* is concerned to leave the hearer/reader in no doubt of Matthew's humility, it also—perhaps more than any other patriarchal biography treated in this book—portrays him as a wonder-worker. According to the *Life*, Matthew performed exorcisms and even raised a workman from the dead.[15] He had the gift of clairvoyance: he knew of events in faraway Ethiopia[16] as well as the secrets of his own flock. "The sins of the people were revealed before [Matthew], as oil in a glass bottle."[17] He was a powerful intercessor for his people, holding regular converse with the Virgin Mary, as well as with the archangel Michael and the equestrian saints Theodore, Mercurius, and George.[18] He had the strange authority to "bind" a saint— in order to learn the identity of a thief, to aid a Coptic notable who had fallen afoul of the authorities, or even to enact vengeance upon an oppressive *amir*.[19] Matthew's authority is not always associated with miraculous power, however. He had, according to the *Life*, great boldness in the face of opposition. On one occasion, he offered his neck to an oppressive *amir* who was threatening him with execution, causing the *amir* to back down and set him free.[20] On another, Matthew successfully faced down a mob bent on destroying the Shahran Monastery.[21] On yet another, he rebuked an *amir* who was enacting discriminatory legislation against Christian women and threatened him with military reprisals at the hands of Christian kings, presumably those of Nubia and Ethiopia.[22]

The first two decades of Matthew's patriarchate correspond closely with the period in which the Circassian Mamluk Barquq held power (1382–1399, though he had effectively ruled since 1378).[23] Although I have not found any "Benjamin–'Amr" accounts of patriarch–ruler encounter in the sources, the *Life* reports that Matthew had a good relationship with the sultan: Barquq "loved this father, and he (Matthew) loved him also."[24] Difficulties came when Barquq was temporarily forced to flee Cairo in 1389, and his usurper arrested and fined the patriarch.[25] Not long after Barquq's death in 1399, Matthew was again arrested and shaken down for funds (by the *amir* Yalbugha al-Salimi, who was collecting funds for his war preparations against the approaching Timur-Lenk).[26] Matthew's third arrest came in 1408 at the hands of the *amir* Jamal al-Din, described by the Muslim historian Ibn Taghribirdi as "irreligious, bloodthirsty, and exceedingly tyrannical."[27] As part of his attempt to concentrate financial power in his hands by any and all possible means, Jamal al-Din accused Matthew of treacherous dealings with the Ethiopian king, hoping thereby to extract a huge ransom from the Coptic community. The *Life* reports that Matthew prayed that he be released from this oppression in such a way that the community not be harmed, and on 31 December 1408, his prayer was answered: he died peacefully at the age of 72. He was buried, in accordance with his instructions, at Dayr al-Khandaq, just outside of Cairo and readily accessible to its people.[28] According to the *Life*, Matthew remained to the end a humble monk, who insisted that his body be wrapped in a woolen shroud like any other monk so that no one should kiss his feet.[29] But he also, for the *Life*, remained a great holy man, whose burial ushered in a year of signs and wonders.[30]

An Orchestra of Holiness? The Principals

Patriarch Matthew is portrayed by his biographer as a fit successor of the greatest of the patriarchs and monastic leaders of the Egyptian church, a holy man who, with great authority and boldness, interceded for, blessed, and protected his community (*and* who efficaciously cursed its oppressors). Matthew, however, was not alone in his work on behalf of the Coptic community. To repeat a metaphor that I have used to describe Patriarchs Michael I (#46, 743–763) and Abraham ibn Zur'ah (#62, 975–978), Matthew may be considered a kind of "conductor" of an "orchestra of holiness."[31]

The principals in this ensemble, besides Matthew himself, were three saints commemorated every day in the Coptic Orthodox Church's *majma' al-qiddisin* ("assembly of the saints"), that is, the litany addressed to the Virgin, the angels, the apostles, the martyrs, and the saints. Patriarch Matthew's three contemporaries are mentioned in succession toward the end of the litany:[32] first, "Abba Tegi," better known as Anba Ruways (1334–1404), who was a close contemporary of Patriarch Matthew; next, "Abba Abra'am the *hegumenos*," that is, *al-Qummus* Ibrahim al-Fani of the Monastery of St. Antony (1321–1396), Matthew's senior by a quarter century; and finally, "our father Abba Markos," that is, Marqus al-Antuni, monk at the monastery of St. Antony and the eldest of the group (1296–1386), forty years older than Patriarch Matthew. Despite the forty-year range in age, the lives of these four overlapped for a full half century (from Matthew's birth in 1336 to Mark's death in 1386); the overlap includes the first eight years of Matthew's patriarchate.

A Holy Monk: Marqus al-Antuni

Patriarch Matthew himself showed the greatest deference to Marqus al-Antuni, one of the great saints of the Monastery of St. Antony.[33] Thanks to the existence of a *Life of Marqus al-Antuni* (composed shortly after his death in the well-known hagiographical form of a *Life* "proper" followed by thirty-four *Miracles*),[34] we can get a vivid picture of his long monastic career (c. 1319–1386)[35]—including his interactions with Patriarch Matthew. According to a story found in the *Life of Marqus* as well as the *Life of Matthew*, the two of them shared adversity in 1365 when, after the sack of Alexandria by Latin Christians based in Cyprus, the *amir* Yalbugha (ruled

1361–1366) was filled with rage against Christians;[36] his men raided the
Monastery of St. Antony, mistreated the monks, and seized everything of
value. The young monk Matthew was savagely beaten; when the much older
monk Marqus protested, Matthew was set free and Marqus beaten instead.
Eventually they and others were led off in fetters across the desert, in the
scorching heat, toward the Nile Valley at Itfih. When their captors refused
to give them water to drink, the *Lives* report, Marqus prayed for relief, and
God sent a downpour of rain. Shortly afterward, word arrived from the
sultan ordering the captives' release and safe return to the monastery.[37]

Matthew regarded Marqus as a kind of spiritual father. He asked
permission from Marqus before leaving the Monastery of St. Antony for
Dayr al-Muharraq,[38] and later begged leave to visit the elders of the
Monastery of St. Antony, "especially the blessed Marqus," before allowing
himself to be consecrated patriarch; these elders encouraged Matthew to
accept his call to service.[39] Within a few years, Patriarch Matthew returned
to the Monastery of St. Antony with a large assembly of Coptic notables
for the consecration of the Church of the Three Young Men in the
monastery garden. Once again, Matthew turned to Marqus, seeking his
support in the midst of the burdens of the patriarchate. Marqus encouraged
the patriarch:

> "Go, my father, and do not be afraid. The Lord, in his mercy
> upon you, has made the heaven earth, and the earth heaven."
> Thus he returned to his [patriarchal] throne in joy, and the
> Church stood upright in his days.[40]

Matthew was by no means the only person to travel to the Monastery
of St. Antony in order to seek the blessing and counsel of Marqus al-Antuni.
Marqus's *Life* and *Miracles* include many accounts of visitors who had traveled
long distances to see him (or whom he visited in miraculous fashion):
people in various kinds of distress, including women disguised as monks;[41]
converts to Islam who desired to repent and return to Christian faith;[42]
even high-ranking financial supervisors from among the "Muslim Copts"
who had run afoul of the authorities.[43] According to his *Life*, Marqus
possessed many of the charisms of a great saint: clairvoyance, prophecy,
bilocation, and the power to heal. He became a spiritual father for many
disciples. But perhaps what is most distinctive about his portrait is the way
in which he struggled for the salvation of souls,[44] and the alacrity with
which he forgave the sinners who came to him seeking a word of absolution
and hope.

A Faithful Disciple: Ibrahim al-Fani

The *qummus* Ibrahim al-Fani makes an early appearance in the *Life of Matthew* as one who had opposed Matthew's ordination at the age of eighteen —until, that is, he came to see Matthew's truly exceptional qualities.[45] A *Life of Ibrahim al-Fani* tells us much more about this rather neglected saint.[46] He began his monastic career at Dayr Abu Fanah (whence his *nisbah* "al-Fani") and lived as a hermit outside of Akhmim[47] before he moved to the Monastery of St. Antony in order to place himself under the supervision of the blessed Marqus.[48] Indeed, we are told that henceforth Ibrahim did nothing without consulting Marqus;[49] that Marqus was his trainer in the struggle against the demons;[50] and that it was Marqus who taught him to receive sinners with joy and to admit them promptly to the Eucharist, without assigning heavy penance.[51] Marqus's insistence on showing mercy to sinners was so great that on one occasion, according to his *Life*, he rebuked Ibrahim for being too harsh;[52] on another, he even admonished his disciples to flee from an image of St. Shenoute, since the stern archimandrite "frequently rejected sinners and cast them into Hell."[53]

When Marqus died in 1386, it was Ibrahim who led the mourning.[54] Up to this point, Ibrahim had lived mostly in the shadow of Marqus, but now he moved to Cairo, where he preached, exhorted Christians to righteous living, and participated in the charitable activities of his spiritual son, the patriarch Matthew.[55] Before Ibrahim died in 1396, he encouraged Matthew much as Marqus had done a decade or more earlier:

> "Do not let your heart be sad and afraid, O my son Matthew, but rather let it be strong, for many crowns are prepared for you with Christ because of the pains that you bear daily on behalf of your people."[56]

Ibrahim returned to his home village of Minyat Bani Khasib shortly before his death, died, and was buried there, although he was mourned both at the Monastery of St. Antony and at the Shahran Monastery south of Cairo, where Patriarch Matthew led the commemoration.[57] While Ibrahim's disciples were surprised that he had not chosen to be buried with the blessed Marqus at the Monastery of St. Antony, they certainly placed the two alongside one another in memory: the *Life of Ibrahim* does its utmost to associate Ibrahim in Marqus's glory.[58]

An Independent Saint: Anba Ruways

Marqus, Ibrahim, and Matthew were connected through the Monastery of St. Antony, which by the late fourteenth century—especially after the Black

Death had decimated the monasteries of Scetis—had become a major center of spiritual energy in the Coptic Orthodox Church.[59] The fourth great saint of the period, however, followed a different path. (Again, we possess a *Life*—or, formally, a *Life* "proper" followed by *Miracles*—that gives a vivid picture of his career.[60]) Furayj was a young Christian of Gharbiyyah who, when his father was forced to convert to Islam in 1354, fled his home (and, presumably, pressures to convert). He became a kind of itinerant fool, a "new Job" who lived in refuse dumps, wore few clothes, ate little food, and spoke few words. At times he enclosed himself in narrow places; at other times he lived exposed to the elements. His identity was a mystery to many: he used the name "Ruways," which had been the name of his affectionate camel, or "Tegi the liar."[61] Once a group of Muslim judges came out to see him, unsure of whether he was a Christian holy man or a Muslim *faqir*.[62] He was granted, his *Life* claims, extraordinary gifts: of prophecy,[63] of seeing heavenly beings,[64] and even of bilocation.[65] He and the blessed Marqus are said to have interacted at a great distance. On one occasion, Marqus told his disciples at the Monastery of St. Antony that Anba Ruways had just (mysteriously) been among them and had taken a blessing from the spring of water.[66] When Marqus died at the same monastery, Anba Ruways was overheard bidding him farewell from his distant hermitage.[67]

Anba Ruways passed through Cairo as early as 1371, some years before Matthew became patriarch.[68] Eventually he established himself in Cairo so that, despite his years of wandering the Egyptian countryside, he is primarily remembered as an urban saint, one who walked the streets of Cairo, visited its churches, and interacted with its folk.[69] He healed the sick and gave counsel and help to Copts in trouble, whether of their own or of others' making.[70] The *Life of Anba Ruways* tells one story in which the saint delivered a Coptic merchant who was just about to be arrested for receiving stolen sugar,[71] and another in which he rebuked a deacon who was planning a murder.[72] In two stories, Anba Ruways rescued Coptic men who had become inappropriately involved with women not their wives (in one case, from the rage of a jealous Muslim husband); both of these Copts repented and became monks at the Monastery of St. Antony.[73]

Inevitably, Anba Ruways's path crossed that of Patriarch Matthew, who bore witness to his capacity for fasting (eleven straight days on one occasion)[74] as well as to his miracles.[75] One wealthy Copt whom Anba Ruways healed of a serious injury, al-Sa'id Barakah ibn Wagh al-Muhr, became a wholehearted participant in the patriarch's charitable programs.[76] Furthermore, Matthew and Anba Ruways looked out for one another during unsettled times. On one occasion, Anba Ruways was arrested and carried off to the house of one of the *amir*s; there, despite a savage beating, he refused to say a word to his tormentors, in imitation of Christ who kept his silence before Pilate. On that occasion it was patriarch Matthew who came and arranged for Ruways's release.[77] Returning the favor, Anba Ruways prayed from his sickbed for the release of Patriarch Matthew during the patriarch's imprisonment in the year 1400, following the death of the sultan Barquq.[78]

A few years later, in 1404, the strange saint died and was buried at Dayr al-Khandaq, in the church commonly known today as the Church of Anba Ruways; his grave would soon be visited by people seeking healing.[79] Four years later, Patriarch Matthew died and was buried in the same church. Thus, two of the greatest saints of the city of Cairo came to the same final resting place, near the city and close to their people.

A Quartet and a Chorus?

Taken together, the ministries of these four saints—Patriarch Matthew, Marqus al-Antuni, Ibrahim al-Fani, and Anba Ruways—represent an extraordinary project of shoring up the Christian community toward the end of a near-disastrous century. In the previous chapter, we reviewed the catastrophes of the early Mamluk period and the recurring episodes of anti-*dhimmi* legislation and anti-Christian rioting that punctuated it. Both the Coptic sacred geography and sacred calendar, space and time, had suffered as churches were destroyed and festivals curtailed.[80] Conversion to Islam—whether the result of coercion, association, calculation, resignation, or conviction—had become commonplace. Matthew and the remarkable individuals clustered about him lived at a time when the Coptic Christian community was experiencing a new "crisis of cohesion," as it hemorrhaged members and prestige.[81] The impression left by their *Lives* is that they faced the crisis with energy, imagination, and courage. There we find them ministering to the basic needs of poor Copts (and Muslims, e.g., Matthew's charitable programs); working to bind elite Copts to the Church (e.g., Ruways and his involvement with urban Copts in various sorts of trouble); cultivating ties with Muslim Copts in government administration (e.g., Marqus and his contacts); and carefully tending relationships with the Muslim authorities (e.g., Matthew and the sultan al-Zahir Barquq). Through such measures, as well as by encouraging the restoration of penitent apostates to the community (e.g., Marqus and Ibrahim and their joyful reception of "sinners"), these saints appear to have been doing their utmost to stabilize a community that had been reeling from the repeated blows dealt it during a terrible period of its history.

There is more to the story, however. Matthew's biography in the Cairo edition of the *History of the Patriarchs* comes to the following rather abrupt conclusion:

> And the number of the martyrs who suffered martyrdom in his time was forty-nine martyrs. May the blessing of his prayer and the prayer of all the Saints be with us. Amen.[82]

Forty-nine martyrs?[83] Fortunately, the full *Life of Matthew* gives a list of their names, where they came from, and occasionally a few notes about the circumstances of their martyrdom:[84] a summary is given in an appendix to this book. The list is rather widely ecumenical: it includes, for example, four *Latin* priests martyred while on pilgrimage to Jerusalem;[85] another Latin priest, an Ethiopian monk, and an Armenian are also mentioned.[86] One of the martyrs was a Muslim convert (from a Muslim family).[87] Most of the names in the list, however, are those of Copts: a small number of Copts who refused to give in to conversion by force;[88] a larger number of Copts who had converted to Islam but then announced their return to Christian faith, and were subsequently executed for apostasy;[89] and many Christians executed for invective preaching against Islam.[90]

A few of the forty-nine martyrs are remembered in the Copto-Arabic *Synaxarion*, which allows us to date some of the martyrdoms to the early 1380s.[91] This information is supplemented by what we find in Islamic sources. For example, the Muslim chronicler al-Maqrizi reports that in Dhu l-Hijjah AH 781 (= March AD 1380)

> a party of men and women came to Cairo and mentioned that they had apostatized from Islam, that before [becoming Muslims] they had been Christians, and that by their apostasy they desired to be brought near to Christ through the shedding of their blood. They were offered Islam several times, but they did not accept it, and said: "We have come to be purified and brought near to the Lord Christ."[92]

They were all beheaded: the men first, and then, after another offer of conversion, the women.[93] The matter did not end there, however. Shortly afterward, a Christian monk appeared and publicly denounced Islam. He was promptly beheaded, at which three female followers exultantly "lifted their voices with the clattering of their tongues as women do at their feasts"—and resumed the monk's invective.[94] On 30 March 1380 they too were executed and their bodies burned, "on account that they had apostatized from Islam."[95] Al-Maqrizi goes on to comment:

> They showed that they did this out of love for the aforementioned monk, who was known as Abu Qufayfah. In the annals of love we have not heard any story stranger than this![96]

We note that with the exception of the monk "Abu Qufayfah" (executed for his preaching against Islam), the other martyrs were put to the sword for apostasy: these were people who had been identified as members of the Muslim community, but who then returned to Christian faith and sought salvation in martyrdom.

While al-Maqrizi's initial group of martyrs does not clearly correlate with the martyr list in the *Life of Matthew*,[97] the second group of martyrs does: al-Maqrizi's "Abu Qufayfah" is almost certainly Ya'qub Abu Muqaytif, who heads the list and is immediately followed by "his [spiritual] daughters, the three truly courageous nuns, who, when they were offered up to the sword, exulted and rejoiced with ululations, as women exult at their feasts and weddings."[98] Moreover, in the *Life of Marqus al-Antuni* we learn that Ya'qub had been Marqus's disciple,[99] and that his "daughters" included women with ties to Marqus: he had encouraged them and foreseen their martyrdom.[100] It appears, then, that Marqus was an influential figure at the beginning of the wave of martyrdoms (which began in 1380, but may have continued into the 1390s).[101] We know that Marqus welcomed penitent apostates: some became monks;[102] others returned to the world. Among those who returned to the world, some were able to live in peace as Christians;[103] others may have hoped for a peaceful life, but, when denounced and hauled before a judge, refused to deny their Christian faith even if that led to their execution.[104] And then there were the *voluntary* martyrs: penitent apostates who returned to the world determined to make public display of their Christian faith and thereby provoke their own martyrdom, joined by other Christians who shared their aspirations and achieved them by defaming Islam.[105]

When a comparable wave of voluntary martyrdoms broke out in Córdoba, al-Andalus (Islamic Spain) in the 850s, the Christian community there was torn between those who honored and supported the martyrs and those who saw their actions as destructive to the community.[106] Nor was the Coptic Orthodox community in the late fourteenth century of a single mind with regard to voluntary martyrdoms. Were these martyrs heroes of the faith who dramatically reclaimed public space, drew clear lines of demarcation between what was Christian and what was not, and in general issued a call to fearless discipleship before a rapt Christian (and formerly Christian) audience?[107] Or were they misguided suicides who by their verbal violence were upsetting prospects for communal peace?[108]

The author of the *Life of Ibrahim* regarded the wave of martyrdoms as something glorious, and was happy to portray Ibrahim and Marqus as giving the voluntary martyrs their encouragement and blessing.[109] In the *Life of Marqus*, however, we have hints that the martyrdoms were controversial, even among the monks of the Monastery of St. Antony.[110] And if this was true in the Eastern Desert, how much more disconcerting the voluntary martyrdoms must have been in Cairo-Misr, where Patriarch Matthew was careful to maintain a good working relationship with Sultan Barquq![111] The *Life of Matthew*, in fact, attributes the end of the wave of martyrdoms to the patriarch's prayers.[112]

If Matthew had misgivings about any of the martyrs of his day, however, the author of his *Life* is eager to include Matthew among them. According to this author, when Matthew died (peacefully, we remember, thereby cheating the tyrant Jamal al-Din of a hostage and victim), he was received into heaven by a great crowd of saints, beginning with the Virgin Mary and the Archangel Michael. The apostles, evangelists, Old Testament patriarchs, and the bishops of the ecumenical councils all came to seat Matthew with his eighty-six predecessors, the popes of the Egyptian church. At the heavenly banquet table he found "his children, the martyrs of his times." Marqus al-Antuni was there, rejoicing; he had prophesied that Matthew would receive a crown like the crown of martyrdom. Anba Ruways also rejoiced with Matthew; he had prophesied that Matthew's soul would be taken up to heaven along with the souls of his children the martyrs.[113]

Whatever controversies may have existed within the Coptic Orthodox Church regarding the voluntary martyrs of Matthew's patriarchate, and whatever turbulent mix of conviction, despair, emotion, and political calculation informed them, the *Life of Matthew* concludes with a vision of perfect harmony. The exemplary patriarch has run his earthly course. A humble monk, holy man, wonder-worker, and bloodless martyr, he is surrounded by the saints and martyrs of his own days, welcomed by the Orthodox saints of all times, and seated with his predecessors—all the patriarchs of the Egyptian church. Just so, the author of the *Life* powerfully asserted Patriarch Matthew's place as one of the greatest patriarchs of the Coptic Orthodox Church, clothed the voluntary martyrs of his day in sanctity, and provided the faithful with an account of a burst of holiness that might inspire and sustain them in difficult days ahead.

Nine

Humility in Action

Gabriel V (#88, 1409–1427)
John XI (#89, 1427–1452)
Matthew II (#90, 1452–1465)
Gabriel VI (#91, 1466–1474)
Michael VI (#92, 1477–1478)
John XII (#93, 1480–1482)
John XIII (#94, 1484–1524)

After the Fireworks

When Patriarch Matthew I died at the end of the year 1408, the last of the remarkable saints treated in the previous chapter had passed from the scene. If a "burst of holiness" had lit up the Coptic community for a time, it had now faded. Anba Ruways had once predicted that people would mourn the passing of "the days of Matthew and Barquq" (from about 1378 to 1399);[1] those days were now slipping into a dim past.

The period of Circassian Mamluk rule post-Barquq was rather grim for the Coptic community—and indeed, for many of the inhabitants of Egypt. If it began (in 1400) with the *amir* Yalbugha al-Salimi arresting and trying to extract money from Patriarch Matthew in order to fund his war preparations against the approaching Timur-Lenk,[2] the last patriarch of the period, John XIII (#94, 1484–1524), was repeatedly pressed for funds in order to finance the wars of Sultan Qaitbay (1468–1496) and his successors against the Ottomans (from 1484) and the Portuguese (from 1501).[3] Those wars would be, finally, in vain: the Portuguese in the Indian Ocean were successful at cutting the spice trade that was the major source of Cairo's wealth, while the Ottomans, after initial setbacks, were finally able to absorb Egypt into their empire in 1517.[4]

119

It should be pointed out that the Christians were not specially singled out by Mamluk revenue collectors (often expert in pillage and torture), any more than they were singled out by the effects of insufficient Nile flooding and famine (as occurred in 1403) or outbreaks of plague (as in 1405 and, on the average, once every eight years thereafter). They *were*, along with the Jewish community, singled out for periodic renewals of anti-*dhimmi* regulations (e.g., in 1417, 1419, 1422, 1442, 1463), including the exclusion of Christians and Jews from the government financial bureaus and rules concerning dress—e.g., blue turbans for Christian men, yellow ones for Jews—and the riding of animals.[5] The fact that these regulations had to be renewed so often is a clear indication that they seldom stayed in force for long, but the constant pressure on the Coptic elite meant ongoing conversions to Islam and, for the Coptic community as a whole, the loss of prominent members and their wealth.[6]

It is against this background that we examine the patriarchs of the fifteenth century. The *History of the Patriarchs* and the patriarchal history attributed to Bishop Yusab have only the briefest of entries for them;[7] searching for portrayals of these patriarchs is a mostly frustrating task. However, a few passages give food for thought, and occasionally we have writings from a patriarch's own hand. In these, the patriarch's humility is a recurring theme: not humility wrapped in signs and wonders (as was the case for Patriarch Matthew I, as we saw in the previous chapter), but humility of a tough, practical sort well suited to the times.

"Listless" and "Lacking in Blessing"?

Matthew's successor as patriarch was a monk and former civil servant who took the name Gabriel V (#88, 1409–1427). According to the *Life of Matthew*, his patriarchate had an auspicious beginning: as he was being ordained *hegumenos* (in preparation for his consecration as patriarch), Matthew himself appeared and participated in the laying on of hands.[8] But if this Christian source affords Gabriel's patriarchate a supernatural blessing at its beginning, an Islamic source gives a rather different picture after its end. In his necrology for the year AH 830 (AD 1426–1427), the Muslim chronicler al-Maqrizi wrote:

> Gabriel, patriarch of the Jacobite Christians, perished on Wednesday, 2 Rabi' I.[9] He was originally from the scribal class, then he rose until he assumed the patriarchate. His days were the worst days through which the Christians had ever passed. He encountered tribulations and the most humiliating

bitterness. He used to walk the roads on foot. When he entered the council ["sitting-place"] of the sultan and the emirs, he would remain standing. He possessed little. He went out to the villages many times in order to beg for alms, but he accomplished little because of the want and poverty that had descended upon them. It used to be that the patriarchs were owed dues by the *hatti*, the king of Ethiopia, and that great wealth would be brought them from him; but this was cut off in the days of this Gabriel because of their contempt and indifference toward him. Their complaint against him was that he had been a scribe [= financial administrator] and in this capacity was involved in acts of injustice against [his own] people. In sum, we have never perceived a patriarch more listless in movement or more lacking in blessing.[10]

Gabriel's days were indeed hard times for the Egyptian Christian community, with blows coming from every direction. From Cairo, the decision was taken (in 1412) to collect the *jizyah* individually, rather than by community: every Christian or Jew would owe from 1 to 4 dinars annually, depending on economic status.[11] Repeated attempts were made to enforce the *ghiyar* regulations that publicly distinguished and humiliated Christians and Jews. From the south (if al-Maqrizi's report is right), aid from the Ethiopian king was being withheld. And one of the rudest shocks (again, if al-Maqrizi is to be trusted) came from the north, when news arrived that Venetian merchants had stolen one of the holiest relics of the Coptic Orthodox Church: the head of St. Mark the Evangelist.[12]

The Copts had long and with great pride guarded the holy relic of the head of St. Mark the Evangelist, ever since (according to the *History of the Patriarchs*) it came into the possession of Patriarch Benjamin soon after the Arab conquest of Egypt.[13] Mawhub ibn Mansur ibn Mufarrij, the original translator–editor of the *History of the Patriarchs*, reports that the holy relic was, at a certain point during the patriarchate of Christodoulos (eleventh century), in danger of confiscation (and sale to the Chalcedonians!). It was saved, in the end, but Mawhub's own father spent thirty-seven days in prison while the governor of Alexandria tried to track down the precious relic.[14] We also know that the relic was ritually visited and wrapped in a rich new cloth by new patriarchs upon their consecration in the city; at least, we have reports to this effect for Patriarchs Mark ibn Zur'ah (in the twelfth century) and Cyril III ibn Laqlaq (in the thirteenth),[15] as well as instructions for the ritual (from the thirteenth and fourteenth centuries).[16] The theft of this material connection to the founder of the Egyptian Church and the first of the Coptic patriarchs was nothing short of an outrage. "The Jacobite Christians were enraged and made a big deal of the matter," reports al-Maqrizi, "and considered it an enfeeblement of their religion."[17]

In the midst of all of Gabriel's tribulations, and despite al-Maqrizi's claim that he was "listless in movement" and "lacking in blessing," he did find occasion and energy for specifically churchly activities. One remarkable achievement was in the liturgical realm: Gabriel oversaw a project of gathering, standardizing, and providing notes and rubrics for the services of the Coptic Orthodox Church. The resulting *Book of Ritual*[18] was approved at a synod held at the Church of St. Mercurius in 1411, and has exercised an influence on the Coptic liturgy down to the present day.[19]

Another accomplishment of Gabriel's patriarchate was the assistance rendered to the *Syrian* Orthodox Church, which had fallen on very hard times as a result of the Mongol invasions and the Mamluk defeat (in 1375) of the regional Christian power, the Armenian kingdom of Cilicia. Among the results of this terrible period in Syrian Orthodox church history was the scattering of Syrian Orthodox Christians to places of (relative) security and the development of parallel Syrian Orthodox patriarchates (of Antioch-Syria and of Mardin, and later, of Tur 'Abdin).[20] In the year 1422, the Syrian Orthodox bishop of Jerusalem, Mar Basilius Shem'un, visited Patriarch Gabriel with the news that Patriarch Philoxenus II (of Antioch and Syria) had died, and requested that he, Mar Basilius, be consecrated patriarch in his place.[21] Gabriel at first demurred, but finally was persuaded by the argument that the bishops in Syria were few in number, subject to harassment, and thus unable to meet in synod. Thus Gabriel and three bishops (two Copts and one Syrian) consecrated Basilius as *Patriarch* Basilius IV. The consecration took place at the Church of St. Mercurius in Misr, after which Basilius was formally enthroned at the Church of the Virgin at Harat al-Zuwaylah, Cairo.[22]

These accomplishments are by no means insignificant. It appears, then, that one must take al-Maqrizi's obituary notice for Patriarch Gabriel with several grains of salt. This "listless" patriarch was responsible for a major work of liturgical scholarship and preservation that has proved its worth to generations of worshippers. And, despite "tribulations" and "humiliating bitterness," he was able to provide aid to a Christian community in even greater need, and opened a new period of fruitful cooperation between the Coptic and the Syrian Orthodox Churches. Al-Maqrizi may have pronounced Patriarch Gabriel "lacking in blessing" and a cause for shame, but the Orthodox faithful may have seen him otherwise: as a humble patriarch who, even in the hardest of times, was able to find opportunities for service to the Church.

Diplomacy and Faithfulness

One of the participants in the service of consecration of Syrian Orthodox Patriarch Basilius IV in 1422 was the priest of the Church of St. Mercurius, one Abu l-Faraj.[23] Perhaps this exposure to matters ecumenical and international was a token of things to come, for, as Patriarch John XI (#89, 1427–1452), the former priest Abu l-Faraj would come to have extensive contacts throughout the Christian world, including correspondence with Roman Catholic Pope Eugene IV (1431–1447) on the one hand, and with the great Ethiopian "King of Kings" Zar'a Ya'qob (1434–1468) on the other.

But first, it was not very long after becoming patriarch that John once again met Syrian Orthodox Patriarch Basilius IV. Together, the two were responsible for the first of only two known occasions during the century on which the holy *myron* was prepared.[24] The visiting patriarch was in need of the chrism,[25] and so the two patriarchs and the metropolitan of Jerusalem prepared it at the Mu'allaqah Church in Misr during Holy Week of 1430. There is no record of any Coptic bishops or clergy in attendance, as the plague was raging in Misr-Cairo at the time.[26]

Plague was just one of many difficulties that the Coptic community experienced during John's patriarchate. Between 1437 and 1439 there were renewed assaults on the Coptic Orthodox 'sacred geography': a church in Shubra was burned, part of the Mu'allaqah Church was destroyed, and churches in Damietta were pillaged.[27] The greatest shock, however, was the destruction in 1438 of Dayr al-Maghtis, the Monastery of the Pool, in the northern Delta.[28] The monastery had by this time become a major pilgrimage site: not only had it become associated with the itinerary of the Holy Family during the Flight into Egypt, but it was also the site of an annual festival, the *'Id al-Zuhur* or "Feast of the Apparition." Every May (21 Bashans), crowds of pilgrims gathered at the monastery church and watched expectantly for the Virgin Mary to make an appearance in a luminous boat.[29]

Dayr al-Maghtis had been a way station for Ethiopian pilgrims to Jerusalem,[30] and it soon came to play a role in Egyptian–Ethiopian relations. The destruction of the monastery came just a few years after Zar'a Ya'qob, who would earn a reputation as one of the greatest monarchs in Ethiopia's history, came to power, taking the throne name Constantine I. He took his role as an Ethiopian Constantine seriously, which meant both building up the Church in Ethiopia (a project in which bishops sent from Egypt assisted) and asserting himself as protector of Orthodox Christians, in Egypt and elsewhere. As early as 1437, he wrote to the Egyptian authorities seeking good relations—but also good treatment of Christians and their churches.[31] In 1443, after Patriarch John had sent him news of the destruction of Dayr al-Maghtis, the request had become a demand.[32]

Zar'a Ya'qob's threats—whether of retaliating against Muslims in Ethiopia if the Copts were ill treated, or of withholding the waters of the Nile—placed his co-religionist and correspondent, the Coptic patriarch, in a delicate position with the governing authorities. In fact, in 1448 Sultan Jaqmaq (1438–1453) had Patriarch John arrested, beaten, imprisoned, and fined. Then he was forced to take an oath that he would henceforth have no contact with the king of Ethiopia in any way whatsoever except by the explicit permission of the sultan. Any infraction of that oath would merit death.[33]

Perhaps unknown to the Mamluk authorities, Patriarch John had already had an exchange of letters and embassies with the pope of Rome, Eugene IV.[34] In 1440 the Roman pope's representative in the east, the Franciscan Alberto de Sarteano, had approached the Coptic patriarch with Pope Eugene's invitation to join the union between Latin and Greek churches that had been proclaimed the previous year at the Council of Florence. Patriarch John received the pope's letter almost as if it were a synodical letter from one patriarch to another with whom he was in communion, and, after translation, had it read aloud during a liturgy at the Church of the Virgin in Harat al-Zuwaylah. He then responded to the pope's letter in kind. In a composition marked by the greatest courtesy and flowery language, including the rhymed prose so typical of Arabic, he confessed the Orthodox faith and offered thanks to and prayers for the pope.[35] What is striking about the letter is that, despite its humble and courteous tone, Patriarch John makes no concessions to major Roman concerns, e.g., papal primacy or the existence of two natures in the incarnate Christ.[36] Nor does it broach any practical, canonical issues of church-to-church relations. This may be, in part, because Patriarch John knew that discussions about union at the practical level would be unwelcome to the Mamluk authorities; but it also reflects the Coptic patriarch's determination to stand his Church's doctrinal and canonical ground—but to do so in a language of love and utmost respect.[37]

Patriarch John appointed the monk Andrea, superior of the Monastery of St. Antony, as his representative to the Council of Florence. Andrea did indeed travel to Florence, and on 4 February 1442 the bull *Cantate Domino* announced the union of the Coptic and Roman churches. The union came to little, however: the Latins understood it as a union under the Roman Pontiff, while the Copts did not understand it as more than a "union of love."[38] With this exchange, a pattern was set for future Coptic Orthodox–

Roman Catholic negotiations (which would be renewed in earnest in the sixteenth and seventeenth centuries).[39] Patriarch John had shown that there could be, underlying a courteous humility and a genuine desire for fellowship, a firmness of identity and unwillingness to compromise Coptic Orthodox faith and culture—even for the sake of winning allies in troubled times.

Quiet Leadership in Difficult Times

We know little about the patriarchs who followed John XI. As mentioned above, the standard histories of the patriarchs give us exceedingly brief entries containing information that can quickly be reduced to a table.[40] But even the data recorded in such sources—the patriarchs' names and places of origin, the monasteries from which they came—are revealing. Both Matthew II (#90, 1452–1465) and John XII (#93, 1480–1482) were monks of Dayr al-Muharraq, near al-Qusiyya in Upper Egypt. Matthew was called "al-Sa'idi," the Upper Egyptian, while Michael VI (#92, 1477–1478), John XII (#93, 1480–1482), and John XIII (#94, 1484–1524) all hailed from Middle or Upper Egyptian towns.[41] When John XIII died, it was Bishop Gabriel of Manfalut who led the mourning. In all this, we see a shift of the center of Egyptian Christian life southward. This had been going on for some time, of course; in the previous chapter we noted the shift of monastic spiritual energy from Scetis to the Red Sea monasteries. During the patriarchate of John XIII, however, the latter fell into ruin: we possess a note in his own hand from the year 1506 in which he laments that the Monastery of St. Antony was "empty, deprived of inhabitants."[42] As the Red Sea monasteries declined, however, monasteries such as Dayr al-Muharraq gained in importance.[43]

After Patriarchs John and Basilius prepared the holy *myron* in 1430, we know of only one more such preparation during Mamluk times—and indeed, only one more occasion until 1703. This took place in 1458, when Patriarch Matthew II prepared the holy chrism at the Church of the Virgin in Harat al-Rum, Cairo. Six bishops were in attendance—a small number, but what is also striking is that only one of them was from the Delta; the others came from well south of Cairo, including the bishop of Qusqam (that is, Dayr al-Muharraq).[44] While we are probably incompletely informed on these matters,[45] we are left with the impression of an impoverished and demographically changing church. Certainly, both the numerical and geographical contrasts between the *myron* consecration of 1305 (described in Chapter Seven) and that of 1458 are striking: for the former, eighteen bishops from both Upper and Lower Egypt gathered at the Monastery of St. Macarius; for the latter, six bishops, five of them from Middle and Upper Egypt, met in Cairo.

The popes of the final decades of Mamluk rule in Egypt will undoubtedly come into greater focus as scholars examine their correspondence and other documentary materials, preserved especially in the Library of the Coptic Patriarchate. Some beginnings have been made.[46] For example, a letter from Patriarch John XIII to his colleague Ignatius Nuh of Lebanon, patriarch of Antioch and Syria (1494–1509), has recently been published.[47] It is a letter of commendation for a Syrian priest named Ibrahim, who had been caught in the complexities of parallel Syrian Orthodox patriarchates: Ibrahim had been consecrated metropolitan of the town of al-Ma'dan by the Syrian Orthodox patriarch of Tur 'Abdin, and not by Patriarch Ignatius Nuh (of Antioch-Syria), who had consecrated his own candidate for the position. In his letter, Coptic Patriarch John attempts to give pastoral advice in the midst of a touchy situation. John concedes that the patriarch of Tur 'Abdin had erred in consecrating a metropolitan for a town outside of his jurisdiction, and insists that the canon of Nicaea stipulating that there cannot be two bishops for the same city must be upheld. Yet he still gives Ibrahim his support, and hopes that Patriarch Ignatius Nuh can do so as well.[48] He counsels his colleague as follows:

> But for the sake of God (may he be exalted!), pass over this matter graciously, and be like the Lord Christ, the Generous, the Longsuffering. Let nothing show that indicates wrath, because of the difficulty of the time.[49]

Patriarch John then invokes the figure of St. Severus of Antioch to remind his successor that the canons of the Church were always intended to be compassionate.

> And likewise it is necessary now as well, because of the great destruction, ruin, and want in every place, that the fathers look to their people with mercy, because of the hour and the time, and that they take care in what they decree for them: [both] that they be able to bear it, given the time, and that they are in need of it. For example, [they should] provide them with certain knowledge by which they may refine their belief and their powers of will, by which their way of life will be made beautiful, their worship complete, and their alms a duty. [They should provide them as well with] leadership by which their life in society may be good and their condition upright, in this world and the next.[50]

Patriarch John XIII was all too aware of "the great destruction, ruin, and want in every place." Just so, the shepherds of the Christian flocks were called to be forgiving, gracious, generous, longsuffering, slow to anger, merciful—so as to bind up the community, and neither cause damage nor give anyone else the opportunity to do so. Their call was to provide the leadership by which Christians' life in society might be "good." These are rather humble goals, rendered in language that is not particularly exalted or stirring. Given the "difficulty of the time," however, they were appropriate. John's letter is a reminder of the sort of quiet, humble, realistic leadership that—perhaps just as much as saintly fireworks—helped the Coptic Orthodox Church through one of its most difficult periods.

Epilogue

Survival

In this book I have attempted to pay close attention to how the medieval Coptic Orthodox patriarchs were portrayed by their biographers, and how these portrayals not only reflected but also helped to define 'Coptic Orthodox' identity during the long centuries between the Arab conquest and that of the Ottoman Turks. The techniques of representation have been many and varied, including the use of biblical echo and allusion, motifs from the *Lives* of saints and martyrs, and even the use of a particular hagiographical literary form (the *Life-Miracles* genre). In these portrayals, the *continuity* of the Coptic Orthodox Church with its great past is continually stressed: we note regular allusions to Saints Mark, Athanasius, and Cyril; the popes are frequently described with the virtues—and occasionally with the thaumaturgic gifts—of the great desert ascetics and 'holy men'. At the same time, the theological *specificity* of the Coptic Orthodox Church in contrast to Chalcedonian (and other) competitors is made clear; it is no accident that mentions of Severus of Antioch, the great theologian of the Cyrillian one-nature Christology, bracket the present volume.[1]

These elements—continuity with the great Egyptian Christian past and theological specificity over against the followers of Chalcedon—were already in evidence in the patriarchal biographies described by Stephen J. Davis in Chapter Four of the first volume in this series, on the two centuries between the Council of Chalcedon and the Arab conquest of Egypt (451–640s).[2] As Egyptian Christians came to be part of the "new world order" of the *Dar al-Islam*, however, what came to be termed 'Coptic Orthodox' identity continued to be constructed, defined, and defended—and the Coptic Orthodox patriarchate with it. As the community came to view itself as the suffering Church "of the Martyrs," patriarchs were portrayed as patient sufferers, sometimes winning "crowns" akin to those of martyrdom.[3] As the community celebrated its specifically Egyptian 'sacred geography' (within the territory controlled by Muslim rulers), patriarchs are described as actively building, rebuilding, and consecrating churches and monasteries, thereby doing their best to maintain (and occasionally to extend) the network of sacred spaces that provided Coptic Orthodox culture its territorial rootedness. As relationships between rulers and patriarchs had again and again to be established, the literary tradition provided an account of mutual assistance and respect—that of the meeting between 'Amr ibn al-'As and Patriarch Benjamin—that remained an ideal template throughout the medieval period. And as lay notables came to play significant roles in negotiating and managing the interface between Muslim authorities and the Church, the patriarchs are sometimes, at least, portrayed as "conductors" of an ensemble in which all manner of gifts are put to work, for the benefit of the community as a whole.[4]

The patriarchs of the medieval period were not merely literary constructions, as significant a role as their portrayals may have had in the definition, description, and elaboration of Coptic Orthodox identity. Behind the portrayals as they have come to us were human beings, many of them quite remarkable, who were active participants in the creation and tending of this identity. They reenacted the connection of the Coptic Orthodox Church to St. Mark through ceremonies of consecration in Alexandria and even, in the later Middle Ages, through visiting the relic of St. Mark's head. They sent synodical letters in which the faith of the Three Ecumenical Councils, as elaborated by Patriarchs Dioscorus and Theodosius of Alexandria and Severus of Antioch, was promulgated. They marked the space and time sacred to the Copts, consecrating churches, celebrating feasts, and traveling the Egyptian 'sacred geography' (with special emphasis on Scetis and the Monastery of St. Macarius). They dealt with government officials as well as with notables within their own community. And, on special occasions (such as the consecration of the holy *myron*), they liturgically enacted the unity of the Church, as clergy and laity gathered about the patriarch at the altar.

The patriarchs' synodical letters spelled out in detail the meaning of 'Orthodox' in the phrase 'Coptic Orthodox Church'. As for the term 'Coptic', it is multivalent, indicating, in the first place, the specifically *Egyptian* character of the Church (with its particular history and geography); in the second place, its *Christian* commitment (in contrast with the Islamic faith of Egypt's rulers); and in addition, its investment in the *Coptic language* as a sign of both. Even as Egyptian Christians lost fluency in Coptic, the medieval patriarchs were active in the attempt to maintain the Church's investment in the language at the same time that the very preservation of Christian faith required an overcoming of resistance to the use of Arabic in theology, catechesis, and even worship. It is part of the greatness of Patriarch Gabriel II ibn Turayk (#70) that he possessed and called for competence in both languages, at the same time that he worked to make the Church's instruction and prayer accessible to Christians who only spoke Arabic. And it is worth noting that one of the last literary monuments of the period covered by this volume is the *Book of Ritual* by Patriarch Gabriel V (#88)—an Arabic-language guide to the proper use of Coptic liturgical texts.

As mentioned in the Preface, some readers will find the story of the medieval Coptic Orthodox Church to be one of tragic loss: loss of a language with its specific cultural possibilities, loss of numbers and position in society, loss of sacred space.[5] The community's relationship to the Coptic language certainly underwent a radical change during the centuries covered here. As for demographic losses, while we have no census numbers for medieval Egypt, the sources consulted for this volume provide some striking indicators. For example, when (according to the *History of the Patriarchs*) Patriarch Simon (#42) convened a synod toward the end of the seventh century, sixty-four bishops were in attendance; when Patriarch Matthew II (#90) consecrated the holy *myron* in 1452, only six bishops were present. In addition, the loss of shrines (e.g., the pilgrimage center of St. Menas, or Dayr al-Maghtis) and the suppression of festivals make for somber reading.

Still, just as the present volume bears witness to a Coptic Orthodox cultural revival *in Arabic*, so it bears witness to the "elasticity" of the Egyptian sacred geography. As Alexandria declined in importance, Misr-Cairo became a great center of the Church; when the monasteries of Scetis fell silent in our sources, the Red Sea monasteries as well as Dayr Shahran and later Dayr al-Muharraq and others rose to new significance; while the shrine of St. Menas fell into ruin, the itinerary of the Holy Family's sojourn in Egypt was gradually elaborated. And while, at the end of the period covered in this volume, Dayr al-Maghtis had been destroyed, there would soon again be a thriving pilgrimage center in the same region of the Delta, one dedicated to St. Dimyanah.[6]

As I complete this book, it is, finally, the *survival* of the Egyptian church, rather than its demographic decline, that makes the greatest impression on me: the Coptic Orthodox Church, with its patriarchs as reflections, exemplars, and actors, developed and tended an identity and culture that was complex, satisfying, and supple enough to withstand serious challenges and to bounce back from especially difficult times. The present volume breaks off after the great literary and artistic renaissance of the thirteenth century had given way to the trials and tribulations of the Mamluk period. This is, however, by no means the end of the story. It is the privilege of the authors of the third volume of this three-volume set to tell the story of the modern patriarchs and their roles in later revivals of the Coptic Orthodox Church—in the eighteenth century, and again in the twentieth.[7]

Appendix

The Forty-Nine Martyrs during the Patriarchate of Matthew I (#87, 1378–1408)[1]

1.   Ya'qub Abu Muqaytif [on or before 30 March 1380][M]
2–4.   Three nuns, his [spiritual] daughters [30 March 1380][M]
5.   Rizq Allah, his disciple [3 Barmudah = 29 March 1380][S]
6.   Iliyya, from the people of Durunkah
7–8.   Sidrak and Fadl Allah, from the Monastery of St. Antony [15 Bashans = 10 May 1383][S]
9.   Da'ud al-Banna', from the Monastery of St. Antony [19 Barmudah = 14 April 1383][S]
10–12. Barakah (called Jirjis), Jirjis, and Jirjis, from the same monastery
13.   Arsaniyus al-Habashi, from Jabal Qusqam (al-Muharraq Monastery) [9 Bashans = 4 May 1380][S]
14.   The priest Quzman al-Kharraz, from Qandul
15.   The priest Abu Faraj, from Gharb Qamulah
16.   The priest Rufa'il, from al-Buhayrah
17.   The priest Yuhanna, from the people of Tukh
18.   A Latin priest martyred outside of Alexandria
19.   The priest Hibat Allah al-Katib, also martyred outside of Alexandria
20–23. Four Latin priests martyred while on pilgrimage to Jerusalem [before 5 November 1393][M]
24–30. The soldier–priest and monk Musa and six companions, also soldiers, martyred between Gaza and Jerusalem
31.   Hadid (or Jadid), from Giza (refused to convert as his grandfather had done)
32–33. Two Coptic youths of Misr, Nasr Allah and Abu Ishaq
34–35. Ya'qub and Yuhanna, from the people of Sunbat

36.   Bulus, from Munyat Bani Khasib
37–38.   Furayj, from Tanan, and his companion Mikha'il, [spiritual] son
           of Ruways
39.   The priest Ya'qub (apostatized under duress but returned to the
           faith the next day)
40–41.   The monks Mansur ibn Butrus and Da'ud the *amnut* (refused to
           convert despite coercion)
42.   Ibrahim al-Suryani (apostate monk who returned to Christianity)
43.   Mikha'il (formerly "Mamadiyus"), convert (refused to renounce
           his Christian faith)
44.   'Isa, an Armenian
45.   Abu l-Faraj al-Banna', from al-Maqs
46.   Ghubriyal, from Huw
47.   Ibrahim, from Shubra
48.   Ya'qub, from al-Manawat
49.   Jirjis, known as Ibn al-Rahibah

[M] = date from Maqrizi, *Suluk*, iii. [S] = date from *Synaxarion* (ed. Forget), ii.

Works Cited

Primary Sources

Abu Qurrah, Theodore. *Theologus Autodidactus* (translator's title). Translated by John C. Lamoreaux, in *Theodore Abu Qurrah*. Library of the Christian East 1. Provo, Utah: Brigham Young University Press, 2005.

Alexander II, Patriarch of Alexandria. *Paschal Letter.* Translated by L. S. B. MacCoull. "The Paschal Letter of Alexander II, Patriarch of Alexandria: A Greek Defense of Coptic Theology under Arab Rule," *Dumbarton Oaks Papers* 44 (1990), 29–34.

Athanasius, Patriarch of Alexandria. *Life of Antony: The Coptic Life and the Greek Life.* Translated by Tim Vivian and Apostolos N. Athanassakis. Cistercian Studies Series 202. Kalamazoo, MI and Spencer, MA: Cistercian Publications, 2003.

Ps.-Athanasius. *Apocalypse.* Sahidic text edited by Bernd Witte, in *Die Sünden der Priester und Mönche: Koptische Eschatologie des 8. Jahrhunderts nach Kodex M 602 pp. 104–154 (ps. Athanasius) der Pierpont Morgan Library*, I: *Textausgabe.* Arbeiten zum spätantiken und koptischen Ägypten 12. Altenberge: Oros Verlag, 2002. Sahidic text and Arabic recension edited and translated by Francisco Javier Martinez, in "Eastern Christian Apocalyptic in the Early Muslim Period: Pseudo-Methodius and Pseudo-Athanasius." Ph.D. dissertation, Catholic University of America, 1985, 247–590.

Benjamin I, Patriarch of Alexandria. *On Cana of Galilee.* Edited and translated by C. Detlef G. Müller, in *Die Homilie über die Hochzeit zu Kana und weitere Schriften des Patriarchen Benjamin I. von Alexandrien.* Abhandlungen der Heidelberger Akademie der

Wissenschaften, Philosophisch-historische Klasse 1968/1. Heidelberg: Carl Winter; Universitätsverlag, 1968. English translation in Mikhail, Maged S. A. "On Cana of Galilee: A Sermon by the Coptic Patriarch Benjamin I," *Coptic Church Review* 23 (2002), 66–93.

Besa. *The Life of Shenoute.* Translated by David N. Bell. Cistercian Studies Series 73. Kalamazoo, MI: Cistercian Press, 1983.

Book of the Chrism. Edited and translated by A. van Lantschoot. "Le ms. Vatican copte 44 et le Livre du Chrême (ms. Paris arabe 100)," *Le Muséon* 45 (1932), 181–234.

Book of Ritual. Edited and translated by Alfonso 'Abdallah, in *L'ordinamento liturgico di Gabriele V–88° patriarca copto, 1409–1427.* Studia Orientalia Christiana: Aegyptiaca. Cairo: Centro Francescano di Studi Orientali Cristiani, 1962.

Christodoulos, Patriarch of Alexandria. *Canons.* Edited and translated by O. H. E. Burmester. "The Canons of Christodoulos, Patriarch of Alexandria (A.D. 1047–1077)," *Le Muséon* 45 (1932), 51–84.

Churches and Monasteries of Egypt and Some Neighboring Countries, Attributed to Abû Sâlih, the Armenian. Edited and translated by B. T. A. Evetts. Oxford: Clarendon Press, 1895; reprint Piscataway, NJ: Gorgias Press, 2001.

Confession of the Fathers. Edited by "a monk of Dayr al-Muharraq," in *I'tirafat al-aba'.* Min Makhtutat Dayr al-Muharraq al-'amir. Cairo: Dayr al-Muharraq, 2002.

Coptic Orthodox Psalmody. Tasbihat nisf al-layl al-sanawi: al-ahad wa-l-ayam. 7th ed. Cairo: Kanisat al-Sayyidah al-'Adhra' Maryam bi-'Izbat al-Nakhl, 1999. Italian translation in Marco Brogi, ed., *La santa salmodia annuale della chiesa copta.* Studia Orientalia Christiana: Aegyptiaca. Cairo: Franciscan Centre for Christian Oriental Studies, 1962.

Copto-Arabic *Synaxarion.* Edited by Jacobus Forget, in *Synaxarium Alexandrinum.* 2 vols. CSCO Ser. III, 18–19. Beirut: E Typographeo catholico, 1905.

Copto-Arabic *Synaxarion.* Edited and translated by René Basset, in *Le Synaxaire arabe jacobite (redaction copte).* PO 1.3, 3.3, 11.5, 16.2, 17.3, 20.5. Paris: Firmin-Didot, 1907–1929.

Copto-Arabic *Synaxarion. Kitab al-Sinaksar: al-Jami' akhbar al-anbiya' wa-l-rusul wa-l-shuhada' wa-l-qiddisin al-musta'mal fi kana'is al-karazah al-marqusiyyah fi ayam wa-ahad al-sanah al-tutiyyah.* 2 vols. Cairo: Maktabat al-Mahabbah, n.d.

Cyriacus, Patriarch of Antioch. *Synodical Letter to Mark II.* Edited and translated by Herman Teule. "La lettre synodale de Cyriaque, patriarche monophysite d'Antioche (793–817)," *Orientalia Lovaniensia Periodica* 9 (1978), 121–40.

Cyril II, Patriarch of Alexandria. *Canons.* Edited and translated by O. H. E. Burmester. "The Canons of Cyril II, LXVII Patriarch of Alexandria," *Le Muséon* 49 (1936), 245–88.

Ethiopic *Synaxarion.* In part edited and translated by Ignazio Guidi (and Sylvain Grébaut), *Le synaxaire éthiopien.* PO 1.5, 7.3, 9.4, 15.5, 26.1. Paris: Firmin-Didot, 1907–1945. Completed, with an index volume, by Gérard Colin, *Le synaxaire éthiopien.* PO 43.3, 44.1, 44.3, 45.1, 45.3, 46.3, 46.4, 47.3, 48.3. Turnhout, Belgium: Brepols, 1986–1999. English translation by E. A. Wallis Budge, *The Book of the Saints of the Ethiopian Church.* 4 vols. Cambridge, UK: Cambridge University Press, 1928.

Eutychius. *Annals.* Edited by Louis Cheikho et al. *Eutychii patriarchae Alexandrini annales.* 2 vols. CSCO 50–51 = ar. 6–7. Louvain: L. Durbecq, 1954 [1906–1909].

Gabriel II ibn Turayk. *Canons* (First Series). Edited and translated by O. H. E. Burmester. "The Canons of Gabriel ibn Turaik, LXX Patriarch of Alexandria (First Series)," *Orientalia Christiana Periodica* 1 (1935), 5–45.

———, *Canons* (Second Series). Edited and translated by O. H. E. Burmester. "The Canons of Gabriel ibn Turaik, LXX Patriarch of Alexandria," *Le Muséon* 46 (1933), 43–54.

———, *Laws of Inheritance.* Edited and translated by O. H. E. Burmester. "The Laws of Inheritance of Gabriel ibn Turaik LXX Patriarch of Alexandria," *Orientalia Christiana Periodica* 1 (1935), 315–27.

———, *Nomocanon.* Edited by Antonios Aziz Mina, in *Le Nomocanon du patriarche copte Gabriel II ibn Turayk (1131–1145).* 2 vols. Patrimoine Arabe Chrétien 12–13. Beirut: CEDRAC, 1993.

Historia Monachorum in Aegypto. Translated by Norman Russell, in *The Lives of the Desert Fatthers: The* Historia Monachorum in Aegypto. London and Oxford: Mowbray and Kalamazoo, MI: Cistercian Publications, 1980.

[*History of the Patriarchs.*] *Severus ibn al-Muqaffaʻ: Alexandrinische Patriarchengeschichte von S. Marcus bis Michael I (61-767), nach der ältesten 1266 geschriebenen Hamburger Handschrift im arabischen Urtext herausgegeben.* Edited by C.F. Seybold. Hamburg: 1912.

History of the Patriarchs of the Coptic Church of Alexandria. Edited and translated by B.T.A. Evetts. PO 1.2; 1.4; 5.1; 10.5. Paris: Firmin-Didot, 1904–1915.

History of the Patriarchs of the Egyptian Church (*History of the Holy Church*). Edited and translated by O. H. E. Burmester et al., Vols. 2.1–3, 3.1–3, 4.1–2. Publications de la Société d'Archéologie Copte, Textes et Documents 3–5, 11–15. Cairo: Société d'Archéologie Copte, 1943–1974.

Holy Jerusalem Voyage of Ogier VIII, Seigneur d'Anglure. Translated by Roland A. Browne. Gainesville: University Presses of Florida, 1975.

Homélie sur l'église du Rocher attribuée à Timothée Ælure. Edited and translated by Anne Boud'hors and Ramez Boutros. PO 49.1 = no. 217. Turnhout, Belgium: Brepols, 2001.

Ibn Iyâs. *Histoire des mamlouks circassiens*, II *(872–906)*. Translated by Gaston Wiet. Textes et traductions d'auteurs orientaux 6. Cairo: Institut Français d'Archéologie Orientale, 1945.

Ibn Kabar, Shams al-Ri'asah Abu l-Barakat. *Misbah al-zulmah fi idah al-khidmah*, Vol. 1. Edited by Samir Khalil Samir. Cairo: [1971].

Ibn Sabba', Yuhanna ibn Abi Zakariyya. *Kitab al-Jawharah al-nafisah fi 'ulum al-kanisah* = Jûhannâ ibn Abî Zakarîâ ibn Sibâ'. *Pretiosa margarita de scientiis ecclesiasticis*. Edited and translated by Vincentio Mistrih. Studia Orientalia Christiana: Aegyptiaca. Cairo: Franciscan Centre of Christian Oriental Studies, 1966.

Ibn Taghribirdi, Abu al-Mahasin Yusuf. *Nujum al-zahirah fi muluk Misr wa-l-Qahirah*. Translated by William Popper, in *History of Egypt, 1382–1469 A.D. Translated from the Arabic Annals of Abu l-Mahâsin ibn Taghrî Birdî*. University of California Publications in Semitic Philology 13–14, 17–19, 22–24. Berkeley and Los Angeles: University of California Press, 1954–1963.

Isaac the Presbyter. *Life of Samuel of Kalamun*. Edited by Anthony Alcock. Warminster [Wiltshire], UK: Aris & Philips, 1983.

John III of Samannud, Patriarch of Alexandria. *Theodore's Questions*. Edited and translated by A. van Lantschoot, in *"Questions de Théodore": Texte sahidique, recensions arabes et éthiopienne*. Studi e Testi 192. Vatican City: Biblioteca Apostolica Vaticana, 1957.

John XI, Patriarch of Alexandria. *Letter to Pope Eugene IV*. Edited and translated by Philippe Luisier. "La lettre du patriarche copte Jean XI au pape Eugène IV: Nouvelle edition," *Orientalia Christiana Periodica* 60 (1994), 87–129.

al-Kindi, Abu 'Umar Muhammad ibn Yusuf. *The Governors and Judges of Egypt, or Kitâb el 'Umara' wa Kitâb el Qudâh of El Kindî*. Edited by Rhuvon Guest. E. J. W. Gibb Memorial Series 19. Leiden: E. J. Brill; London: Luzac and Co., 1912.

Life of Abraham the Syrian, Patriarch of Alexandria. Edited and translated by L. Leroy. "Histoire d'Abraham le Syrien, patriarche copte d'Alexandrie," *Revue de l'Orient Chrétien* 14 (1909), 380–99, and 14 (1910), 26–41.

Life of Anba Ruways. MS Paris, Bibliothèque Nationale, arabe 282, ff. 82–139.

Life of Benjamin (fragment). Edited and translated by C. Detlef G. Müller, in *Homilie über die Hochzeit zu Kana und weitere Schriften des Patriarchen Benjamin I. von Alexandrien.* Abhandlungen der Heidelberger Akademie der Wissenschaften. Philosophisch-historische Klasse 1968/1, 295–300. Heidelberg: Carl Winter; Universitätsverlag, 1968.

Life of Ibrahim al-Fani. MS Monastery of St. Antony, Hist. 75 (old catalogue).

Life of John Hegumenos. Edited by Ugo Zanetti. "La vie de saint Jean higoumène de Scété au VIIe siècle," *Analecta Bollandiana* 114 (1996), 273–405.

Life of Marqus al-Antuni. MS Monastery of St. Paul, Hist. 115.

Life of Matthew. MSS Paris, Bibliothèque Nationale, arabe 132, ff. 32–58, and Bibliothèque Nationale, arabe 145, ff. 77–143.

Livre de la consécration du sanctuaire de Benjamin. Edited and translated by René-Georges Coquin. Bibliothèque d'études coptes 13. Cairo: Institut Français d'Archéologie Orientale du Caire, 1975.

al-Maqrizi. *History of the Copts* (from *Kitab al-mawaʿiz wa-l-iʿtibar fi dhikr al-khitat wa-l-athar*). Edited and translated by Ferdinand Wüstenfeld, in *Macrizi's Geschichte der Copten: Aus den Handschriften zu Gotha und Wien mit Übersetzung und Anmerkungen.* Abhandlungen der Königlichen Gesellschaft der Wissenschaften zu Göttingen 3. Göttingen: in der Dieterichschen Buchhandlung, 1845; reprint Hildesheim and New York: Georg Olms Verlag, 1979.

———, *Kitab al-suluk li-maʿrifat duwal al-muluk.* Vols. 1 (in 3 parts) and 2 (in 2 parts). Edited by Muhammad Mustafa Ziyadah. Cairo: Lajnat al-Taʾlif wa-l-Tarjamah wa-l-Nashr, 1934–1942; Vols. 3 (in 3 parts) and 4 (in 3 parts). Edited by Saʿid ʿAbd al-Fattah ʿAshur. Cairo: Dar al-Kutub, 1970–1973.

Martyrdom of John of Phanijoit. Edited and translated by Jason R. Zaborowski, in *The Coptic Martyrdom of John of Phanijoit: Assimilation and Conversion to Islam in Thirteenth-Century Egypt.* HCMR 3. Leiden and Boston: Brill, 2005.

Mena of Nikiou. *The Life of Isaac of Alexandria and The Martyrdom of Saint Macrobius.* Translated by David N. Bell. Cistercian Studies Series 107. Kalamazoo, MI: Cistercian Publications, 1988.

Michael, Patriarch of Antioch. *Chronicle.* Edited and translated by J.-B. Chabot, *Chronique de Michel le Syrien, Patriarche Jacobite d'Antioche (1166–1199).* 4 vols. Paris: Ernest Leroux, 1899–1910; reprint, Brussels: Culture et Civilisation, 1963.

Mikha'il, Metropolitan of Damietta. *Al-Sunan allati infaradat biha al-qibt* (*Usages that Distinguish the Copts*). German translation by Georg Graf, in *Ein Reformversuch innerhalb der koptischen Kirche im zwölften Jahrhundert*. Collectanea Hierosolymitana 2, 147–80. Paderborn: Ferdinand Schöningh, 1923.

al-Mufaddal ibn Abi al-Fada'il. *History of the Mamluk Sultans*. Edited by E. Blochet. *Moufazzal ibn Abil-Fazail: Histoire des sultans mamlouks*. PO 12.3, 14.3, and 20.1. Paris: Firmin-Didot, 1919–1929.

Palladius, *The Lausiac History*. Translated by Robert T. Meyer. Ancient Christian Writers 34. New York and Mahwah, NJ: Paulist Press, 1964.

Rite of Consecration of the Patriarch of Alexandria (Text according to MS. 253 Lit., Coptic Museum). Edited and translated by O. H. E. Khs-Burmester. Cairo: Société d'archéologie copte, 1960.

al-Safi ibn al-'Assal. *On the Trinity and the Incarnation*. Edited by Samir Khalil Samir, in *Brefs chapitres sur la Trinité et l'Incarnation*. PO 42.3 = No 192. Turnhout, Belgium: Brepols, 1985.

al-Sakhawi, Muhammad ibn 'Abd al-Rahman. *Kitab al-tibr al-masbuk fi dhayl al-Suluk*. Edited by Sa'id 'Abd al-Fattah 'Ashur, Najwa Mustafa Kamil, and Labibah Ibrahim Mustafa. 4 vols. Cairo: Dar al-Kutub, 2002–2007.

Ps.-Samuel of Kalamun. *Apocalypse*. Edited and translated by J. Ziadeh. "L'apocalypse de Samuel, supérieur de Deir-el-Qalamoun," *Revue de l'Orient Chrétien* 20 (1915–1917), 374–407.

(Ps.-) Sawirus ibn al-Muqaffa'. *The Book of Elucidation (Kitab al-idah)*. MS Paris, Bibliothèque Nationale, arabe 170. Edited by Marqus Jirjis (non-critical edition), *Kitab al-durr al-thamin fi idah al-din*. Cairo: 1925.

al-Shabushti, Abu l-Hasan 'Ali ibn Muhammad. *Book of the Monasteries*. Edited and translated by Aziz Suryal Atiya. "Some Egyptian Monasteries according to the Unpublished MS of al-Shabushti's '*Kitab al-diyarat*,'" *Bulletin de la Société d'Archéologie Copte* 5 (1939), 1–28.

Ps.-Shenoute, *Apocalypse*. Arabic version edited and translated by E. Amélineau, in *Monuments pour servir à l'histoire de l'Égypte chrétienne aux IVe et Ve siècles*. Mémoires publiés par les members de la Mission archéologique française au Caire 4, 338–51. Paris: Ernest Leroux, 1888.

Sibylline Prophecy. Copto-Arabic recension edited and translated by R.Y. Ebied and M. J. L. Young. "A Newly-Discovered Version of the Arabic Sibylline Prophecy," *Oriens Christianus* 60 (1976), 83–94.

al-Tabari, Abu Ja'far Muhammad ibn Jarir. *Tarikh al-rusul wa-al-muluk*. Extracts translated by Joel L. Kramer, *The History of al-Tabari*, Vol. 34: *Incipient Decline*. Albany: SUNY Press, 1989.

Texts Relating to St. Menas. Edited and translated by James Drescher, in *Apa Mena: A Selection of Coptic Texts Relating to St. Menas.* Cairo: Société d'Archéologie Copte, 1946.

Ps.-Yusab of Fuwwah. *Tarikh al-aba' al-batarikah li-l-anba Yusab usquf Fuwwah* [*History of the Fathers, the Patriarchs*]. Edited by Samu'il al-Suryani and Nabih Kamil, [Cairo]: [Institute of Coptic Studies], [1987].

Secondary Sources

Abbot, Nabia. *The Kurrah Papyri from Aphrodito in the Oriental Institute.* The Oriental Institute of the University of Chicago, Studies in Ancient Oriental Civilization 15. Chicago: University of Chicago Press, 1938.

Alcock, Anthony. "Samu'il of Qalamun, Saint," in *CE*, vii, 2092–93.

Ambraseys, N. N., C. P. Melville, and R. D. Adams. *The Seismicity of Egypt, Arabia and the Red Sea: A Historical Review.* Cambridge, UK: Cambridge University Press, 1994.

Armanios, Febe Y. "Coptic Christians in Ottoman Egypt: Religious Worldview and Communal Beliefs." Ph.D. dissertation, Ohio State University, 2003.

Atiya, Aziz Suryal, ed. *The Coptic Encyclopedia.* 8 vols. New York: Macmillan, Toronto: Collier Macmillan Canada, and New York: Maxwell Macmillan International, 1991.

Atiya, Aziz S. "Patriarchs, Dates and Succession of," in *CE*, vi, 1913–20.

Bagnall, Roger S., and Klaas A. Worp. *Chronological Systems of Byzantine Egypt.* 2nd ed. Leiden and Boston: Brill, 2004.

Basilios, Archbishop. "Fasting," in *CE*, iv, 1093–97.

Baumeister, Theofried. *Martyr Invictus: Der Märtyrer als Sinnbild der Erlösung in der Legende und im Kult der frühen koptischen Kirche.* Forschungen zur Volkskunde 46. Münster, Regensberg: 1972.

Bcheiry, Iskandar. "Lettera del patriarca copto Yuhanna XIII al patriarca siro Nuh libanese," *Parole de l'Orient* 30 (2005), 383–409.

———, "Due patriarchi siri-ortodossi consacrati in Egitto?" *Parole de l'Orient* 31 (2006), 257–67.

Becker, C. H. "Badr al-Djamali," in *EI* (new ed.), i, 869–70.

Bianquis, Thierry. "Autonomous Egypt from Ibn Tulun to Kafur, 868–969," in *The Cambridge History of Egypt*, i, 86–119.

Bierman, Irene A. *Writing Signs: The Fatimid Public Text.* Berkeley, Los Angeles, and London: University of California Press, 1998.

Bigoul al-Suriany. "New Elements in the History of the Pope Gabriel III the 77th (1268–1270 AD)," in *Actes du huitième congrès international*

d'études coptes, Paris, 28 juin–3 juillet 2004, 2 vols., edited by
N. Bosson and A. Boud'hors. Vol. 1, 15–23. Orientalia Lovaniensia
Analecta 163. Louvain: Peeters, 2007.

Bilaniuk, Petro B. T. "Coptic Relations with Rome," in *CE*, ii, 609–11.

Bolman, Elizabeth S., ed. *Monastic Visions: Wall Paintings in the Monastery
of St. Antony at the Red Sea*. Cairo: American Research Center in
Egypt; New Haven and London: Yale University Press, 2002.

———, "Theodore, 'The Writer of Life,' and the Program of 1232/1233," in
Bolman, ed., *Monastic Visions*, 37–76.

Boud'hors, Anne, and Ramez Boutros. "La Sainte Famille à Gabal al-Tayr et
l'Homélie du Rocher," in *Études Coptes VII: Neuvième journée d'études,
Montpellier 3–4 juin 1999*, edited by N. Bosson, 59–76. Cahiers de la
Bibliothèque Copte 12. Paris, Louvain, and Sterling VA: Peeters, 2000.

Boud'hors, Anne, and Denyse Vaillancourt, eds. *Huitième congrès international d'études coptes (Paris 2004): I. Bilans et perspectives 2000–2004.*
Collections de l'Université Marc-Bloch–Strasbourg, Études
d'archéologie et d'histoire ancienne; Cahiers de la Bibliothèque
Copte 15. Paris: De Boccard, 2006.

Brakmann, Heinzgerd. "Zum Pariser Fragment angeblich des koptischen
Patriarchen Agathon: Ein neues Blatt der Vita Benjamins I," *Le
Muséon* 93 (1980), 299–309.

Brogi, Marco, ed. *La santa salmodia annuale della chiesa copta*. Studia
Orientalia Christiana: Aegyptiaca. Cairo: Franciscan Centre of
Christian Oriental Studies, 1962.

Brown, Peter. "The Rise and Function of the Holy Man in Late Antiquity,"
Journal of Roman Studies 61 (1971), 80–101. Reprinted in Peter
Brown, *Society and the Holy in Late Antiquity*, 103–52. Berkeley, Los
Angeles, and Oxford: University of California Press, 1982.

———, *The World of Late Antiquity, AD 150–750*. London: Thames and
Hudson, 1971.

Bulliet, Richard W. *Conversion to Islam in the Medieval Period: An Essay
in Quantitative History*. Cambridge, MA, and London: Harvard
University Press, 1979.

Burmester, O. H. E., Khs-. *The Egyptian or Coptic Church: A Detailed
Description of Her Liturgical Services and the Rites and Ceremonies
Observed in the Administration of Her Sacraments*. Cairo: Publications
de la Société d'Archéologie Copte, 1967.

Butler, Alfred J. *The Arab Conquest of Egypt and the Last Thirty Years of the
Roman Dominion*. 2nd ed. Edited by P. M. Fraser. Oxford: Clarendon
Press, 1978.

Cahen, Claude. "Le régime des impôts dans le Fayyum," *Arabica* 3 (1956), 8–30.

———, "Ayyubids," in *EI* (new ed.), i, 796–807.

Canard, M. "Al-Hakim bi-Amr Allah," in *EI* (new ed.), iii, 76–82.

Cerulli, Enrico. *Il libro etiopico dei miracoli di Maria.* Studi Orientali pubblicati a cura della Scuola Orientale 1. Rome: Giovanni Bardi, 1953.

Chamberlain, Michael. "The Crusader Era and the Ayyubid Dynasty," in *The Cambridge History of Egypt,* i, 211–41.

Charfi, Abdelmajid. "La fonction historique de la polémique islamochrétienne à l'époque abbaside," in *Christian Arabic Apologetics during the Abbasid Period (750–1258),* edited by Samir Khalil Samir and Jørgen S. Nielsen, 44–56. Leiden, New York, and Cologne: E. J. Brill, 1994.

Clarysse, Willy. "The Coptic Martyr Cult," in *Martyrium in Multidisciplinary Perspective: Memorial Louis Reekmans,* edited by M. Lamberigts and P. van Deun, 377–95. Louvain: University Press and Peeters, 1995.

Cohen, Mark R., and Sasson Somekh. "Interreligious Majalis in Early Fatimid Egypt," in Lazarus-Yafeh et al., eds., *The Majlis,* 128–36.

Conti Rossini, C. "Aethiopica (Serie II)," *Rivista degli Studi Orientali* 10 (1923–1925), 481–520.

Coope, Jessica A. *The Martyrs of Córdoba: Community and Family Conflict in an Age of Mass Conversion.* Lincoln, NE and London: University of Nebraska Press, 1995.

Coquin, René-Georges. "Abraham and George of Scetis, Saints," in *CE,* i, 12–13.

———, "Barsum the Naked, Saint," in *CE,* ii, 348–49.

———, "Dayr al-Maghtis," in *CE,* iii, 818–19.

———, "Matthew the Poor, Saint," in *CE,* v, 1571–72.

Coquin, René-Georges, and Maurice Martin. "Dayr Shahran," in *CE,* iii, 862–63.

Crum, W. E. "Barsaumâ the Naked," *Proceedings of the Society of Biblical Archaeology* 29 (1907), 135–49, 187–206.

Dadoyan, Seta B. "The Phenomenon of the Fatimid Armenians," *Medieval Encounters* 2 (1996), 193–213.

Davis, Stephen J. "Ancient Sources for the Coptic Tradition," in Gabra, ed., *Be Thou There: The Holy Family's Journey in Egypt,* 133–62.

———, *The Early Coptic Papacy: The Egyptian Church and Its Leadership in Late Antiquity.* The Popes of Egypt, Vol. 1. Cairo and New York: American University in Cairo Press, 2004.

———, *Coptic Christology in Practice: Incarnation and Divine Participation in Late Antique and Medieval Egypt.* Oxford: Oxford University Press, 2008.

———, "Variations on an Egyptian Female Martyr Legend: History, Hagiography, and the Gendered Politics of Medieval Arab Religious Identity," in *Writing 'True Stories': Historians and Hagiographers in the Late-Antique and Medieval Near East*, edited by Arietta Papaconstantinou, Muriel Debié, and Hugh Kennedy. Cultural Encounters of Late Antiquity and the Middle Ages 9. Turnhout, Belgium: Brepols, forthcoming.

Décobert, Christian. "Sur l'arabisation et l'islamisation de l'Égypte médiévale," in *Itinéraires d'Égypte: Mélanges offerts au père Maurice Martin, S.J.*, edited by Christian Décobert, 273–300. Cairo: Institut Français d'Archéologie Orientale du Caire, 1992.

——, "Maréotide médiévale: Des bédouins et des chrétiens," in *Alexandrie médiévale 2*, edited by Christian Décobert, 127–67. Études alexandrines 8. Cairo: Institut Français d'Archéologie Orientale du Caire, 2002.

Den Heijer, Johannes. "History of the Patriarchs of Alexandria," in *CE*, iv, 1238–42.

——, "Mawhub ibn Mansur ibn Mufarrij al-Iskandarani," in *CE*, v, 1573–74.

——, "Sawirus Ibn al-Muqaffa', Mawhub Ibn Mansur Ibn Mufarrig et la genèse de *l'Histoire des Patriarches d'Alexandrie*," *Bibliotheca Orientalis* 41 (1984), 336–47.

——, *Mawhub ibn Mansur ibn Mufarrig et l'historiographie copto-arabe: Étude sur la composition de* l'Histoire des Patriarches d'Alexandrie. CSCO 513 = subsidia 83. Louvain: E. Peeters, 1989.

——, "Une liste d'évêques coptes de l'année 1086," in *Itinéraires d'Égypte: Mélanges offerts au père Maurice Martin, S.J.*, edited by Christian Décobert, 147–65. Cairo: Institut Français d'Archéologie Orientale du Caire, 1992.

——, "Apologetic Elements in Coptic-Arabic Historiography: The Life of Afraham ibn Zur'ah, 62nd Patriarch of Alexandria," in *Christian Arabic Apologetics during the Abbasid Period (750–1258)*, edited by Samir Khalil Samir and Jørgen S. Nielsen, 192–202. Leiden, New York, and Cologne: E. J. Brill, 1994.

——, "Coptic Historiography in the Fatimid, Ayyubid and Early Mamluk Periods," *Medieval Encounters* 2 (1996), 67–98.

——, "Considérations sur les communautés chrétiennes en Égypte fatimide: l'État et l'Église sous le vizirat de Badr al-Jamali (1074–1094)," in *L'Égypte fatimide, son art et son histoire: Actes du colloque organisé à Paris le 28, 29 et 30 mai 1998*, edited by Marianne Barrucand, 569–78. Paris: Presses de l'Université de Paris–Sorbonne, 1999.

——, "La conquête arabe vue par les historiens coptes," in *Valeur et distance: Identités et sociétés en Égypte*, edited by Christian Décobert, 227–45.

Paris: Maisonneuve et Larose; [Aix-en-Provence]: Maison méditerranéenne des sciences de l'homme, 2000.

——, "Le patriarcat copte d'Alexandrie à l'époque fatimide," in *Alexandrie médiévale 2*, edited by Christian Décobert, 83–97. Cairo: Institut Français d'Archéologie Orientale du Caire, 2002.

——, "Wadi al-Natrun and the *History of the Patriarchs of Alexandria*," *Coptica* 2 (2003), 24–42.

——, "Les patriarches coptes d'origine syrienne," in *Studies on the Christian Arabic Heritage in Honour of Father Prof. Dr. Samir Khalil Samir S.I. at the Occasion of his Sixty-Fifth Birthday*, edited by Rifaat Ebied and Herman Teule, 45–63. Eastern Christian Studies 5. Leuven, Paris, and Dudley, MA: Peeters, 2004.

——, "Relations between Copts and Syrians in the Light of Recent Discoveries at Dayr as-Suryan," in *Coptic Studies on the Threshold of a New Millennium: Proceedings of the Seventh International Congress of Coptic Studies, Leiden, 27 August–2 September 2000*, edited by Mat Immerzeel and Jacques van der Vliet. 2 vols. Orientalia Lovaniensia Analecta 133. Vol. 2, 923–38. Leuven, Paris, and Dudley, MA: Peeters, 2004.

Dennett, Daniel C. *Conversion and the Poll Tax in Early Islam.* Cambridge, MA: Harvard University Press, 1950.

Derat, Marie-Laure. "Dabra Metmaq," in *Encyclopaedia Aethiopica*, edited by Siegbert Uhlig, ii, 34–35. Wiesbaden: Harrassowitz, 2003–.

Dols, Michael W. *The Black Death in the Middle East.* Princeton, NJ: Princeton University Press, 1977.

Elli, Alberto. *Storia della chiesa copta.* 3 vols. Studia Orientalia Christiana Monographiae 12–14. Cairo: Franciscan Centre of Christian Oriental Studies; Jerusalem: Franciscan Printing Press, 2003.

Evelyn White, Hugh G. *The Monasteries of the Wadi 'n Natrûn.* 3 vols. Part I: *New Coptic Texts from the Monastery of Saint Macarius.* Part II: *The History of the Monasteries of Nitria and of Scetis*, edited by Walter Hauser. Part III: *The Architecture and Archaeology*, edited by Walter Hauser. Publications of the Metropolitan Museum of Art. Egyptian Expedition 2, 7, 8. New York: The Metropolitan Museum of Art, 1926, 1932, 1933.

Fahmy, Aly Mohamed. *Muslim Naval Organisation in the Eastern Mediterranean: From the Seventh to the Tenth Century A.D.* 2nd ed. Cairo: National Publication and Printing House, 1966.

Faltas, Joseph Moris. "Athanasius the Great as Source of the Theology of Bulus al-Bushi (13th c.)" [in Greek]. Ph.D. dissertation, University of Athens, 1994.

Fattal, Antoine. *Le statut légal des non-musulmans en pays d'Islam.* Recherches publiées sous la direction de l'Institut de lettres orientales de Beyrouth 10. Beirut: Imprimerie Catholique, 1958.

Fiey, J. M. "Coptes et Syriques: Contacts et échanges," *Studia Orientalia Christiana Collectanea* 15 (1972–1973), 295–365.

Fowden, Garth. *Empire to Commonwealth: Consequences of Monotheism in Late Antiquity.* Princeton, NJ: Princeton University Press, 1993.

Frankfurter, David, ed. *Pilgrimage and Holy Space in Late Antique Egypt.* Religions in the Graeco-Roman World 134. Leiden and Boston: Brill, 1998.

————, "The Perils of Love: Magic and Countermagic in Coptic Egypt," *Journal of the History of Sexuality* 10 (2001), 480–500.

Gabra, Gawdat. "Über die Flucht der Heiligen Familie nach koptischen Traditionen," *Bulletin de la Société d'Archéologie Copte* 38 (1999), 29–50.

————, ed. *Be Thou There: The Holy Family's Journey in Egypt.* Cairo and New York: American University in Cairo Press, 2001.

————, "Perspectives on the Monastery of St. Antony: Medieval and Later Inhabitants and Visitors," in Bolman, ed., *Monastic Visions*, 173–83.

————, "New Research from the Library of the Monastery of St. Paul," in Lyster, ed., *The Cave Church of Paul the Hermit*, 94–105.

Garcin, Jean-Claude. "The Regime of the Circassian Mamluks," in *The Cambridge History of Egypt*, i, 290–317.

Gaudeul, Jean-Marie. *Encounters and Clashes: Islam and Christianity in History.* 2 vols. Rome: Pontificio Istituto di Studi Arabi e Islamici, 1990.

Geary, Patrick J. *Furta Sacra: Thefts of Relics in the Central Middle Ages.* Rev. ed. Princeton, NJ: Princeton University Press, 1990.

Gibb, H. A. R., et al., eds. *Encyclopedia of Islam* (new ed.). 13 vols. Leiden: Brill, 1954–2008.

Gibb, H. A. R., and P. Kraus. "Al-Mustansir," in *EI* (new ed.), vii, 729–32.

Girgis, Magdi, Michael Shelley, and Nelly van Doorn-Harder. *The Emergence of the Modern Coptic Papacy.* The Popes of Egypt, Vol. 3. Cairo and New York: American University in Cairo Press, forthcoming.

Goehring, James. "2005 NAPS Presidential Address: Remembering Abraham of Farshut: History, Historiography, and the Fate of the Pachomian Tradition," *Journal of Early Christian Studies* 14 (2006), 1–26.

Gottschalk, H. L. "Awlad al-Shaykh," in *EI* (new ed.), i, 765–66.

Grabar, Oleg. *The Shape of the Holy: Early Islamic Jerusalem.* Princeton, NJ: Princeton University Press, 1996.

Graf, Georg. *Ein Reformversuch innerhalb der koptischen Kirche im zwölften Jahrhundert.* Collectanea Hierosolymitana 2. Paderborn: Ferdinand Schöningh, 1923.

———, "Zwei dogmatische Florilegien der Kopten," *Orientalia Christiana Periodica* 3 (1937), 345–402.

———, *Geschichte der christlichen arabischen Literatur.* 5 vols. Studi e Testi 118, 133, 146, 147, 172. Vatican City: Biblioteca Apostolica Vaticana, 1944–1953.

Griffith, Sidney H. "Comparative Religion in the Apologetics of the First Christian Arabic Theologians," *Proceedings of the PMR Conference* (Villanova, PA) 4 (1979), 63–87. Reprinted in Sidney H. Griffith, *The Beginnings of Christian Theology in Arabic: Muslim-Christian Encounters in the Early Islamic Period,* Essay I. Variorum Collected Studies Series CS746. Aldershot, Hampshire and Burlington, VT: Ashgate Variorum, 2002.

———, "The *Kitab Misbah al-'Aql* of Severus ibn al-Muqaffaʻ: A Profile of the Christian Creed in Arabic in Tenth-Century Egypt," *Medieval Encounters* 2 (1996), 15–42.

———, "The Monk in the Emir's *Majlis*: Reflections on a Popular Genre of Christian Literary Apologetics in Arabic in the Early Islamic Period," in Lazarus-Yafeh et al., eds., *The Majlis*, 13–65.

———, "The *Life of Theodore of Edessa*: History, Hagiography, and Religious Apologetics in Mar Saba Monastery in Early Abbasid Times," in *The Sabaite Heritage in the Orthodox Church from the Fifth Century to the Present,* edited by Joseph Patrich, 147–69. Orientalia Lovaniensia Analecta 98. Louvain: Uitgeverij Peeters and Departement Oosterse Studies, 2001.

———, *The Church in the Shadow of the Mosque: Christians and Muslims in the World of Islam.* Princeton, NJ and Oxford: Princeton University Press, 2008.

Grossmann, Peter. "The Pilgrimage Center of Abû Mîna," in Frankfurter, ed., *Pilgrimage and Holy Space in Late Antique Egypt*, 281–302.

Grypeou, Emmanuela, Mark N. Swanson, and David Thomas, eds. *The Encounter of Eastern Christianity with Early Islam.* HCMR 5. Leiden and Boston: Brill, 2006.

Harmless, William. *Desert Christians: An Introduction to the Literature of Early Monasticism.* Oxford and New York: Oxford University Press, 2004.

Hoyland, Robert G. *Seeing Islam as Others Saw It: A Survey and Evaluation of Christian, Jewish and Zoroastrian Writings on Early Islam.* Studies in Late Antiquity and Early Islam 13. Princeton, NJ: Darwin Press, 1997.

Innemée, Karel C. *Ecclesiastical Dress in the Medieval Near East.* Studies in Textile and Costume History 1. Leiden and New York: E. J. Brill, 1992.

Innemée, Karel C, and Lucas van Rompay. "La présence des syriens dans le Wadi al-Natrun (Égypte)," *Parole de l'Orient* 23 (1998), 167–202.

Innemée, Karel C, and Lucas van Rompay, and Elizabeth Sobczynski. "Deir al-Surian (Egypt): Its Wall-paintings, Wall-texts, and Manuscripts," *Hugoye: Journal of Syriac Studies* [online journal] 2:2 (July 1999).

Irwin, Robert. *The Middle East in the Middle Ages: The Early Mamluke Sultanate, 1250–1382.* Carbondale and Edwardsville, IL: Southern Illinois University Press, 1986.

Jenkins, Philip. *The Lost History of Christianity: The Thousand-Year Golden Age of the Church in the Middle East, Africa, and Asia—and How It Died.* New York: HarperOne, 2008.

Johnson, David W. "Further Remarks on the Arabic History of the Patriarchs of Alexandria," *Oriens Christianus* 61 (1976), 7–17.

Kennedy, Hugh. "Egypt as a Province in the Islamic Caliphate, 641–868," in *The Cambridge History of Egypt*, i, 62–85.

Lane-Poole, Stanley. *A History of Egypt in the Middle Ages.* 2nd rev. ed. London: Methuen & Co., 1914. Reprint, Karachi: S. M. Mir, 1977.

Lapidus, Ira. "The Conversion of Egypt to Islam," *Israel Oriental Studies* 2 (1972), 248–62.

Lazarus-Yafeh, Hava, et al., eds. *The Majlis: Interreligious Encounters in Medieval Islam.* Studies in Arabic Language and Literature 4. Wiesbaden: Harrassowitz, 1999.

Leclercq, H. "Ère," in *Dictionnaire d'archéologie chrétienne et de liturgie* V, 2, cols. 351–53. Paris: Librairie Letouzey et Ané, 1923.

el-Leithy, Tamer. "Coptic Culture and Conversion in Medieval Cairo, 1293–1524 A.D." Ph.D. dissertation, Princeton University, 2005.

Levi della Vida, Giorgio. "A Christian Legend in Moslem Garb," *Byzantion* 15 (1940–1941), 144–57.

Life of Saint Sim'an the Cobbler (the "Tanner"). *Sirat al-qiddis Sim'an al-Kharraz "al-Dabbagh."* 2nd ed. Cairo: Church of St. Sim'an the Tanner, 1993.

Little, Donald P. "Coptic Conversion to Islam under the Bahri Mamluks, 692–755/1293–1354," *Bulletin of the School of Oriental and African Studies* 39 (1976), 552–69.

——, "Coptic Converts to Islam during the Bahri Mamluk Period," in *Conversion and Continuity: Indigenous Christian Communities in Islamic Lands, Eighth to Eighteenth Centuries*, edited by Michael Gervers and Ramzi Jibran Bikhazi, 263–88. Papers in Medieval Studies 9. Toronto: Pontifical Institute of Medieval Studies, 1990.

Luisier, Philippe. "La lettre du patriarche copte Jean XI au pape Eugène IV: Nouvelle édition," *Orientalia Christiana Periodica* 60 (1994), 87–129.

———, "Jean XI, 89ème patriarche copte: Commentaire de sa lettre au pape Eugène IV, suivi d'une esquisse historique sur son patriarcat," *Orientalia Christiana Periodica* 60 (1994), 519–62.

———, "De Pilate chez les Coptes," *Orientalia Christiana Periodica* 62 (1996), 411–25.

Lutfi, Huda. "Coptic Festivals of the Nile: Aberrations of the Past?" in *The Mamluks in Egyptian Politics and Society*, edited by Thomas Philipp and Ulrich Haarmann, 254–82. Cambridge Studies in Islamic Civilization. Cambridge, UK and New York: Cambridge University Press, 1998.

Lyster, William, ed. *The Cave Church of Paul the Hermit at the Monastery of St. Paul, Egypt*. Cairo: American Research Center in Egypt; New Haven, CT and London: Yale University Press, 2008.

MacCoull, Leslie S. B. "Three Cultures under Arab Rule: The Fate of Coptic," *Bulletin de la Société d'Archéologie Copte* 27 (1985), 61–70. Reprinted in MacCoull, *Coptic Perspectives on Late Antiquity*, Essay XXV.

———, "The Strange Death of Coptic Culture," *Coptic Church Review* 10 (1989), 35–45. Reprinted in MacCoull, *Coptic Perspectives on Late Antiquity*, Essay XXVI.

———, "The Paschal Letter of Alexander II, Patriarch of Alexandria: A Greek Defense of Coptic Theology under Arab Rule," *Dumbarton Oaks Papers* 44 (1990), 27–40. Reprinted in MacCoull, *Coptic Perspectives on Late Antiquity*, Essay XIX.

———, *Coptic Perspectives on Late Antiquity*. Variorum Collected Studies Series CS398. Aldershot, Hampshire and Brookfield, VT: Variorum, 1993.

———, "A Note on the Career of Gabriel III, Scribe and Patriarch of Alexandria," *Arabica* 43 (1996), 357–60.

Magued, A. M. "Al-Hafiz," in *EI* (new ed.), iii, 54–55.

Martin, Maurice P. "Une lecture de *l'Histoire des Patriarches d'Alexandrie*," *Proche-Orient Chrétien* 35 (1985), 15–36.

———, "Le Delta chrétien à la fin du XIIe s.," *Orientalia Christiana Periodica* 63 (1997): 181–99.

Martinez, Francisco Javier. "Eastern Christian Apocalyptic in the Early Muslim Period: Pseudo-Methodius and Pseudo-Athanasius." Ph.D. dissertation, Catholic University of America, 1985.

al-Masri, Iris Habib. *Qissat al-kanisah al-qibtiyyah*. Vol. 3. Alexandria: Matba'at al-Karnak, 1981.

Matanic, Athanasio G. "Tavelic, Nicola e III compagni," in *Bibliotheca sanctorum*, xii, 148–51. Rome: Città Nuova, 1961–1970.

Meinardus, Otto F. A. "An Examination of the Traditions Pertaining to the Relics of St. Mark," *Orientalia Christiana Periodica* 36 (1970), 348–76.

———, *Christian Egypt, Ancient and Modern*. 2nd rev. ed. Cairo: American University in Cairo Press, 1977.

———, "About the Coction and Consecration of the Holy Myron in the Coptic Church," *Coptic Church Review* 12 (1991), 78–86.

———, "Notes on New Saints in the Coptic Church," *Coptic Church Review* 25 (2004), 2–26.

Meyer, Marvin, and Richard Smith, eds. *Ancient Christian Magic: Coptic Texts of Ritual Power*. San Francisco: HarperSanFrancisco, 1994.

Mikhail, Maged S.A. "Egypt from Late Antiquity to Early Islam: Copts, Melkites, and Muslims Shaping a New Society." Ph.D. dissertation, University of California, Los Angeles, 2004.

Miles, George C. "The Earliest Arab Gold Coinage," *American Numismatic Society Museum Notes* 13 (1967), 203–29 and Plates XLV–XLVII.

Miller, Daniel Earl. "From Catalogue to Codes to Canon: The Rise of the Petition to 'Umar among Legal Traditions Governing Non-Muslims in Medieval Islamicate Societies." Ph.D. dissertation, University of Missouri–Kansas City, 2000.

Moawad, Samuel. "Zur Originalität der Yusab von Fuwah zugeschriebenen Patriarchengeschichte," *Le Muséon* 199 (2006), 255–70.

Monferrer-Sala, Juan Pedro, ed. *Eastern Crossroads: Essays on Medieval Christian Legacy*. Gorgias Eastern Christianity Studies 1. Piscataway, NJ: Gorgias Press, 2007.

Müller, C. Detlef G. "Stellung und Haltung der koptischen Patriarchen des 7. Jahrhunderts gegenüber islamischer Obrigkeit und Islam," in *Acts of the Second International Congress of Coptic Study: Roma, 22–26 September 1980*, edited by Tito Orlandi and Frederik Wisse, 203–13. Rome: C.I.M., 1985.

———, "Gabriel II. Ibn Turaik, 70. Papst und Patriarch des Missionsbereiches des Heiligen Markos," *Oriens Christianus* 74 (1990), 168–86.

Munier, Henri. *Recueil des listes épiscopales de l'église copte*. Cairo: Société d'Archéologie Copte, 1943.

Nadal Cañellas, Juan, and Stefano Virgulin, eds. *Bibliotheca sanctorum orientalium. Enciclopedia dei santi: Le chiese orientali*. 2 vols. Rome: Città Nuova, 1998–1999.

Nakhlah, Kamil Salih. *Sirat al-baba Ghubriyal ibn Turayk, al-batriyark al-sab'in*. Cairo: Maktabat al-Mahabbah al-Qibtiyyah, 1947.

———, *Silsilat tarikh al-babawat batarikat al-kursi al-Iskandari*. 5 fascicles. 2nd ed. Cairo: Dayr al-Suryan, 2000 [1951–1954].

Northrup, Linda S. "The Bahri Mamluk Sultanate, 1250–1390," in *The Cambridge History of Egypt*, i, 242–89.

Papaconstantinou, Arietta. *Le culte des saints en Égypte des byzantins aux abbasides: L'apport des inscriptions et des papyrus grecs et coptes*. Paris: CNRS Editions, 2001.

———, "Historiography, Hagiography, and the Making of the Coptic 'Church of the Martyrs' in Early Islamic Egypt," *Dumbarton Oaks Papers* 60 (2006), 65–86.

———, "'They Shall Speak the Arabic Language and Take Pride in It': Reconsidering the Fate of Coptic after the Arab Conquest," *Le Muséon* 120 (2007), 273–99.

Papaconstantinou, Arietta, and Muriel Debié, and Hugh Kennedy, eds. *Writing 'True Stories': Historians and Hagiographers in the Late-Antique and Medieval Near East*. Cultural Encounters of Late Antiquity and the Middle Ages 9. Turnhout, Belgium: Brepols, forthcoming.

Pearson, Birger A. "The Coptic Inscriptions in the Church of St. Antony," in Bolman, ed., *Monastic Visions*, 217–39, 267–70.

Pelikan, Jaroslav. *The Spirit of Eastern Christendom (600–1700)*. The Christian Tradition: A History of the Development of Doctrine, Vol. 2. Chicago and London: University of Chicago Press, 1974.

Petry, Carl F., ed. *The Cambridge History of Egypt*. Vol. 1: *Islamic Egypt, 640–1517*. Cambridge, UK and New York: Cambridge University Press, 1998.

Reinink, Gerrit J. "Early Christian Reactions to the Building of the Dome of the Rock in Jerusalem," *Xristianskij Vostok* 2 (2000), 227–41.

Rubenson, Samuel. "Translating the Tradition: Some Remarks on the Arabization of the Patristic Heritage in Egypt," *Medieval Encounters* 2 (1996), 4–14.

Saad, Saad Michael, and Nardine Miranda Saad. "Electing Coptic Patriarchs: A Diversity of Traditions," *Bulletin of Saint Shenouda the Archimandrite Coptic Society* 6 (2001), 20–32.

Saleh, Marlis J. "Government Relations with the Coptic Community in Egypt during the Fatimid Period (358–567 A.H./969–1171 C.E.)." Ph.D. dissertation, University of Chicago, 1995.

Samir Khalil. "Gabriel V," in *CE*, iv, 1130–33.

———, "Gabriel VI," in *CE*, iv, 1133.

———, "Yannah, dans l'onomastique arabo-copte," *Orientalia Christiana Periodica* 45 (1979), 166–70.

———, "Gabriel II, patriarche copte d'Alexandrie (1131–1145)," in *Dictionnaire d'histoire et de géographie ecclésiastiques*, edited by Alfred Baudrillart et al., vol. 19, 1981, cols. 528–39. Paris: Letouzey et Ané, 1912.

Samir, Khalil. Introduction to Antonios Aziz Mina, ed., *Le Nomocanon du patriarche copte Gabriel II ibn Turayk (1131–1145).* 2 vols. Vol. 1, 23–164. Patrimoine Arabe Chrétien 12–13. Beirut: CEDRAC, 1993.

Samir, Samir Khalil. "Vie et oeuvre de Marc ibn al-Qunbar," in *Christianisme d'Égypte: Hommages à René-Georges Coquin*, 123–58. Cahiers de la Bibliothèque Copte 9. Paris and Louvain: Peeters, 1995.

———, "The Role of Christians in the Fatimid Government Services of Egypt to the Reign of al-Hafiz," *Medieval Encounters* 2 (1996), 177–92.

———, "Un traité nouveau de Sawirus ibn al-Muqaffa': La Lettre à Abu al-Yumn Quzman ibn Mina," *Parole de l'Orient* 25 (2000), 567–641.

Sanders, Paula. *Ritual, Politics, and the City in Fatimid Cairo.* Albany: State University of New York Press, 1994.

Shaban, M. "Conversion to Early Islam," in *Conversion to Islam*, edited by Nehemiah Levtzion, 24–29. New York and London: Holmes and Meier, 1979.

Shenouda, Maryann M. "Displacing *Dhimmi*, Maintaining Hope: Unthinkable Coptic Representations of Fatimid Egypt," *International Journal of Middle East Studies* 39 (2007), 587–606.

Sidarus, Adel Y. *Ibn ar-Rahibs Leben und Werk: Ein koptisch-arabischer Enzyklopädist des 7./13. Jahrhunderts.* Islamkundliche Untersuchungen 36. Freiburg im Breisgau: Klaus Schwarz Verlag, 1975.

———, "Medieval Coptic Grammars in Arabic: The Coptic *Muqaddimat*," *Journal of Coptic Studies* 3 (2001), 63–79.

———, "The Copto-Arabic Renaissance in the Middle Ages: Characteristics and Socio-Political Context," *Coptica* 1 (2002), 141–60.

———, "La pré-renaissance copte arabe du Moyen Âge (deuxième moitié du XIIe/début du XIIIe siècle)," in Monferrer-Sala, ed., *Eastern Crossroads*, 191–216.

Skreslet, Stanley H. "The Greeks in Medieval Islamic Egypt: A Melkite *Dhimmi* Community under the Patriarch of Alexandria (640–1095)." Ph.D. dissertation, Yale University, 1988.

Stewart, Randall. "Barsanuphians," in *CE*, ii, 347–48.

Suermann, Harald. "Copts and the Islam of the Seventh Century," in Grypeou et al., eds., *Encounter of Eastern Christianity with Early Islam*, 95–109.

Swanson, Mark N. "The Specifically Egyptian Context of a Coptic Arabic Text: Chapter Nine of the *Kitab al-Idah* of Sawirus ibn al-Muqaffa'," *Medieval Encounters* 2 (1996), 214–27.

———, "A Copto-Arabic Catechism of the Late Fatimid Period: 'Ten Questions that One of the Disciples Asked of His Master,'" *Parole de l'Orient* 22 (1997), 474–501.

——, "'These Three Words Will Suffice': The 'Jesus Prayer' in Coptic Tradition," *Parole de l'Orient* 25 (2000), 67–80.

——, "Two Vatican Manuscripts of 'The Book of the Master and the Disciple' (Eight Chapters) of Mark ibn al-Qunbar," *Orientalia Christiana Periodica* 66 (2000), 185–93.

——, "The Martyrdom of 'Abd al-Masih, Superior of Mount Sinai (Qays al-Ghassani)," in *Syrian Christians under Islam: The First Thousand Years*, edited by David Thomas, 107–29. Leiden and Boston: Brill, 2001.

——, "'Our Brother, the Monk Eustathius': A Ninth-Century Syrian Orthodox Theologian Known to Medieval Arabophone Copts," *Coptica* 1 (2002), 119–40.

——, "The Christian al-Ma'mun Tradition," in *Christians at the Heart of Islamic Rule: Church Life and Scholarship in 'Abbasid Iraq*, edited by David Thomas, 63–92. HCMR 1. Leiden and Boston: Brill, 2003.

——, "Folly to the *Hunafa*': The Crucifixion in Early Christian-Muslim Controversy," in Grypeou et al., eds., *Encounter of Eastern Christianity with Early Islam*, 237–56.

——, "Telling (and Disputing) the Old, Old Story: A Soteriological Exchange in Late Twelfth-Century Egypt," *Coptica* 5 (2006), 69–82.

——, "'Our Father Abba Mark': Marqus al-Antuni and the Construction of Sainthood in Fourteenth-Century Egypt," in Monferrer-Sala, ed., *Eastern Crossroads*, 217–28.

——, "The Monastery of St. Paul in Historical Context," in Lyster, ed., *The Cave Church of Paul the Hermit*, 42–59.

——, "Sainthood Achieved: Coptic Patriarch Zacharias according to *The History of the Patriarchs*," in Papaconstantinou et al., eds., *Writing 'True Stories'*.

——, "George the Archdeacon," in *CMR*1, 234–38.

——, "John the Deacon," in *CMR*1, 317–21.

——, "John the Writer," in *CMR*1, 702–05.

——, "The Coptic Patriarch and the Apostate Scribe at Dayr al-Tin: An Incident from the Career of Pope Gabriel II ibn Turayk (#70, 1131–1145)," in the Proceedings of the 8th Conference on Arab Christian Studies, Granada, 26–27 September 2008, forthcoming in *Parole de l'Orient*.

Thomas, David, and Barbara Roggema, eds. *Christian-Muslim Relations: A Bibliographical History*, Vol. 1 (600–900). HCMR 11. Leiden and Boston: Brill, 2009.

Thomas, David. "'Ali l-Tabari," in *CMR*1, 669–74.

——, "Al-Jahiz," in *CMR*1, 706–12.

Trombley, Frank R. "Sawirus ibn al-Muqaffaʿ and the Christians of Umayyad Egypt: War and Society in Documentary Context," in *Papyrology and the History of Early Islamic Egypt*, edited by Petra M. Sijpesteijn and Lennart Sundelin, 199–226. Islamic History and Civilization: Studies and Texts 55. Leiden and Boston: Brill, 2004.

Troupeau, Gérard. *Catalogue des manuscrits arabes*. Première partie: *Manuscrits chrétiens*. 2 vols. Paris: Bibliothèque Nationale, 1972–1974.

Van Lent, Jos. "Les apocalypses coptes de l'époque arabe: Quelques réflexions," in *Études coptes V: Sixième journée d'études, Limoges 18–20 juin 1993, et Septième journée d'études, Neuchâtel 18–20 mai 1995*, edited by M. Rassart-Debergh. Cahiers de la Bibliothèque Copte 10. Paris and Louvain: Peeters, 1998.

———, "Coptic Apocalyptic Prophecies from the Islamic Period." Ph.D. dissertation, University of Leiden, forthcoming.

———, "The Apocalypse of Shenute," in *CMR*1, 182–85.

Varguese, Baby. *Les onctions baptismales dans la tradition syrienne*. CSCO 512 = subs. 82. Louvain: Peeters, 1989.

Vermeulen, Urbain. "The Rescript of al-Malik as-Salih Salih against the Dimmis (755 AH/1354 AD)," *Orientalia Lovaniensia Periodica* 9 (1978), 175–84.

Vivian, Tim. "St. Antony the Great and the Monastery of St. Antony at the Red Sea, ca. AD 251 to 1232/1233," in Bolman, ed., *Monastic Visions*, 3–17.

Voile, Brigitte. "Barsum le Nu: Un saint copte au Caire à l'époque mamelouke," in *Saints orientaux*, edited by Denise Aigle, 151–68. Hagiographies Médiévales Comparées 1. Paris: De Boccard, 1995.

———, "Les miracles des saints dans la deuxième partie de *l'Histoire des Patriarches d'Alexandrie*: Historiographie ou hagiographie?" in *Miracle et Karama*, edited by Denise Aigle, 317–30. Hagiographies Médiévales Comparées 2. Bibliothèque de l'École des Hautes Études Sciences Religieuses 109. Tournhout, Belgium: Brepols, 2000.

Wadi Abuliff. "Abramo l'Egumeno," in *BSSOr*, i, 19.

———, "Barsauma il Nudo," in *BSSOr*, i, 360–62.

———, "Marco l'Antoniano," in *BSSOr*, ii, 410–13.

———, "Matteo il Vasaio," in *BSSOr*, 468–69.

———, "Quarantanove martiri," in *BSSOr*, ii, 866–68.

———, "Ruways," in *BSSOr*, ii, 889–92.

Wadi, A. "Vita di Sant' Atanasio in una traduzione araba inedita," *SOC Collectanea* 28 (1995), 145–60.

———, *Studio su al-Muʾtaman Ibn al-ʿAssal*. Studia Orientalia Christiana Monographiae 5, 44–65. Cairo: The Franciscan Centre of Christian Oriental Studies; Jerusalem: Franciscan Printing Press, 1997 [in Arabic].

Wadi A. "Homilies on the Voyage of the Holy Family: Printed Works and Manuscripts" [in Arabic], in *Ninth Coptic Studies Week: Special File on the Flight of the Holy Family into Egypt, 1999/1716*, 87–104. Cairo: Church of the Virgin in Rawd al-Farag, 2002.

Walker, Paul E. "The Isma'ili Da'wa and the Fatimid Caliphate," in *The Cambridge History of Egypt*, i, 120–50.

Werthmuller, Kurt James. "An In-Between Space: An Archival and Textual Study of Coptic Identity and Ayyubid Politics in Egypt, 1171–1250 CE." Ph.D. dissertation, University of California, Santa Barbara, 2007.

Witte, Bernd. "The Apocalypse of Pseudo-Athanasius," in *CMR*1, 274–80.

Wolf, Kenneth Baxter. *Christian Martyrs in Muslim Spain*. Cambridge, UK: Cambridge University Press, 1988.

Youssef, Youhanna Nessim. "Notes on the Traditions Concerning the Flight of the Holy Family into Egypt," *Coptic Church Review* 20 (1999), 48–55.

Yusuf, 'Abd al-Tawwab. *Al-Hilal wa-l-salib* [The Crescent and the Cross]. Cairo: Maktabat Ruz al-Yusuf, 1980.

Zaborowski, Jason R. *The Coptic Martyrdom of John of Phanijoit: Assimilation and Conversion to Islam in Thirteenth-Century Egypt*. HCMR 3. Leiden and Boston: Brill, 2005.

Zakhari, Wadi' Farajallah. *Babawat al-Kanisah al-Mu'allaqah*. Cairo: Kanisat al-'Adhra' wa-l-shahidah Dimyanah—al-Mu'allaqah, 1994.

Zanetti, Ugo. "Le livre de Marc Ibn Qunbar sur la confession retrouvé," *Orientalia Christiana Periodica* 49 (1983), 426–33.

———, "Matarieh, la Sainte Famille et les baumiers," *Analecta Bollandiana* 111 (1993), 21–68.

———, "La vie de saint Jean higoumène de Scété au VIIe siècle," *Analecta Bollandiana* 114 (1996), 273–405.

Notes

Editors' Introduction

1. Aziz S. Atiya, ed., *The Coptic Encyclopedia*, 8 volumes (New York: Macmillan, 1991).

2. Gawdat Gabra, "Christian Arabic Literature of the Copts: Notes on the State of Research, 1988–1992," in *Acts of the Fifth International Congress of Coptic Studies I. Reports on Recent Research*, ed. T. Orlandi (Rome: C.I.M., 1993), 51–54.

3. Mark N. Swanson, "Recent Developments in Copto-Arabic Studies, 1996–2000," in *Coptic Studies on the Threshold of a New Millennium: Proceedings of the Seventh International Congress of Coptic Studies, Leiden, 27 August–2 September 2000*, ed. Mat Immerzeel and Jacques van der Vliet, vol. 1 (Louvain: Peeters, 2004); idem, "Recent Developments in Copto-Arabic Studies, 2000–2004," in *Actes du Huitième congrès international d'études coptes (Paris 2004). I. Bilans et perspectives*, ed. A. Boud'hors and D. Vaillancourt (Cahiers de la Bibliothèque Copte 15; Paris: De Boccard, 2006) 261–78; idem, "Copto-Arabic Studies: Bibliography, 2004–2008," paper presented at the Ninth International Congress for Coptic Studies, Cairo, Egypt, 11 September 2008 (text available at http://rmcisadu.let. uniroma1.it/~iacs/bibswan.pdf). With respect to Christian–Muslim relations and early Christian Arabic literature, see also his contributions to *Christian-Muslim Relations: A Bibliographical History, Vol. 1 (600–900)*, ed. David Thomas and Barbara Roggema (History of Christian-Muslim Relations 11; Leiden and Boston: Brill, 2009).

Author's Preface

1. Davis, *The Early Coptic Papacy*, xiv.
2. See, for example, Johnson, "Further Remarks," and den Heijer, *Mawhub*. A convenient summary is den Heijer, "History of the Patriarchs of Alexandria."
3. The closest thing we have to such a comprehensive history is now the appropriate chapters in Elli, *Storia della chiesa copta*.
4. One may attempt to keep up by following the reports on progress in various subfields of Coptic studies, accompanied by extensive bibliographies, given at each International Congress of Coptic Studies (held every four years) and subsequently published. For example, for reports on progress in Coptic studies during the years 2000–2004, see Boud'hors and Vaillancourt, eds., *Huitième congrès international d'études coptes*. The publication of reports for the years 2004–2008, given at the Ninth International Congress of Coptic Studies in Cairo, September 2008, is forthcoming; some bibliographies may be accessed at the website of the International Association of Coptic Studies, http://rmcisadu.let. uniroma1.it/~iacs/, under "Congress 2008" (accessed 5 September 2009).
5. I have been encouraged in this regard by the work of Fr. Maurice Martin, in whose elegant articles literary depictions and archaeological data work hand in hand to produce provocative sketches of the history of the Coptic community. An essay that was particularly helpful to me as I began work on the present volume was Martin, "Une lecture de *l'Histoire des Patriarches d'Alexandrie*."
6. See den Heijer, *Mawhub*, 14–80.
7. I have not had access to the one partial (*Lives* #1–46) edition of the "primitive" recension: *History of the Patriarchs* (ed. Seybold, 1912).
8. As I do, for example, in Chapter Six, in which I considered it best to make my own English translations of the Arabic text in *HPEC* 4.1–2. When citing this source, I give the page numbers of the Arabic text first, and then those of the editors' English translation.
9. For example, for Isaac, the forty-first patriarch, I have followed Zakhari and Meinardus and dated his patriarchate to 690–692. Atiya, "Patriarchs," p. 1915, gives 686–689 as the dates for Isaac's patriarchate. In this particular case, an explanation of some of the issues involved may be found in Mena of Nikiou, *Life of Isaac* (trans. Bell), 22–26.
10. Zakhari, *Babawat al-Kanisah al-Mu'allaqah*, 64–80.
11. Meinardus, *Christian Egypt*, 55–66.

Abbreviations

1.   According to my photocopy of the relevant pages of this manuscript, it is labeled Hist. 75 (at f. 3v, according to the Coptic cursive pagination). This may be the *old* catalog number; the manuscript appears to correspond to Hist. 69 in the present catalog. I am grateful to Fr. Wadi A., ofm, of the Franciscan Centre of Oriental Studies in Cairo, for his assistance in this matter.

Chapter One:
Continuity and Reinvention

1.   On St. Antony, see Athanasius of Alexandria, *Life of Antony* (trans. Vivian and Athanassakis), esp. Vivian's introduction, pp. xxiii–lxvi; and Harmless, *Desert Christians*, Chapters 3, 4, and 6. On the Monastery of St. Antony, see Bolman, *Monastic Visions*; for photographs of the wallpaintings of the patriarchs, see pp. 70 (Mark, Ill. 4.36), 94 (Athanasius, Ill. 6.8), 112 (Severus and Dioscorus, Ill. 7.14), and 76 (Dioscorus, Theophilus, Peter, and Benjamin, Ill. 4.43).

2.   Pearson, "Coptic Inscriptions," 234.

3.   See Bolman, "Theodore," 37–76.

4.   For their stories, see Davis, *The Early Coptic Papacy*.

5.   The page is preserved as MS Paris, Bibliothèque Nationale, copte 129[14]. Edition and translation in *Life of Benjamin* (ed. Müller), 295–300. For a discussion that warns us against claiming too much certainty about this text (e.g., with regard to the attribution of authorship to Benjamin's successor Agathon, or the localization of the vision at the Monastery of St. Macarius), see Brakmann, "Zum Pariser Fragment."

6.   *Life of Benjamin* (ed. Müller), 298.

7.   On this shaping of something *new* (and the importance of martyrdom to the project), see Papaconstantinou, "Historiography."

8.   On George, see den Heijer, *Mawhub*, 142–45, or Swanson, "George the Archdeacon," in *CMR* 1, 234–38.

9.   In Evetts's edition and translation of the *History of the Patriarchs*, the section for which George is the principal source is found in PO 1.4, 445–518 and PO 5.1, 3–48.

10.   See Davis, *The Early Coptic Papacy*, 112–21.

11.   A good explanation of the Christological issues at stake is Pelikan, *The Spirit of Eastern Christendom*, Chapter Two, "Union and Division in Christ."

12.   The standard account of the Arab conquest of Egypt is still Butler, *The Arab Conquest of Egypt*.

13. PO 1.4, 502–503.
14. PO 1.4, 503. On this "crown" language and its connection to martyrdom, see below.
15. See, for example, M. Shaban, "Conversion to Early Islam," 24–29. The conquering Arabs saw the conquered provinces as "a garden protected by our spears," and saw no need to replace the gardeners; Brown, *The World of Late Antiquity*, 196.
16. See Fattal, *Le statut legal*.
17. He received advice in this from Shenoute, the duke of Antinoë, who was an anti-Chalcedonian; PO 1.4, 495–96.
18. PO 1.4, 501. See also Kennedy, "Egypt as a Province," 67.
19. The terms *jizyah* and *kharaj* were often used interchangeably for "taxes," although their specific meanings, as poll tax and land tax respectively, have some early attestation; Dennett, *Conversion and the Poll Tax*, 12–13, 65–115; Mikhail, "Egypt from Late Antiquity to Early Islam," 177–78.
20. Taxes were exacted for "the sailors in the fleet"; PO 5.1, 5. The naval buildup began under 'Abd Allah ibn Sa'd ibn Abi Sarh in 645, and the Muslim navy showed its effectiveness when it defeated the Byzantines at the so-called Battle of the Masts in 654; Kennedy, "Egypt as a Province," 67. For details on the naval buildup, see Fahmy, *Muslim Naval Organisation*.
21. The question of the attitudes of the Copts toward the Arab conquerors has generated some controversy; recent literature displays a reaction to the generalization that the Copts, motivated by a sense of "nationalism," welcomed the Arabs as liberators from the Byzantine yoke; see, e.g., Mikhail, "Egypt from Late Antiquity to Early Islam." On this question, see Davis, *The Early Coptic Papacy*, 122–23.
22. For an overview of Christian apocalyptic literature from the early Islamic period, see Hoyland, *Seeing Islam as Others Saw It*, Chapter Eight, "Apocalypses and Visions." Also see below, Chapter Two, at notes 12–15.
23. George the Archdeacon speaks quite favorably about the Arab Muslims (at least as far as his text is preserved in the "primitive recension" of the *History of the Patriarchs*): den Heijer, "La conquête arabe."
24. *Livre de la consécration du sanctuaire de Benjamin*, 106–109.
25. Most of Peter's nine-year reign (644/45–653/54) was spent in exile, and after his death the Chalcedonian patriarchate remained vacant until the election of Cosmas I in c. 742; Skreslet, "The Greeks in Medieval Islamic Egypt," 59.
26. See Skreslet, "The Greeks in Medieval Islamic Egypt," 81–91.
27. See Davis, *The Early Coptic Papacy*, esp. 98–108.

28. In brief: (a) The *akephaloi* were the "headless ones" or *aposchistai*, "separatists," who renounced their allegiance to Patriarch Peter III Mongus (#27, 477–490); Davis, *The Early Coptic Papacy*, 93–98. (b) "Phantasaists" was a name given to the followers of Julian of Halicarnassus by his opponents. Julian had taught that Christ's body was immune from corruption (*aphthartos*); his opponents claimed that this made Christ's sufferings a mere appearance or "fantasy;" Davis, *The Early Coptic Papacy*, 100–101. (c) The Gaianites were the followers of Gaianus, a rival to Patriarch Theodosius (#36, 536–566), who gathered support from the movements just named; Davis, *The Early Coptic Papacy*, 101–102. (d) "Barsanuphians" is a name for an early separatist movement or group of *akephaloi* among the monks; see Stewart, "Barsanuphians." For a helpful visual overview, see the chart in Davis, *The Early Coptic Papacy*, Appendix 3.

29. One bishop who refused to return, Victor of al-Fayyum (see PO 1.4, 491 and 497) is singled out as a "Judas" in Benjamin's sermon, *On Cana of Galilee*; Müller, *Die Homilie über die Hochzeit zu Kana*, 84–85; English translation in Maged S. A. Mikhail, "On Cana of Galilee," 78.

30. The Chalcedonian historian (and later patriarch) Sa'id ibn Bitriq (Eutychius) claimed that, during the first century of Islamic rule, "the Jacobites had seized all the churches in Misr and Alexandria"; Eutychius, *Annals* (ed. Cheikho), ii, 46. While this claim is exaggerated, it no doubt reflects the vigor with which the anti-Chalcedonian patriarchs pressed their claims on existing churches.

31. PO 5.1, 9.

32. PO 5.1, 18–19.

33. PO 5.1, 45–46.

34. PO 5.1, 34. Around this time a single Chalcedonian bishop remained in Egypt, in Misr; Eutychius, *Annals* (ed. Cheikho), ii, 46.

35. PO 1.4, 498.

36. The *History of the Patriarchs* later tells stories about (a) recovering the head after it had come into the possession of a Turkish *amir* (during the patriarchate of Zacharias, #64, 1004–1032), *HPEC* 2.2, 201; (b) hiding the head in Alexandria and keeping it from falling into the hands of the governor (during the patriarchate of Christodoulos, #66, 1046–1077), *HPEC* 2.3, 264–67. For the twelfth through the fifteenth centuries we have witnesses to the role that visiting the head and wrapping it in a new cloth played in the rite of consecration and enthronement of a new patriarch; see, e.g., the reference to this ceremony in a fourteenth-century manuscript: *Rite of Consecration of the Patriarch of Alexandria* (ed. Burmester), 46 (Coptic text), 83 (English translation). For all this see Otto F. A. Meinardus, "An

Examination of the Traditions," 348–76, as well as below, Chapter Nine, notes 16–17.

37. PO 1.4, 495, 498–500. According to the story, when the captain of a ship stole St. Mark's head and then tried to set sail, his ship refused to leave harbor.

38. PO 1.4, 500; PO 5.1, 18. Even so, the other major church of Alexandria, the Angelicon, remained the Great Church. It was rebuilt under Patriarch Isaac, and had a greater number of clergy than the Church of St. Mark at the time of the patriarchal election of 692; PO 5.1, 25–26.

39. PO 5.1, 21.

40. PO 1.4, 496–97.

41. The story of 'Amr and Benjamin is told, for example, in a children's book on national unity in Egypt: Yusuf, *al-Hilal wa-l-salib*, 20.

42. C. Detlef G. Müller, "Stellung und Haltung," 204.

43. PO 5.1, 13–14. For more on this episode, see below.

44. PO 5.1, 16–17.

45. He was influenced and aided in this by his two anti-Chalcedonian secretaries, Athanasius and Isaac; PO 5.1, 12; Mena of Nikiou, *Life of Isaac* (trans. Bell), 56, 61, 65–67, notes 60 and 110. For further bibliography, see Mikhail, "Egypt from Late Antiquity to Early Islam," 109.

46. A fragment of the Coptic text has been preserved, and is edited and translated in Evelyn White, *The Monasteries of the Wadi 'n Natrûn*, i, 171–75. An Arabic recension is preserved in (for example) MS Paris, Bibliothèque Nationale, arabe 215, ff. 186r–202v. On this text, see Suermann, "Copts and the Islam of the Seventh Century," 104–106; but watch for the forthcoming edition of the Arabic recension by Stephen J. Davis, Bilal Orfali, and Samuel Noble.

47. Evelyn White, *The Monasteries of the Wadi 'n Natrûn*, i, 175. The patriarch's argument for the reality of the crucifixion depends on a miraculous demonstration: a fragment of the True Cross did not burn when thrown into the fire.

48. MS Paris, Bibliothèque Nationale, arabe 215, f. 202v. A more reliable indication of Patriarch John's theological capacities is probably provided by his answers to the questions of one Theodore: John III of Samannud, Patriarch of Alexandria, *Questions de Théodore* (ed. Van Lantschoot).

49. This phrase was coined by Sidney H. Griffith. See his "The Monk in the Emir's *Majlis*," 13–65.

50. See below. The interreligious situation pictured here is also characteristic of the early Islamic period. With the removal of Byzantine power and the state church, Christians of different confessions and Jews came to occupy a level playing field, in which interreligious argument was possible and offered opportunities to the skilled debater.

51.   Mena of Nikiou, *Life of Isaac* (trans. Bell), 67–68.
52.   Mena of Nikiou, *Life of Isaac* (trans. Bell), 68–69.
53.   Mena of Nikiou, *Life of Isaac* (trans. Bell), 71.
54.   Mena of Nikiou, *Life of Isaac* (trans. Bell), 72.
55.   Mena of Nikiou, *Life of Isaac* (trans. Bell), 72.
56.   PO 5.1, 24–25. The reference to Abyssinia is not entirely clear. In *Life of Isaac* the quarrel is between the king of Makouria and the "king of Maurotania"; Mena, *Life of Isaac* (trans. Bell), 72–75.
57.   PO 5.1, 25. In *Life of Isaac*, the patriarch is able to explain matters to the governor's satisfaction—but he is accompanied into the audience hall by the apostle Peter and Mark the Evangelist! Mena of Nikiou, *Life of Isaac* (trans. Bell), 74–75.
58.   PO 5.1, 43.
59.   PO 5.1, 36.
60.   PO 5.1, 36–42.
61.   Mikhail stresses the importance of the involvement of the governor, which resulted in al-Fustat (and environs) becoming a center of influence in church affairs; Mikhail, "Egypt from Late Antiquity to Early Islam," 279–82.
62.   PO 5.1, 22–23.
63.   The text regularly uses "Misr" to refer to the medieval Christian city at "Old Cairo" plus adjacent Fustat, founded by the Muslim conquerors.
64.   PO 5.1, 23–24. George the Archdeacon assures his readers that "the matter was from God," but it is still striking that the Muslim governor in effect overturned a patriarchal election, however irregular it might have been.
65.   PO 5.1, 28. Emphasis added.
66.   See Papaconstantinou, *Le culte des saints en Égypte*; Frankfurter, *Pilgrimage and Holy Space*, 281–302.
67.   See Gabra, *Be Thou There*.
68.   PO 1.4, 500.
69.   PO 1.4, 490.
70.   PO 1.4, 504–18; *Livre de la consécration* (ed. Coquin).
71.   *Livre de la consécration* (ed. Coquin), 80–97; the expression "holy land" is at pp. 88–89.
72.   PO 1.4, 507–10; *Livre de la consécration* (ed. Coquin), 112–133.
73.   PO 1.4, 511; *Livre de la consécration*, 138–41.
74.   Most of the patriarchs from Michael I (#46, 743–767) to Shenoute II (#65, 1032–1046) came from the Monastery of St. Macarius.
75.   On the role of the Monastery of St. Macarius in the consecration of patriarchs in the Fatimid period, see den Heijer, "Wadi al-Natrun," esp. 28–29, 32–34.

76.   Grossmann, "The Pilgrimage Center of Abû Mîna," 281–302.

77.   *Apa Mena: Coptic Texts Relating to St. Menas* (ed. Drescher).

78.   The *Encomium* hails the role of the emperors Zeno and Anastasius, both favorably inclined to the anti-Chalcedonians, as well as that of the anti-Chalcedonian patriarch Timothy (Aelurus), the "confessor-archbishop;" *Apa Mena*, 146–48. Theophanes the Chalcedonian is mentioned at PO 5.1, 13 and 18.

79.   On John's charitable projects, see PO 5.1, 18–20.

80.   A number of studies on the Holy Family tradition appeared around the year 2000. In addition to the essays in Gabra, *Be Thou There*, see, for example: Gabra, "Über die Flucht der Heiligen Familie"; Youssef, "Notes on the Traditions"; Wadi Abullif, "Homilies on the Voyage of the Holy Family."

81.   Davis, "Ancient Sources for the Coptic Tradition."

82.   Davis, "Ancient Sources for the Coptic Tradition," 154–55. Wadi Abullif, "Homilies on the Voyage of the Holy Family," 90–95.

83.   The preserved fragments of the Coptic text and Arabic recensions have been edited and translated: *Homélie sur l'église du Rocher*. A study that goes with these editions is Boud'hors and Boutros, "La Sainte Famille à Gabal al-Tayr et l'Homélie du Rocher."

84.   See the lists in the Appendix to Davis, "Ancient Sources for the Coptic Tradition," 154–55; or in Wadi Abuliff, "Homilies on the Voyage of the Holy Family," 95–99. The oldest accessible manuscripts list (but not with entire consistency): Pelusium, Tell Basta, al-Mahammah, Bilbays, Minyat Janah, Burullus, al-Matla', Bilad al-Sibakh, Bikha Isous or Dayr al-Maghtis, Jabal al-Natrun, al-Matariyyah, Abu Sarjah, Kanisat al-Kaff, al-Ashmunayn, and Qusqam.

85.   *Livre de la consécration* (ed. Coquin), 110–11.

Chapter Two:
Patient Sufferers

1.   I normally use the Anglicized form of the patriarch's name as found in the *Coptic Encyclopedia*. In the case of the six medieval patriarchs (#46, 53, 56, 68, 71, and 92) named Kha'il or Mikha'il = Michael, however, *CE* has three entries under "Kha'il" (I–III) and three under "Michael" (IV–VI). Other lists of patriarchs distinguish between Kha'il and Mikha'il in other ways. In this work I will refer to all six of these patriarchs as Michael, from Michael I to Michael VI.

2.   L. S. B. MacCoull, "Paschal Letter," 33.

3.   Of course, the patriarch had secretaries who may have been responsible for drafting the letter. *The Life of Isaac* relates that the young Isaac spent one month a year writing the paschal letters for Patriarch John III (#40, 680–689); Mena of Nikiou, *Life of Isaac* (trans. Bell), 55.

4.   Following MacCoull's suggestion for the dating. The other possibilities, based on the day on which Easter fell, are 713 and 719.

5.   This is a useful reminder that those we call "Coptic Christians" continued to use Greek well into the eighth century, and indeed, into the ninth. On this, see Mikhail, "Egypt from Late Antiquity to Early Islam," 131–51.

6.   MacCoull, "Paschal Letter," 31–33. The "Manichaean insanity of the docetists" is a polemical reference to the conviction of the followers of Julian of Halicarnassus that the body of Christ was *aphthartos*, incorruptible; see Davis, *The Early Coptic Papacy*, 100–101.

7.   We note, for example, the patriarch's words: "the wisdom of this world has done very well to reject the boast of the mystery of Christ, and it treats as of no effect His death, which through His Cross has become life-giving for us, thinking not to value it as something divine but rather to despise it"; MacCoull, "Paschal Letter," 33. These words take on a certain sharpness against the background of the Qur'anic denial that Jesus was crucified (Q 4:157).

8.   MacCoull, "Paschal Letter," 33.

9.   On the significance of the Dome of the Rock, see, e.g., Grabar, *The Shape of the Holy*; or briefly in Fowden, *Empire to Commonwealth*, 141–43. On Christian reactions to its building, see Reinink, "Early Christian Reactions," as well as my comments below on *The Apocalypse of Shenoute*.

10.   Compare the coins pictured in Fowden, *Empire to Commonwealth*, 154–55 (Plate 9) with that at page 127 (Plate 6). For more details about 'Abd al-Malik's new coins, see Miles, "The Earliest Arab Gold Coinage."

11.   Al-Kindi, *The Governors and Judges of Egypt*, 58–59.

12.   On the Copto-Arabic apocalypses, see Hoyland, *Seeing Islam as Others Saw It*, 278–94; van Lent, "Les apocalypses coptes de l'époque arabe," 181–95; and watch for van Lent, "Coptic Apocalyptic Prophecies from the Islamic Period," forthcoming.

13.   See van Lent, "The Apocalypse of Shenute," in *CMR*1, 182–85. The apocalypse, which appears as an interpolation in the Arabic recension of Besa's *Life of Shenoute*, has not been preserved in Coptic. The Arabic text translated here is found in Ps.-Shenoute, *Apocalypse* (ed. Amélineau), 341.

14.   See Witte, "The Apocalypse of Pseudo-Athanasius."

15.   English translation of the *Apocalypse of Pseudo-Athanasius* IX.9 by Martinez, "Eastern Christian Apocalyptic," 529–30. A new edition of the

Sahidic text, with a German translation, has been prepared by Witte: Ps.-Athanasius, *Apocalypse*; for this passage, see pp. 184–85. The number 666 is the sum of the numerical values of the letters in "Mametios," a free (!) Coptic transliteration of "Muhammad."

16. See den Heijer, *Mawhub*, 145–46; Swanson, "John the Deacon," in *CMR1*, 317–21.

17. PO 5.1, 89.

18. PO 5.1, 48.

19. As we shall see, even the 'Abbasid revolt is very much a part of the divine Plan.

20. PO 5.1, 67.

21. A very few pages into his account, John tells his readers that "Satan stirred up strife against the bishops"; PO 5.1, 50. This is the first of many references to Satan and his schemes.

22. We are told, in particular, that God hears the prayers of the patriarchs (PO 1.5, 62, 98), the monks (pp. 71, 183), and the bishops (p. 116).

23. See below.

24. This is very clear in John's portrayal of Patriarch Alexander II; in spite of many trials, "he gave thanks to God, and was bravely patient"; PO 5.1, 67.

25. It is worth noting that Patriarch Simon (#42) had died in AD 700, and that it was nearly four years before his successor was named. According to the *History of the Patriarchs*, the prominent Upper Egyptian bishop Gregory of Qays was delegated by the governor 'Abd al-'Aziz to oversee the financial responsibilities of the Church during the interregnum, and it was not until 704 that an assembly of the people, together with bishops, priests, and government secretaries, agreed on the holy monk Alexander of the Ennaton (Dayr al-Zujjaj) as their next patriarch; PO 5.1, 48–50. It is not impossible that the mention of "government secretaries" (*kuttab al-diwan*; PO 5.1, 50) gives us a clue as to the delay: with their proximity to the center of power in Egypt, the Coptic notables in Misr may have been claiming a larger role in the selection of the patriarch. See Martin, "Une lecture de *l'Histoire des Patriarches d'Alexandrie*," 18.

26. Kennedy, "Egypt as a Province," esp. p. 65.

27. In addition to Fahmi, *Muslim Naval Organisation*, see Trombley, "Sawirus ibn al-Muqaffa'."

28. The *History of the Patriarchs* claims that the restrictions on movement imposed by Usamah ibn Zayd led to economic stagnation: "At last the roads were made impassable, and no man could travel or sell or buy. The fruits of the vineyards were wasted, and there was no one to buy them for a single dirhem..."; PO 5.1, 69. For the "Coptic revolts," see below; or for a synthetic treatment, see Mikhail, "Egypt from Late Antiquity to Early Islam," 195–211.

29. The *History of the Patriarchs* reports, for example, the census and cadastre ordered by 'Ubayd Allah ibn Habhab when he became *sahib al-kharaj* after 724: "he commanded that the people and the cattle should be numbered, and the lands and vineyards measured with measuring lines"; PO 5.1, 74–75. Stringent restrictions on movement, including the requirement that every traveler have a *sijill* or passport, are ascribed to Usamah ibn Zayd a decade earlier; PO 5.1, 68–70.
30. Martinez, "Eastern Christian Apocalyptic," 530–31.
31. PO 5.1, 50–51. In general, monks were considered exempt from *jizyah* for most of the Umayyad period.
32. PO 5.1, 52.
33. PO 5.1, 52–53.
34. Examples will be given below. For the story of a young Muslim who stabbed a wall-painting of the crucified Christ (PO 5.1, 149–50), see Swanson, "Folly to the *Hunafa*," 240–43.
35. PO 5.1, 56.
36. PO 5.1, 56.
37. Abbot, *The Kurrah Papyri*, with a biography of Kurrah at pp. 57–69.
38. PO 5.1, 54–55, 58–59; the quotation is from p. 61.
39. See Trombley, "Sawirus ibn al-Muqaffa'," 203–207. According to the *History of the Patriarchs*, under the financial official Usamah ibn Zayd (who came to authority after the death of Qurrah), restrictions on travel became so great that the flow of goods was drastically curtailed, causing considerable economic damage; PO 5.1, 69. But "God took away his life . . . in a grievous and painful manner, as he deserved;" 71.
40. PO 5.1, 72.
41. PO 5.1, 73.
42. PO 5.1, 73.
43. PO 5.1, 76. On this revolt, see also al-Kindi, *The Governors and Judges of Egypt*, 73–74.
44. PO 5.1, 77.
45. PO 5.1, 88.
46. PO 5.1, 101–103. In this connection John the Deacon relates a story about an Arab who spat on a cross at a monastery near Tinnis, and the divine vengeance that befell him; pp. 102–103. For reflections on the significance of the story, see Christian Décobert, "Maréotide médiévale," 134–35.
47. PO 5.1, 86.
48. PO 5.1, 95–96.
49. PO 5.1, 97–98.
50. PO 5.1, 104–105.

51.   PO 5.1, 105–13.

52.   PO 5.1, 109–12.

53.   PO 5.1, 113.

54.   Eutychius, *Annals* (ed. Cheikho), ii, 45–46.

55.   PO 5.1, 119–32. At the same time that the issue of ownership of the shrine of St. Menas was being litigated, negotiations were taking place for the union of the churches. These, however, appear to have foundered on the role that Chalcedonian clergy would play in the newly united Church; pp. 126–29.

56.   PO 5.1, 148–49.

57.   PO 5.1, 132–33.

58.   PO 5.1, 140–43.

59.   PO 5.1, 143–46.

60.   PO 5.1, 116–17.

61.   PO 5.1, 134.

62.   PO 5.1, 134–39.

63.   PO 5.1, 156–57.

64.   For more details, see below.

65.   PO 5.1, 158–88.

66.   PO 5.1, 150–54. On John's remarkable portrayal of the 'Abbasid rebels' God-given victory, see Swanson, "Folly to the *Hunafa*," 240–43.

67.   PO 5.1, 187.

68.   PO 5.1, 181.

69.   PO 5.1, 189.

70.   PO 5.1, 189.

71.   PO 5.1, 192.

72.   PO 5.1, 193.

73.   PO 5.1, 193.

74.   PO 5.1, 136.

75.   George the Archdeacon does say that Dioscorus, who died in exile, had earned the "crown of martyrdom"; PO 1.4, 444.

76.   Said of both Severus of Antioch and Theodosius of Alexandria; PO 1.4, 458, 468.

77.   Said of Benjamin; PO 1.4, 496.

78.   Said of Benjamin after Athanasius, Severus, and Theodosius had been mentioned; PO 1.4, 502–503.

79.   PO 1.4, 491–42.

80.   PO 5.1, 13–16.

81.   PO 5.1, 14. A similar expression is found later in the *History of the Patriarchs* when Bishop Musa of Awsim refuses, even when threatened with violence,

to be separated from Patriarch Michael: "Do whatever thou desirest"; PO 5.1, 175.

82. PO 5.1, 15.

83. Matthew 27:19 (Revised Standard Version).

84. 'Abd al-'Aziz came to be regarded favorably in George's account, as in other Coptic sources. One might recall, however, that stories of the repentance and martyrdom of Pontius Pilate have been popular in Egypt: there was a church named for him in the twelfth century, and there are reports of Copts named "Pilate" as late as the eighteenth; Luisier, "De Pilate chez les Coptes," esp. 414–15.

85. We hear little, for example, about attempts to reconcile communities of Christians not in communion with him, with the exception of the progress made by a Christian civil servant who received permission from governor Qurrah to charge those Christians not in communion with Patriarch Alexander double the normal *jizyah*—which encouraged many (Gaianites, Barsanuphians, Julianists) to return to the true faith. PO 5.1, 62–63.

86. PO 5.1, 54–79.

87. PO 5.1, 162.

88. PO 5.1, 162–63.

89. PO 5.1, 171. Psalm 38:11, which is echoed in the narrative of Jesus's passion at Luke 23:49 ("And all his acquaintances . . . stood at a distance . . ."), is explicitly quoted here.

90. PO 5.1, 172.

91. PO 5.1, 173.

92. Cf. Mark 15:1–5 and parallels.

93. The major study of this feature of Coptic martyrology is Baumeister, *Martyr Invictus*. For a brief summary, see Clarysse, "The Coptic Martyr Cult," esp. p. 391.

94. PO 5.1, 187–88.

95. PO 5.1, 176.

96. PO 5.1, 177.

97. PO 5.1, 180.

98. PO 5.1, 181.

99. PO 5.1, 167.

100. PO 5.1, 184.

101. Clarysse, "The Coptic Martyr Cult," 395.

102. PO 5.1, 162–64. For the tradition history of this story, see Levi della Vida, "A Christian Legend in Moslem Garb"; and now see Davis, "Variations on an Egyptian Female Martyr Legend."

103. PO 5.1, 174.

104. Indeed, the Church as a whole came to see itself as the Church "of the martyrs." See Papaconstantinou, "Historiography." On the spread of reckoning time in the Coptic era "of the Martyrs" (from about the ninth century), see Bagnall and Worp, *Chronological Systems of Byzantine Egypt*, esp. 67–68.

105. John regularly gives the patriarchs the title "saint," *qiddis*. For emphasis, in one passage he refers to Patriarch Alexander II as "a saint indeed" (*al-qiddis bi-l-haqiqah*); PO 5.1, 79.

106. PO 5.1, 79.

107. Wadi Abullif, "Matteo il Vasaio"; Coquin, "Matthew the Poor, Saint." The *History of the Patriarchs* tells the story of how at his prayers the earth opened up and swallowed a pregnant woman who had been brought to him, who, it turns out, was the victim of her two brothers' incestuous desires; PO 5.1, 79–81. This rather distasteful story may be compared with the *Synaxarion*'s entry for the commemoration of Matthew on 7 Kiyahk, in which the woman confesses her sin and is healed; e.g., Copto-Arabic *Synaxarion* (Cairo ed.), i, 177–78.

108. See Zanetti, "La vie de saint Jean"; Coquin, "Abraham and George of Scetis, Saints." The notice in the *History of the Patriarchs* is somewhat anachronistic since John probably died around 675, Abraham in 693, and George shortly after that—well before Alexander II became patriarch in 704. John's young disciple Epimachus of Arwat, however, was indeed Alexander's contemporary; Zanetti, "La vie de saint Jean," 277. Other saints to emerge from the circle of John the *hegumenos* at the Monastery of St. Macarius include Agathon the stylite, Bishop Zacharias of Sakha, the patriarch Isaac, Bishop Menas of Tmui, and Ptolemy; Evelyn White, *The Monasteries of the Wâdi 'n Natrûn*, ii, 275–86.

109. For the Monastery of St. Shenoute, see PO 5.1, 81 (Abba Seth), 95–97 (miracles at the monastery in the time of al-Qasim), and 205–206 (on Bishop Paul of Akhmim, who had been second-in-command at the monastery). For the Monastery of St. Macarius, see the previous note, as well as PO 5.1, 182–83 (where God hears the prayers offered up at St. Macarius).

110. This is reminiscent of stories about a woman who had been turned into a mare in the *Historia Monachorum*, 21 and the *Lausiac History*, 17; see Frankfurter, "The Perils of Love."

111. PO 5.1, 202–206.

112. See PO 5.1, 133–34 (Musa as healer), 165–67, 180–81, 194 (as prophet).

113. PO 5.1, 197–98.

Chapter Three:
Crisis of Cohesion

1. The expression is that of Christian Décobert in his "Maréotide médiévale," 152, n. 101. His point will be discussed below.

2. PO 10.5, 472–73.

3. See den Heijer, *Mawhub*, 146–49; Swanson, "John the Writer," in *CMR* 1, 702–705. In fact, it is not entirely certain that this scribe's name was John, but it is convenient to call him that.

4. This monastery was a new foundation in the ninth century. See Evelyn White, *The Monasteries of the Wâdi 'n Natrûn*, ii, 305–308.

5. PO 10.5, 531–32; *HPEC* 2.1, 49. One wonders whether John needed such a prophecy in order to legitimate his literary activity.

6. PO 10.5, 360.

7. PO 10.5, 533–34.

8. PO 10.5, 543.

9. PO 10.5, 360; *HPEC* 2.1, 76. John describes his call (by means of a dream) to write the biographies of the patriarchs in *HPEC* 2.1, 49–50.

10. This is a constant theme of John's history from its first pages (beginning at PO 10.5, 362).

11. *HPEC* 2.1, 17.

12. John quotes or alludes to Matthew 16:18, Christ's statement that "the gates of Hell" shall not prevail against the Church, at least five times: PO 10.5, 371, 399, 512, 522; *HPEC* 2.1, 71.

13. PO 10.5, 473.

14. *HPEC* 2.1, 12.

15. See, for example, *HPEC* 2.1, 77–81, where John goes into gory detail about the arrest, multiple beatings, mistreatment by fellow prisoners, and grotesque disease suffered by a deacon who had been responsible for the arrest and imprisonment of an already ailing Patriarch Shenoute. Shenoute, as always, accepts his trials as the consequences of his own sins, forgives his persecutor, and prays for him; *HPEC* 2.1, 75–77, 81.

16. We have already seen the connection made by the (anonymous) author of the *Apocalypse of Athanasius* between Muhammad and the Beast of Revelation 13; see above, Chapter Two. The (likewise) anonymous thirteenth-century *Martyrdom of John of Phanijoit*, written in Coptic, attempts to strengthen the Christian community by characterizing the Muslim community as immoral; see Zaborowski, *The Coptic Martyrdom of John of Phanijoit*, esp. 28–31.

17. See *HPEC* 2.1, 10, 12, 34–35.

18. See PO 10.5, 465 ('Abd Allah ibn Tahir is "a good and merciful man in his religion" who "loved justice and hated tyranny"); *HPEC* 2.1, 61 (Governor

Muzahim [ibn Khaqan] was "a man who was pious and continent in his sect, knowing the precepts of his religion, and just in his ways"); *HPEC* 2.1, 66 (the replacement for the tyrant Ibn al-Mudabbir was "a man careful for his soul, and known for his goodness in the religion of Islam. He . . . began to do good. . . .").

19.   See the nine-page chart of the governors (and other chief officials) of Egypt under the 'Abbasids in Lane-Poole, *A History of Egypt*, 50–58.

20.   PO 10.5, 507.

21.   PO 10.5, 369–70. I have emended the spelling of the patriarch's name, "Mennas" in Evetts's translation.

22.   This text is later quoted by Patriarch Yusab; PO 10.5, 488–89.

23.   PO 10.5, 500; see similar statements by the same patriarch at pp. 504, 514, and 529.

24.   *HPEC* 2.1, 38.

25.   PO 5.1, 190.

26.   PO 10.5, 404. I have regularized the transliteration of an Arabic word in Evetts's translation: *diwan* rather than Divan. The *diwan* here is a register of government officials.

27.   PO 10.5, 381. The Greek/Coptic word *oikonomos* is transliterated rather than translated into Arabic: *uqnum*.

28.   PO 10.5, 385.

29.   PO 10.5, 383: "it was granted to him to be acceptable to all princes and governors, like Joseph the Truthful, . . . to whom he gave grace and wisdom before Pharaoh."

30.   PO 10.5, 383–92.

31.   PO 10.5, 406–408. The entire scene, in which Patriarch Mark prays for the governor, who "admired the sweetness of Abba Mark's voice and his gracious words and the grace with which he was surrounded" (p. 407), is reminiscent of the meeting of Patriarch Benjamin and 'Amr ibn al-'As; see above, Chapter One.

32.   PO 10.5, 419. His building projects included: rebuilding the churches of Fustat-Misr (p. 408), rebuilding one of the churches of the repentant Barsanuphians (p. 415), and rebuilding the Church of the Savior (the *Soter*) in Alexandria (pp. 418–20).

33.   PO 10.5, 483. His guardian's name was Theodore, whose title was *mutawalli kurat Misr* (prefect for the district of Misr).

34.   PO 10.5, 485.

35.   PO 10.5, 538.

36.   *HPEC* 2.1, 27–28.

37.   *HPEC* 2.1, 2.

38. *HPEC* 2.1, 3–5, 16; the quoted phrases are on p. 4.
39. Mikhail, "Egypt from Late Antiquity to Early Islam," 195–211. Mikhail rejects the usual distinction between "Coptic" and "Arab" revolts, and counts a total of nineteen revolts in the following years (where boldface type indicates revolts in which there was significant Egyptian Christian participation: 712, **725**, 739–740, **750** (two revolts), **752**, **767**, 773, 784, 793, 801, 806, 809, **811**, 813, **818–819**, 829, **831**, 832.
40. The south was ruled by al-Sari ibn al-Hakam and the north by 'Abd al-'Aziz al-Jarawi in conjunction with the Yemeni tribes of Lakhm and Judham. Both men were recent arrivals in Egypt. For a very helpful outline of events during the troubled years 806–831, see Kennedy, "Egypt as a Province," 79–83.
41. John's account of events is found in PO 10.5, 427–39.
42. PO 10.5, 429. John the Writer reports that Patriarch Mark purchased six thousand captives, set them free, and gave them the choice of returning home or settling down with the Christians of Egypt.
43. PO 10.5, 430.
44. PO 10.5, 431–34. The official, Macarius, obtained security guarantees for the patriarch from 'Abd al-'Aziz al-Jarawi.
45. PO 10.5, 438–39, 440–41; for more on this "fifth sack of Scetis," see Evelyn White, *The Monasteries of the Wadi 'n Natrûn*, ii, 297–98.
46. The "Paradise of God": PO 10.5, 404, 453, 538. The "Garden of Eden" or the "Holy of Holies": PO 10.5, 438. The "Holy Jerusalem": *HPEC* 2.1, 66.
47. Patriarch Mark speaks of himself as living "in exile" in his letter to Patriarch Dionysius of Antioch; PO 10.5, 436. In the same place, John the Writer explicitly links the patriarch's laments to those traditionally attributed to Jeremiah: "Such were the thoughts he expressed, because these events were like that which is written concerning Jerusalem in the Lamentations of the prophet Jeremiah." The patriarch's laments may be found throughout an extensive passage, PO 10.5, 432–39.
48. PO 10.5, 436. Patriarch Mark's lament echoes Psalm 79:1–3 (a psalm of lament), which he had quoted earlier; PO 10.5, 432.
49. PO 10.5, 438–39. Here and in the previous quotation, I have reformatted the text of Evetts's translations in order to emphasize the passages' similarity to biblical lament.
50. The first four lines of the quoted passage come from Psalm 39:3–4. For the image of the place inhabited only by wild animals, see the prophetic oracles against Babylon in Isaiah 13:19–22 and Jeremiah 50:39.
51. PO 10.5, 440–43. After he became patriarch, Jacob rebuilt the Church of St. Macarius; PO 10.5, 459–60.

52. PO 10.5, 451; see also p. 469.

53. PO 10.5, 465.

54. This situation reflects a new (and oppressive) arrangement for governing Egypt: the local authorities reported to a "super-governor" in Baghdad, who in this case was none other than the caliph's brother, the future caliph al-Mu'tasim. See Kennedy, "Egypt as a Province," 82–83.

55. PO 10.5, 469. John reports that the governor (here 'Isa ibn Yazid al-Juludi) returned the vessels to the patriarch, but still "demanded the taxes with greater severity than before."

56. This revolt is well documented in both Christian and Muslim sources; see Mikhail, "Egypt from Late Antiquity to Early Islam," 207. John the Writer singles out two especially cruel tax gatherers who were responsible for driving their victims to desperate violence: Ahmad ibn al-Asbat and Ibrahim ibn Tamim; PO 10.5, 486–87.

57. PO 10.5, 488–89 (Yusab's preaching before Dionysius's arrival), 493–94 (Yusab and Dionysius together try to dissuade the rebels).

58. PO 10.5, 494.

59. This was the judgment of al-Maqrizi, writing in the fifteenth century, and modern historians have repeated it: "Egypt now became, for the first time, an essentially Mohammadan country"; Lane-Poole, *A History of Egypt*, 38. This may oversimplify matters; see below.

60. The edict has been preserved by al-Tabari, *History* (trans. Kramer), 89–91.

61. *HPEC* 2.1, 6. Translation slightly modified. (See the Preface, "Technical Notes," on the regular modifications I have made to English translations from *HPEC*.)

62. *HPEC* 2.1, 6. John the Writer curiously calls him *al-Ghayr 'Abd al-Masih* ibn Ishaq, "Not-a-servant-of-Christ," son of Isaac. This appears to indicate that John regarded the governor as a Christian named 'Abd al-Masih, perhaps a convert.

63. The semantron, a flat piece of metal beaten to produce a gong-like noise.

64. *HPEC* 2.1, 7–8.

65. On the history of development of the "Covenant of 'Umar," see now Miller, "From Catalogue to Codes to Canon."

66. See below, Chapter Four.

67. See below, Chapters Seven–Nine. An interesting feature in the various decrees is the changing significance of particular colors. In al-Mutawakkil's decrees, yellow is the color that marks the *ahl al-dhimmah*, while in al-Hakim's it is black. Under the Mamluks yellow was reserved for Jews, and blue for Christians. For a detailed discussion, see Miller, "From Catalogue to Codes to Canon," 115–19.

68. *HPEC* 2.1, 8. Translation slightly modified. See Matthew 10:22, Mark 13:10.
69. Ibn al-Mudabbir Ahmad ibn Muhammad al-Rastisani, "the most hated man in Egypt, which explains the escort of 100 young guardsmen who accompanied him on all occasions," according to Bianquis, "Autonomous Egypt," 92.
70. *HPEC* 2.1, 34–35.
71. *HPEC* 2.1, 35–37.
72. *HPEC* 2.1, 39. Even a five-fold increase in the *diyariyah* (a church tax originally intended to support the monasteries) was insufficient to meet Ibn al-Mudabbir's demands.
73. *HPEC* 2.1, 45–46. John mentions the well-known monasteries of St. Shenoute and of al-Qalamun, as well as a monastery of St. Pachomius in the district of Taha.
74. *HPEC* 2.1, 52–60.
75. *HPEC* 2.1, 60.
76. *HPEC* 2.1, 68. The new monastery of St. John Kame appears to have been built with a wall. Fortified enclosures were no doubt created for the other monasteries of Scetis during the last third of the ninth century.
77. PO 10.5, 420–22.
78. PO 10.5, 451–52. The deacon had demanded the usual payments for the churches of Alexandria at precisely the time that, because of disruptions to the pilgrimage to the shrine of St. Menas, funds were short.
79. PO 10.5, 477–79.
80. PO 10.5, 496–97, 502.
81. PO 10.5, 519–522.
82. PO 10.5, 522.
83. PO 10.5, 362–80. Peter presumed on the support of the caliph to the extent that he threatened the governor of Egypt, who clapped him in irons and threw him into a dungeon for three years; pp. 375–76.
84. *HPEC* 2.1, 92–98.
85. PO 10.5, 490–92.
86. PO 10.5, 497–98.
87. PO 10.5, 498–501.
88. On the name of this bishop (which Evetts read as Banah), see Samir, "Yannah, dans l'onomastique arabo-copte."
89. PO 10.5, 523–27.
90. This reconciliation between the two communities took place in 616. See Davis, *The Early Coptic Papacy*, 111–12.
91. Michael, Patriarch of Antioch, *Chronique* (ed. Chabot), iii, 63.
92. PO 10.5, 440.

93. PO 10.5, 429.
94. PO 10.5, 483.
95. *HPEC* 2.1, 91.
96. *HPEC* 2.1, 24. This appears to be a community of "Phantasiasts," who denied the sufferings of Christ.
97. *HPEC* 2.1, 30. "God died in the flesh" would be an orthodox statement, but not that *the Divinity* died.
98. *HPEC* 2.1, 40. The teaching of Cyril of Alexandria is, of course, central to Coptic Orthodox theology. See Davis, *The Early Coptic Papacy*, 70–84.
99. *HPEC* 2.1, 48–49. Shenoute defends the traditional Alexandrian chronology of the fifth-century monk Annianos, according to which the world was created on 25 March 5492 BC, the Annunciation took place exactly 5500 years later, and the Resurrection thirty-three years after that. See Leclercq, "Ère."
100. *HPEC* 2.1, 30.
101. Décobert, "Maréotide médiévale," 152, n. 101.
102. Décobert's article makes this case for Mareotis, where an "economy of miracle" (based on the shrine of St. Menas) was made progressively more fragile and finally destroyed by a mechanism of government control that was "the first moment in a long and slow process of Islamization"; Décobert, "Maréotide médiévale," 159–60.
103. The caliph 'Umar II (717–720) was the exception to this rule, as we noted in Chapter Two.
104. See Charfi, "La fonction historique de la polémique islamochrétienne."
105. Notably al-Jahiz and 'Ali al-Tabari. See Gaudeul, *Encounters and Clashes*, i, 39–48; ii, 24–39, 216–29, 314–21, 328–31, 348–55. See also the entries for them in *CMR* 1: Thomas, "Al-Jahiz," and Thomas, "'Ali l-Tabari."
106. See above, note 68.
107. PO 10.5, 378.
108. PO 10.5, 379. I have added the quotation marks around the biblical quotations; these are from Matthew 10:33 and a conflation of Matthew 22:13 and Mark 9:48.
109. Décobert, "Sur l'arabisation et l'islamisation," 278. The two stelae, numbers 59 and 330 respectively of the Muslim necropolis of Aswan, are dated respectively to AD 857 and 920; Décobert reasons that the fathers may have converted to Islam a half-century or so earlier. It may be, however, that Muhammad and Abu l-Harith Bilal themselves are the converts, having changed their names upon conversion.
110. Bulliet, *Conversion to Islam in the Medieval Period*.
111. Mikha'il, "Egypt from Late Antiquity to Early Islam," 70–71. The contract is preserved in the Egyptian National Library and is known to papyrologists

as P.Cair.Arab.I.56. The marriage contract of this same mixed couple is preserved in P.Cair.Arab.I.48; see Mikha'il, "Egypt from Late Antiquity to Early Islam," 65.

112. On the story of Peter/Abu l-Khayr, see the comments of Mikhail, "Egypt from Late Antiquity to Early Islam," 69–70.

113. See the studies mentioned above (Mikhail, Bulliet, Décobert), as well as Lapidus, "The Conversion of Egypt to Islam." Lapidus, who works especially with the Christian chroniclers including the *History of the Patriarchs*, refers to "the massive turning to Islam which finally occurred in the middle and later decades of the ninth century"; p. 256. At the same time, he recognizes that it was in the Mamluk period that the Copts were "reduced to the small minority they are today in Egypt"; ibid., 262.

114. Throughout this work I (rather inconsistently) use the more recognizable transliteration of Greek for the singular, *archon*, along with the Arabic broken plural, *arakhinah*.

115. PO 10.5, 433–34.

116. *HPEC* 2.1, 4–5, 16.

117. *HPEC* 2.1, 46–47.

118. PO 10.5, 507.

119. Ibid., 503–11.

120. John the Writer mentions exchanges of synodical letters (or personal visits) between:
John IV (777–799) and George I (758–790): PO 10.5, 382–83.
John IV and Cyriacus (793–817): PO 10.5, 392–95.
Mark II (799–819) and Cyriacus: PO 10.5, 408–10; another letter is quoted at p. 417.
Mark II and Dionysius I (818–845): PO 10.5, 435–37.
Jacob (819–830) and Dionysius I: personal visit by Dionysius, PO 10.5, 465–67.
Yusab I (831–849) and Dionysius I: personal visit by Dionysius, PO 10.5, 492–96.
Yusab I and John III (846–873): PO 10.5, 534–35.
Cosmas II (851–858) and John III: *HPEC* 2.1, 5.
Shenoute I (859–880) and John III: *HPEC* 2.1, 25–26.

121. 1. Synodical letter of John IV to Cyriacus: *Confession of the Fathers* (ed. Dayr al-Muharraq), 262–73. 2. Synodical letter of Cyriacus to Mark II: *Confession of the Fathers*, 274–80; Cyriacus, Patriarch of Antioch, "La letter synodale de Cyriaque"(ed. Teule). 3. Letter of Mark II to Cyriacus: PO 10.5, 417–18.

122. The most thorough study of this connection is Fiey, "Coptes et Syriques."

123. The "Monastery of the Theotokos of Bishoi" may have come into existence at a short distance from the original monastery of St. Bishoi in the early

sixth century, when "Severan" monks separated themselves from the "Julianists." On the period, see Davis, *The Early Coptic Papacy*, 101–108.

124. On the discoveries in the old church at Dayr al-Suryan and their significance, see: Innemée and van Rompay, "La présence des syriens"; Innemée, van Rompay, and Sobczynski, "Deir al-Surian"; den Heijer, "Relations between Copts and Syrians."

125. See the Excursus, "The Library of the Syrian Monastery," in Evelyn White, *The Monasteries of the Wadi 'n Natrûn*, ii, 437–58. The library continued to expand throughout the first half of the tenth century under the care of a remarkable abbot, Moses of Nisibis.

126. Excursus, "The Library of the Syrian Monastery," in Evelyn White, *The Monasteries of the Wadi 'n Natrûn*, ii, 437–58. While the most significant Syriac manuscripts were carried off to London in the nineteenth century and are now found in the British Library, the Syrian Monastery still preserves a fine collection of Arabic manuscripts. A number of important contributions to Arabic Christian studies in recent years have involved the publication of texts transcribed from manuscripts at the Syrian Monastery.

127. PO 10.5, 402–40. "He loved good works and the building of churches," p. 419; on his writings, p. 440.

128. PO 10.5, 440–75. On his visions, p. 442; prophecies, pp. 458–59; healing miracles, pp. 460–61, 471–72; cursing, pp. 449, 451–52; "intercessor for the land of Egypt," p. 487.

129. PO 10.5, 476–547. A healing, pp. 533–34; prayers for vengeance, pp. 514–15, 517, 521–22, 530 (and 544–45), 537 (and 546).

130. *HPEC* 2.1, 18–99. On his pastoral ministry, pp. 23–31; his humility and weeping, pp. 21–22; his seeking forgiveness for foes, pp. 33–34, 43, 72, 75, 81–82, 97.

131. For examples of *jihad* language see, e.g., PO 10.5, 376, 380 (Menas I); 393 (John IV); 446, 545–46 (Yusab I); *HPEC* 2.1, 98 (where "champion" translates *mujahid*) (Shenoute I).

132. Likewise the Muslim 'Abd al-'Aziz, who offered Patriarch Mark protection, may be compared with the magistrate Dorotheus of Sakha who gave Patriarch Severus lodging; PO 10.5, 433–34.

133. PO 10.5, 446–47, 474. In addition to these references to Severus of Antioch, on one occasion Patriarch Jacob performs an exorcism using oil from the lamp illuminating Severus's relics; PO 10.5, 471.

Chapter Four:
Saints and Sinners

1. Michael's autobiographical notes are scattered throughout his contribution: *HPEC* 2.2, 102, 168, 195, 202, 235, 240–41. See also den Heijer, *Mawhub*, 150–53.

2. Michael reports the rumors that Shenoute "was desirous of" the patriarchate —something which, of course, no proper patriarch was supposed to be. *HPEC* 2.2, 230.

3. Shenoute quotes Ps. 99:1, "The Lord reigns, let the people tremble," to the *arakhinah* of Misr who had previously opposed his appointment as bishop there; *HPEC* 2.2, 232.

4. *HPEC* 2.2, 232.

5. Michael reports how Shenoute went back on agreements with the Alexandrians, with the saintly *archon* Buqayrah, and with the troublemaking bishop Yu'annis of al-Farama (Pelusium); *HPEC* 2.2, 234–37.

6. *HPEC* 2.2, 239.

7. *HPEC* 2.2, 230. Bishop Michael does not display any doubt about the veracity of the dream.

8. *HPEC* 2.2, 239.

9 See, e.g., Chapter Three above.

10. For a historical overview, see Bianquis, "Autonomous Egypt."

11. See Walker, "The Isma'ili Da'wa."

12. *HPEC* 2.2, 103–107.

13. *HPEC* 2.2, 104–105. Patriarch Michael speaks to Ibn Tulun with language typical of the martyrs: "Now I am before thee. Do what thou wilt. Thou hast domination over my body, but my soul is in the hand of its Creator"; p. 105.

14. *HPEC* 2.2, 105, 107.

15. *HPEC* 2.2, 109–13. We learn that Patriarch Michael managed to gather the first installment of ten thousand dinars, and that the second installment was cancelled after Ibn Tulun died—as was foretold by a poor monk, just as the patriarch was beginning a fundraising tour.

16. Bishop Michael reports on Khumarawayh's visit to the Monastery of St. Macarius, where the body of St. Macarius opened his eyes in Khumarawayh's face, and where the image of St. Theodore caught a sprig of basil that was thrown to him; *HPEC* 2.2, 113–14. According to the *History of the Churches and Monasteries of Egypt*, Khumarawayh built a *manzarah* at the Melkite monastery of al-Qusayr where he went for recreation; see *HCME* (ed. Evetts), 145–53. On the *History of the Churches and Monasteries of Egypt*, attributed sometimes to

Abu Salih al-Armani and sometimes (and more persuasively) to Abu l-Makarim Sa'd Allah ibn Jirjis ibn Mas'ud, see den Heijer, "Coptic Historiography," 77–80.

17. Bishop Michael tells us about Bishop Pachomius of Taha, who had a small private militia and provided military intelligence to the *amir* on the movements of potential foes in the west; *HPEC* 2.2, 114.

18. *HPEC* 2.2, 116–18.

19. *HPEC* 2.2, 118–21. Patriarch Cosmas is commemorated in the Copto-Arabic *Synaxarion* on 3 Baramhat (27 February), although the abbreviated *Life* presented there presents little beyond Bishop Michael's account; e.g., Copto-Arabic *Synaxarion* (Cairo ed.), ii, 12–13.

20. *HPEC* 2.2, 121–22. The text adds that Macarius reacted to his mother's words without understanding, but with "embarrassment and shame."

21. Patriarch Macarius is commemorated in the Copto-Arabic *Synaxarion* (on 24 Baramhat = 20 March) as a saint of the Church! The *Life* presented there softens his mother's rebuke so that the main point of her speech becomes the tremendous responsibility that the patriarch carries for his flock. In this version of the story, Macarius takes her words to heart and becomes an exemplary pastor; Copto-Arabic *Synaxarion* (Cairo ed.), ii, 63–64; Copto-Arabic *Synaxarion* (ed. Basset), PO 16.2, 251–53; Copto-Arabic *Synaxarion* (ed. Forget), ii, 40–41.

22. *HPEC* 2.2, 123–24.

23. *HPEC* 2.2, 124–28.

24. *HPEC* 2.2, 133–35. *HCME* (ed. Evetts), 195–96.

25. See above, Chapter Three.

26. *HPEC* 2.1, 22–23, 26.

27. *HPEC* 2.2, 109. The *History of the Churches and Monasteries* reports that Patriarch Michael also sold land (for a cemetery) and a church—to this day the Jewish synagogue in Old Cairo—to the Jewish community; *HCME* (ed. Evetts), 136. That source also mentions the sale of the herds of camels belonging to the monks of St. Macarius.

28. *HPEC* 2.2, 109. According to Bishop Michael, "none of the patriarchs had sojourned in Alexandria" after Michael II sold the patriarchate's property; *HPEC* 2.2, 121. One possible exception is the elderly Theophanius, who did not remain in his position for long.

29. *HPEC* 2.2, 117.

30. *HPEC* 2.2, 117. Later, Patriarch Abraham would have to renegotiate the agreement and reduce the annual payment to five hundred dinars (*HPEC* 2.2, 146), while Shenoute II would reduce it to three hundred and fifty (*HPEC* 2.2, 234).

31. *HPEC* 2.2, 109. The sum is not specified. Later, Patriarch Shenoute
    II would take six hundred dinars for the consecration of a bishop;
    HPEC 2.2, 233.
32. *HPEC* 2.2, 110.
33. *HPEC* 2.2, 117. Translation slightly modified.
34. The phrase "the ritual city" comes from Paula Sanders's study of Fatimid
    ceremonial, *Ritual, Politics, and the City in Fatimid Cairo*. The Fati-
    mid "public text" is studied in Bierman, *Writing Signs: The Fatimid
    Public Text*.
35. Samir, "The Role of Christians," 177–78.
36. Samir, "The Role of Christians." See also Saleh, "Government Relations,"
    esp. Chapter Four, "Christian Employment in the Fatimid Government."
37. We find details about certain monasteries as attractive places for the caliph's
    recreation in the *Book of Monasteries* by Abu l-Hasan 'Ali ibn Muhammad
    al-Shabushti, who was the librarian and boon companion of the caliph
    al-'Aziz; see al-Shabushti, *Book of Monasteries* (ed. Atiya). We also find
    relevant notices scattered in the *History of the Churches and Monasteries of
    Egypt*: e.g., Dayr Nahya was favored by the caliphs al-Mu'izz and al-Amir
    while Dayr Shahran was favored by the caliph al-Hakim; *HCME*
    (ed. Evetts), 180–84 and 142–43, respectively.
38. *HCME* (ed. Evetts), 15, where it is stated that 915 feddans of land had
    come into the possession of the churches and monasteries through gifts
    from the Fatimid caliphs.
39. *HCME* (ed. Evetts), 15. The *History of the Churches and Monasteries of
    Egypt* gives the fullest account of the churches and monasteries in the
    Fatimid period.
40. Samir, "The Role of Christians," 189–91; Saleh, "Government Relations,"
    214–21.
41. This is a fast of forty-three days beginning on 25 November. The three days
    beyond the traditional forty are in commemoration of the period of fasting
    and prayer that preceded the great miracle. See Basilios, "Fasting," 1095.
42. See the entry in the Copto-Arabic *Synaxarion* under this date; e.g.,
    Synaxarion (Cairo ed.), i, 173–77.
43. The development of this complex coincides with the rise of the cult of the
    other hero of the story (along with the patriarch), Sim'an the Tanner, whose
    feast is celebrated on 28 Abib = 4 August. The first church named for him
    was built in the Zabbalin (garbage-collectors) village in Muqattam in 1974,
    and his relics were discovered in 1991 and soon afterward proclaimed
    authentic. See *Life of Saint Sim'an;* Meinardus, "Notes on New Saints in
    the Coptic Church," 12–13, 25.

44.   On the various forms of the name (Afraham, Abra'am, etc.), see den Heijer, "Les patriarches coptes d'origine syrienne," 55–57.

45.   *HPEC* 2.2, 135–50.

46.   On the biography and its elaborations, see den Heijer, "Apologetic Elements." On the functioning of the story as found in the Copto-Arabic Synaxarion, see Maryann M. Shenouda, "Displacing *Dhimmi*," 587–606.

47.   Den Heijer points out that we have evidence of a connection between Abraham and the Syrian Monastery in the form of a Syriac manuscript that he gave to the monastery; den Heijer, "Les patriarches coptes d'origine syrienne," 50, n. 24.

48.   *HPEC* 2.2, 136–37.

49.   On holy men as effective cursers, see Peter Brown, "The Rise and Function of the Holy Man in Late Antiquity," 122–23.

50.   *HPEC* 2.2, 146. The *archon*'s name was Abu l-Surur al-Kabir. Bishop Michael prefaces this report with *wa-yuqal*, "and it is said ...," making clear that he has no compelling evidence for it.

51.   *HPEC* 2.2, 137.

52.   The *wazir* (vizier) was the top government minister, charged with carrying out the orders of the caliph. The precise nature of the *wizarah* (vizierate), and the amount of power it possessed, varied greatly throughout Egypt's history. For the Fatimid period, see Saleh, "Government Relations," 117–27.

53.   *HPEC* 2.2, 147. Quzman was the recipient of a treatise by Sawirus ibn al-Muqaffa': see Samir, "Un traité nouveau"; information about Quzman is collected at pp. 580–84.

54.   According to Abu l-Makarim, he also gave two thousand dinars to the monasteries in Scetis before his departure, and asked for the prayers of the monks; *HCME* (ed. Evetts), 118–19.

55.   *HPEC* 2.2, 148–50.

56.   *HPEC* 2.2, 137–39.

57.   On Ibn Killis's involvement in and sponsorship of religious debates, see Cohen and Somekh, "Interreligious Majalis in Early Fatimid Egypt."

58.   On Sawirus, see Samir, "Un traité nouveau," and Griffith, "The *Kitab Misbah al-'Aql*," with further bibliography.

59.   Most notably the *History of the Patriarchs* itself, although Johannes den Heijer has persuasively argued that the attribution to Sawirus is late and false; den Heijer, "Sawirus Ibn al-Muqaffa'"; den Heijer, *Mawhub*, 81–86, 93–95. Another work regularly attributed to Sawirus in the manuscript tradition, but probably falsely, is the popular catechetical work *Kitab al-Idah*, "The Book of Elucidation." See Swanson, "'Our Brother, the Monk

Eustathius,'" with notes on Sawirus and the works attributed to him at pp. 120–23. This article, incidentally, demonstrates Sawirus's debt to an earlier *Syrian* Orthodox theologian who wrote in Arabic.

60. This Musa is in fact a well-known figure: the caliph's physician Musa ibn El'azar, known as Paltiel; Griffith, "The *Kitab Misbah al-'Aql*," 18.

61. The quotation here is from the Revised Standard Version. The verse as quoted in the text (which adds "and be cast into the sea") is a conflation of Matthew 17:20 and Mark 11:23.

62. *HPEC* 2.2, 140. It is important to note that when the caliph states that the consequence of failure is that "I shall destroy you with the sword," "you" is plural; on the next page it is glossed as "all the inhabitants of the Christian Religion in the land of Misr."

63. *HPEC* 2.2, 140. Translation slightly revised.

64. *Life of Abraham the Syrian*, ed. Leroy, i, 395 (Arabic text), 385 (French translation). The statement later in this recension (preserved in MS Paris, Bibliothèque Nationale, syriaque 65) that "the Jews have been mistaken for 1,300 years in their evaluation" [of Christ's Messianic claims] may point to a fourteenth-century date; ii, 27. By this time the patriarchate was well-established in Cairo-Misr, and so were convents of nuns.

65. Bishop Michael makes a point of telling us that while some of the monks broke their fast at night with bread, salt, and a little water, Patriarch Abraham did not; *HPEC* 2.2, 140–41.

66. *HPEC* 2.2, 141–42.

67. "And if your eye causes you to sin, pluck it out and throw it away; it is better for you to enter life with one eye than with two eyes to be thrown into the hell of fire" (RSV). Bishop Michael's story tells us nothing about the object of his lust, but details are supplied by later elaborations of the text; see *Life of Abraham the Syrian* (ed. Leroy), i, 386–87.

68. *HPEC* 2.2, 142–43. The later recension published by Leroy gives his name, Sim'an, and a number of details about his life; *Life of Abraham the Syrian* (ed. Leroy), i, 386. Still, it is only in recent years that a cult of this saint has developed; see above, note 43.

69. *HPEC* 2.2, 144. The later recension edited by Leroy is considerably elaborated; in it, the mountain moves *toward* the assembled people rather than up and down; *Life of Abraham the Syrian* (ed. Leroy), i, 388.

70. *HPEC* 2.2, 144–46.

71. In the recension of the story published by Leroy, as well as in the *History of the Churches and Monasteries of Egypt*, the moving of the mountain became an interreligious contest: the Muslims and the Jews prayed to God to move the mountain, but in vain, adding to the apologetic impact of

the Christians' success; *Life of Abraham the Syrian* (ed. Leroy), i, 377–78; *HCME* (ed. Evetts), 116–17. Saleh ("Government Relations," 291) notes how the story echoes the contest of Elijah with the priests of Baal in 1 Kings 18:17–40. John the Deacon had narrated a similar interreligious contest during the patriarchate of Michael I (#46, 743–767), in which the three communities took it in turn to beseech God to raise the level of the Nile; PO 5.1, 193–97.

72.   For the text of this discussion, see *Life of Abraham the Syrian* (ed. Leroy), i, 388–89; ii, 26–30; summary in den Heijer, "Apologetic Elements," 197. On arguments for the "true religion" in Arabic Christian apologetics and the importance of evidentiary miracles within them, see Griffith, "Comparative Religion."

73.   See *Life of Abraham the Syrian* (ed. Leroy), ii, 30–32, for the conversion and baptism of al-Mu'izz, as well as Samir, "The Role of Christians," 180 and den Heijer, "Apologetic Elements," 199–201, for comment on the development of this legend.

74.   One may compare the stories that were told in the Melkite world about the conversion of the 'Abbasid caliph al-Ma'mun: see Griffith, "The *Life of Theodore of Edessa*"; or Swanson, "The Christian al-Ma'mun Tradition."

75.   See above, Chapter Two.

76.   *HPEC* 2.2, 150–74; the story of al-Wadih ibn al-Raja' takes up pp. 151-70! For his apologetic works, see Graf, *GCAL*, ii, 318–19.

77.   The one priestly act Bishop Michael reports him as having performed was the consecration of the monk Daniel of the Monastery of St. Macarius as metropolitan for Ethiopia; *HPEC* 2.2, 171–72.

78.   *HPEC* 2.2, 150–51.

79.   He was Philotheus's spiritual (or biological?) father John, who had been passed over for the patriarchate because "he was an exceedingly old man, already stricken in years, and . . . not fit for this charge"; *HPEC* 2.2, 150.

80.   Bishop Michael gives details on Philotheus's daily schedule, which seems to have involved no more than a couple of hours of work in the morning, in between bathtime and mealtime; *HPEC* 2.2, 170. His stroke is presented as a divine punishment.

81.   *HPEC* 2.2, 174.

82.   *HPEC* 2.2, 169–70. Translation slightly modified, including the adjustment of punctuation and avoidance of a euphemism.

83.   See any edition of the Copto-Arabic *Synaxarion* under 13 Hatur. For an extended discussion of Patriarch Zacharias and his portrayal as a saint, see Swanson, "Sainthood Achieved."

84.   *HPEC* 2.2, 176.

85. Bishop Michael notes that "it was the turn of the Alexandrians this time to appoint the patriarch" (*HPEC* 2.2, 175), although it is not clear when or how this arrangement, with Alexandria and Misr-Cairo taking turns in choosing the patriarch, was established. Patriarch Philotheus had been chosen by a synod meeting in Misr (*HPEC* 2.2, 150).
86. *HPEC* 2.2, 174–76.
87. *HPEC* 2.2, 181. Translation slightly modified.
88. *HPEC* 2.2, 177. Translation slightly modified. A *wali* is a governor or ruler.
89. *HPEC* 2.2, 180. Translation slightly modified.
90. The immediate cause was the malice of a monk named Yu'annis who had been frustrated in his ambition to become a bishop. (The patriarch's handlers scorned him because of his inability to pay, while the patriarch gave him assurances that he was unable or unwilling to keep.) Yu'annis then complained to al-Hakim. *HPEC* 2.2, 181–82, 192–93.
91. Al-Hakim's reign is treated in *HPEC* 2.2, 183–209. For the chronology of his anti-Christian measures, see Canard, "Al-Hakim bi-Amr Allah"; or for greater detail, Saleh, "Government Relations," 58–67.
92. Bishop Michael tells us of ten Christian civil servants who were commanded to embrace Islam; of the ten, six died as martyrs; *HPEC* 2.2, 184–86. One wonders about the extent to which al-Hakim's often arbitrary executions have been reinterpreted as martyrdoms. See the comments of Saleh, "Government Relations," 300–302.
93. *HPEC* 2.2, 188; Saleh, "Government Relations," 59.
94. On al-Hakim's *ghiyar* regulations, Saleh, "Government Relations," 98–105.
95. On the destruction of churches, Saleh, "Government Relations," 81–89. One infamous destruction was that of the Church of the Resurrection in Jerusalem, sometime between AD 1007 and 1010.
96. *HPEC* 2.2, 192–93. We later meet a Nubian monk named Shishih who came through the lions' den with the patriarch; *HPEC* 2.2, 228.
97. Yahya ibn Sa'id al-Antaki, as quoted in Samir, "The Role of Christians," 183.
98. *HPEC* 2.2, 195. Translation slightly modified.
99. *HPEC* 2.2, 184–86.
100. *HPEC* 2.2, 195–99. Among his other pious acts, Buqayrah purchased the head of St. Mark the Evangelist from a Turkish *amir* who had acquired it, and brought it to the Monastery of St. Macarius; *HPEC* 2.2, 201.
101. *HPEC* 2.2, 202–204.
102. Saleh, "Government Relations," 155, 164.
103. *HPEC* 2.2, 199.
104. Daniel 6.

105. *HPEC* 2.2, 204–205.
106. *HPEC* 2.2, 205.
107. *HPEC* 2.2, 206.
108. See above, Chapter One.
109. *HPEC* 2.2, 208.
110. *HCME* (ed. Evetts), 135.
111. An earlier draft of this sentence had "Bishop Michael" as its subject, but that failed to take into account den Heijer's observations about the history of the shaping of Patriarch Zacharias's biography (den Heijer, *Mawhub*, 209-12). Den Heijer shows that the biography's brief collection of Patriarch Zacharias's miracles was added by Mawhub ibn Mansur ibn Mufarrij, and that a yet later editor was responsible for the arrangement of the biography as we have it in the printed edition. This provides a salutary reminder— of which I took inadequate notice in Swanson, "Sainthood Achieved"— that the Coptic sources for the *History of the Patriarchs* have not merely been translated into Arabic, but have also been edited in a variety of ways.
112. *HPEC* 2.2, 211–24. Bishop Michael claims to have met John of Antioch when bringing the synodical letter from Patriarch Christodoulos, but this must have been John VIII (1049–1057); p. 215.
113. *HPEC* 2.2, 226–27. Patriarch Zacharias fasted along with the penitent.
114. We shall encounter the *Life-Miracles* form of hagiographical biographies again in Chapter Five and Chapter Eight.
115. *HPEC* 2.2, 231–32.
116. *HPEC* 2.2, 195–202.
117. *HPEC* 2.2, 234–36.
118. *HPEC* 2.2, 233.
119. *HPEC* 2.2, 235.
120. *HPEC* 2.2, 228–29. In Shenoute's case, Buqayrah was able to get a dispensation from the normal fee.
121. *HPEC* 2.2, 231. Shenoute had also agreed to pay the trouble-making monk Yu'annis (see above, note 90), now bishop of Pelusium, the sum of thirty dinars per year. Shenoute later went back on this agreement. *HPEC* 2.2, 231, 237.
122. *HPEC* 2.2, 233.
123. *HPEC* 2.2, 239.

Chapter Five:
Transitions

1. On Samuel, see Alcock, "Samu'il of Qalamun, Saint"; or *Life of Samuel of Kalamun* (ed. Alcock).

2. That is, the Muslims. Jos van Lent makes a number of persuasive arguments that *hajarah* (plural of *hâjarî or hajarî*) and not *hijrah* is the correct reading here; see van Lent, "Coptic Apocalyptic Prophecies from the Islamic Period."

3. Translated from the Arabic text in Samuel of Kalamun, *Apocalypse*, 379, 384.

4. The irony is pointed out in MacCoull, "Three Cultures under Arab Rule," 66. MacCoull quotes some of the same sentences of the *Apocalypse of Samuel* translated here.

5. See, for example, Papaconstantinou, "'They Shall Speak the Arabic Language and Take Pride in It,'" and the literature cited there.

6. See den Heijer, "Mawhub ibn Mansur ibn Mufarrij al-Iskandarani"; den Heijer, *Mawhub*.

7. His chief collaborator was the deacon Abu Habib Mikha'il ibn Badir al-Damanhuri; see den Heijer, *Mawhub*, 95–108.

8. This is den Heijer's terminology; *Mawhub*, 2–9 ("la première partie"). For an overview of the *History of the Patriarchs*, see den Heijer, "History of the Patriarchs of Alexandria."

9. See *HPEC* 2.3, 245–369.

10. *HPEC* 2.3, 369–99; *HPEC* 3.1; *HPEC* 3.2.

11. "La deuxième partie" according to den Heijer, *Mawhub*, 9–11.

12. This was the important observation of Rubenson, "Translating the Tradition," 8–10.

13. Christodoulos, *Canons* (ed. Burmester); and Cyril II, *Canons* (ed. Burmester).

14. See Graf, "Zwei dogmatische Florilegien der Kopten." This older study is a helpful guide to the recent edition *Confession of the Fathers* (ed. Dayr al-Muharraq).

15. See Gibb and Kraus, "Al-Mustansir."

16. *HPEC* 2.3, 267–70, 303–304.

17. *HPEC* 2.3, 267–68.

18. *HPEC* 2.3, 270. Mawhub goes on to report on other opponents of the Christians who were likewise "smitten."

19. *HPEC* 2.3, 303.

20. *HPEC* 2.3, 276–80.

21. *HPEC* 2.3, 276–77. For the earthquake of 18 March 1068 see Ambraseys, Melville, and Adams, *The Seismicity of Egypt, Arabia and the Red Sea*, 30–31.

22.   *HPEC* 2.3, 278–79. The Lawatah Berbers were in alliance with Nasir al-Dawlah ibn Hamdan (active in the 1060s–1073), who was aspiring to supreme power in Egypt. For more on the Copts and Nasir al-Dawlah's rebellion, see den Heijer, "Le patriarcat copte," esp. pp. 93–96.

23.   "The Terror" = *al-hawl. Sibylline Prophecy*, Copto-Arabic recension (ed. Ebied and Young).

24.   *HPEC* 2.3, 314. On Badr, see Becker, "Badr al-Djamali." On his relationship to the Christian community, see den Heijer, "Considérations."

25.   See, e.g., Dadoyan, "The Phenomenon of the Fatimid Armenians."

26.   *HPEC* 2.3, 344–46.

27.   *HPEC* 2.3, 247; 322–23.

28.   *HPEC* 2.3, 249.

29.   *HPEC* 2.3, 260–61.

30.   *HPEC* 2.3, 269.

31.   *HPEC* 2.3, 319.

32.   *HPEC* 2.3, 256. We have already noted the use of the *Life-Miracles* genre in the biography of Patriarch Zacharias (#64); see above, Chapter Four.

33.   *HPEC* 2.3, 256.

34.   *HPEC* 2.3, 257. Emphasis added.

35.   Mawhub characterizes Bishop Abraham as "the cause of every trouble," *HPEC* 2.3, 348.

36.   *HPEC* 2.3, 332–33; 365. Mawhub's evaluation is backed up by his continuator, Yuhanna ibn Sa'id al-Qulzumi, who reports on a long theological conversation he had with Patriarch Cyril; *HPEC* 2.3, 365–68.

37.   See above, Chapter One.

38.   *HPEC* 2.3, 316–17.

39.   *HPEC* 2.3, 337.

40.   We have encountered this pattern especially in the portrayals of Patriarch Michael I (#46) and of Patriarch Abraham ibn Zur'ah (#62), Chapters Two and Four respectively.

41.   Mawhub's catalog of the "many wonders and miracles" performed by "saintly fathers and monks" in the days of Patriarch Christodoulos is found in *HPEC* 2.3, 284–300; the ten miracles of Bisus occupy pp. 286–96. Mawhub relates two more miracles of Bisus in his biography of Cyril II, *HPEC* 2.3, 362–63.

42.   *HPEC* 2.3, 276–77 (weeping icons); 284–85 (a luminous icon of the Virgin Mary); 289–90 (sweating pillars and pictures); 302–303 (a bleeding icon of Mar Mina).

43.   E.g., *HPEC* 2.3, 275 (St. George kills a Muslim official who spends the night in his church); 285–86 (St. Victor strikes down an oppressive muezzin).

44. *HPEC* 2.3, 334–36. On this list, see den Heijer, "Une liste d'évêques coptes." Den Heijer notes the possibility that the list is an interpolation in Mawhub's text.

45. *HPEC* 2.3, 358–62.

46. *HPEC* 2.3, 361. For a comparison of this list of Flight into Egypt sites with others, see the Appendix in Gabra, *Be Thou There*, 154–55.

47. Indeed, it is from Cyril's patriarchate that the patriarchal residence was definitively relocated to Misr-Cairo, where it has remained until the present day. See den Heijer, "Considérations," 573–74; or den Heijer, "Le patriarcat copte," 84–87, 91–93.

48. Among other references to his family, Mawhub relates how his father was imprisoned for a time when the governor of Alexandria was attempting to confiscate the community's great relic, the head of St. Mark the Evangelist; *HPEC* 2.3, 264–67. Later, Mawhub tells us that he took the head to his own house and had a dream in which the saint appeared to him and informed him of his brother's doubts about the head's authenticity. Mawhub confronted his brother, who repented of his doubts; *HPEC* 2.3, 275–76.

49. *HPEC* 2.3, 286–89. Voile, "Les miracles des saints," 321.

50. Voile made this point; "Les miracles des saints," 325.

51. *HPEC* 2.3, 303.

52. Their biographies are found respectively in *HPEC* 2.3, 370–99; and *HPEC* 3.1, 1–39.

53. *HPEC* 2.3, 387, 395–97.

54. See Chapter One, as well as Davis, *The Early Coptic Papacy*, 119–20. Bishop Sanhut's flight to the southern monasteries also echoes the story of earlier exiles such as St. Athanasius.

55. *HPEC* 2.3, 386–88.

56. *HPEC* 2.3, 395–96.

57. *HPEC* 2.3, 397.

58. *HPEC* 3.1, 12–24.

59. For orientation to the sources introduced here, see den Heijer, "Coptic Historiography."

60. Mark's contribution may be found in *HPEC* 3.1, 39–96.

61. Ps.-Yusab of Fuwwah, *Tarikh al-aba' al-batarikah li-l-anba Yusab usquf Fuwwah*. Henceforth I shall refer to this work as *HPYusab*.

62. See Samuel Moawad, "Zur Originalität."

63. See Swanson, "The Coptic Patriarch and the Apostate Scribe."

64. The part of the work most relevant to us here has long been available with an English translation: *The Churches and Monasteries of Egypt and Some*

Neighboring Countries, Attributed to Abû Sâlih, the Armenian, ed. B. T. A. Evetts. Henceforth I shall refer to this work as *HCME* (ed. Evetts).

65.   Patriarch Gabriel has received a fair amount of attention from twentieth-century authors. See especially Nakhlah, *Sirat al-baba Ghubriyal ibn Turayk*; Müller, "Gabriel II. Ibn Turaik" ; Samir, "Gabriel II, patriarche copte d'Alexandrie (1131–1145)"; Samir, introduction to Mina, *Le Nomocanon du patriarche copte Gabriel II ibn Turayk (1131–1145)*.

66.   See Gabriel II ibn Turayk, *Canons* (First Series) (ed. Burmester); *Canons* (Second Series) (ed. Burmester); *Laws of Inheritance* (ed. Burmester); *Nomocanon* (ed. Mina).

67.   See, e.g., Magued, "Al-Hafiz."

68.   *HPEC* 3.1, 45–46.

69.   *HPEC* 3.1, 50–51.

70.   *HPYusab*, 149.

71.   *HPEC* 3.1, 41–42. Note that we find the same motif in the life of St. Athanasius: Wadi, "Vita di Sant' Atanasio," p. 151.

72.   *HPYusab*, 145.

73.   *HPEC* 3.1, 56.

74.   *HPEC* 3.1, 56–59.

75.   *HPEC* 3.1, 57–58. Compare the scene in the *Life* of Abraham of Farshut in which he was visited by Saints Pachomios, Petronius, and Shenoute, who predicted his death [after six months]; Goehring, "2005 NAPS Presidential Address," p. 23.

76.   *HPYusab*, 146.

77.   *HPYusab*, 149.

78.   *HPYusab*, 149.

79.   See van Lent, "Coptic Apocalyptic Prophecies from the Islamic Period."

80.   Swanson, "The Specifically Egyptian Context," 218–20.

81.   See, for example, Meyer and Smith, eds., *Ancient Christian Magic*.

82.   *HPYusab*, 151.

83.   *HPEC* 3.1, 54–55; the English translation is mine from the Arabic text, pp. 33–34. Emphasis added.

84.   On the monastery, see *HCME* (ed. Evetts), 195.

85.   *HPEC* 3.1, 55–56; *HPYusab*, 148–49; *HCME* (ed. Evetts), 127–28.

86.   What follows is a synoptic and, to a certain extent, harmonizing reading. See Swanson, "The Coptic Patriarch and the Apostate Scribe." A synopsis of the texts is already provided by Nakhlah, *Sirat al-baba Ghubriyal ibn Turayk*, 55–57.

87.   The scribe's precise name is a puzzle. "Abu l-Yumn" is found in *HPEC* and *HPYusab*, and "Yahya" in *HCME*. These three sources give the scribe's

nisbah as al-'Amidi, al-'Ibri, and al-'Ubaydi respectively. The matter is discussed in Swanson, "The Coptic Patriarch and the Apostate Scribe."

88. *HPYusab*, 148. The *History of the Churches and Monasteries* supports Yusab's claim that the scribe employed a Muslim baker. Here one must consult the Arabic text; the published English translation has: "he treacherously allowed many Muslims to attend the liturgies," but this should refer to "his damage in [enlisting] the help of the Muslims in the Eucharistic loaves." *HCME* (ed. Evetts), 127 (English), 50 (Arabic).

89. *HPEC* 3.1, 55–56; *HPYusab*, 148–49; *HCME* (ed. Evetts), 127–28.

90. *HPYusab*, 149.

91. *HPEC* 3.1, 57; but here the translation is my own from the Arabic text on p. 34 (Arabic pagination).

92. Samir, "Gabriel II, patriarche copte d'Alexandrie (1131-1145)," col. 531.

93. *HPYusab*, 148.

94. Gabriel II ibn Turayk, *Nomocanon* (ed. Mina), 79.

95. *HPEC* 3.1, 40. Emphasis added.

96. *HPYusab*, 148.

97. *HPYusab*, 148.

98. Gabriel II ibn Turayk, *Canons* (First Series) (ed. Burmester), 28–29.

99. Gabriel II ibn Turayk, *Canons* (First Series) (ed. Burmester), 18–19.

100. My translation from MS Paris, Bibliothèque Nationale, arabe 170, f. 5r; see Swanson, "The Specifically Egyptian Context," 216.

101. *Fard*, "unique," is commonly used in Islamic theology to refer to God's unicity. *Al-Samad* is an attribute of God found in Q 112, which goes on to say that "He has not begotten or been begotten."

102. My translation, slightly altered from that in Swanson, "The Specifically Egyptian Context," 216.

103. For another witness to this catechetical deficit and an attempt to respond, see Swanson, "A Copto-Arabic Catechism," 474–501; and Swanson, "'These Three Words Will Suffice.'"

104. Michael, Patriarch of Antioch, *Chronique* (ed. Chabot), iii, 235. Emphasis added.

105. *HPEC* 3.1, 42–43.

106. My translation of the Arabic text in *HPEC* 3.1, 27 (Arabic text, with its own pagination); the published English translation is at p. 43 (with *its* own pagination). Emphasis added.

107. *HPYusab*, 148. Emphasis added.

108. *HPYusab*, 148. Emphasis added.

109. According to *HPYusab*, 149, they said: "Then were the fathers, the patriarchs, who preceded you misguided and lacking in knowledge?"

192 *Notes*

110. *HPYusab*, 149.
111. *HPYusab*, 150–51.
112. *HPYusab*, 149–50.
113. Gabriel II ibn Turayk, *Nomocanon* (ed. Mina).
114. The monk was known as Mikha'il ibn Dinishtiri in Arabic; *Dinishtiri* is a deformation of Coptic *tinishti nri*, "the Great Cell" (at the Monastery of St. Macarius).
115. *HPEC* 3.1, 63.
116. *HPEC* 3.1, 65.
117. *HPEC* 3.1, 64–65. On the history and eventual demise of this festival, see Lutfi, "Coptic Festivals of the Nile," 263–68.
118. The fullest detail of Yu'annis ibn Kadran's bid to become patriarch is found in Yusab: *HPYusab*, 153–54.
119. *HPYusab*, 154; *HPEC* 3.1, 61–62. The paper with Christ's name on it was equivalent to "None of the above." If drawn, three new candidates would be sought.
120. On selection of the patriarch by lots, as well as other methods, see Saad and Saad, "Electing Coptic Patriarchs."
121. *HPYusab*, 154. As in the case of the biography of Gabriel ibn Turayk, Yusab preserves a considerable amount of colorful detail not found in Mark ibn Zur'ah's account in the *History of the Patriarchs*.
122. *HPEC* 3.1, 67–68.
123. *HPEC* 3.1, 68–69.
124. For the patriarchs mentioned here, Yusab is mostly dependent upon the *History of the Patriarchs* and offers little additional material.
125. *HPEC* 3.1, 66–96.
126. *HPEC* 3.2.
127. *HPEC* 3.2, 164–65.
128. *HPEC* 3.2, 165. Translation slightly modified.
129. *HPEC* 3.2, 166.
130. See *HCME* (ed. Evetts), 8–9, 119–20, 134–35, 138–39, 143–44 (for churches restored/rededicated in the days of Mark III); 95–96,123–24, 139 (for those restored/rededicated in the days of John VI).
131. This generalization is not entirely fair to Patriarch John VI. He was a wealthy merchant before becoming patriarch, and was admired for abolishing simony, canceling the *diyariyat* church taxes, and spending his entire fortune of seventeen thousand dinars on the poor and the Church; *HPEC* 3.2, 167; *HPYusab*, 159; Maqrizi, *Suluk*, i, 183.
132. *HPEC* 3.1, 91–92.
133. Stephen Davis notes that the Coptic term *reftanho*, "life-giving," is found elsewhere in the Coptic liturgy and was frequently added to the liturgy of

St. Gregory as it was translated from Greek into Coptic; Davis, *Coptic Christology in Practice*, 93, 98.

134. *HPEC* 3.1, 92–93.
135. *HPEC* 3.1, 93–95.
136. *HPEC* 3.1, 92.
137. The presentation of Marqus ibn al-Qunbar found in the following pages is adapted from my article: Swanson, "Telling (and Disputing) the Old, Old Story," 75–78. For more on Marqus ibn al-Qunbar, see Graf, *Ein Reformversuch*; and Samir, "Vie et oeuvre de Marc ibn al-Qunbar." These are the main sources for the biographical information that follows.
138. The Muslim historian al-Maqrizi referred to them as *al-Qanabirah*, "the Qunbarites;" al-Maqrizi, *Geschichte der Copten* (ed.Wüstenfeld), 28 (Arabic text), 68 (German translation).
139. These convictions pervade Marqus's writings. See, for example, the chapter headings of his *Book of the Master and the Disciple (8 Chapters)*, in Swanson, "Telling (and Disputing) the Old, Old Story," 81–82, or Zanetti, "Le livre de Marc Ibn Qunbar," 430–33.
140. For the example that follows, see Swanson, "Two Vatican Manuscripts," 190–93.
141. In fact, we find this analogy in a work of the early ninth-century Melkite theologian Theodore Abu Qurrah (who, however, does not give the name of the son); see Abu Qurrah, *Theologus Autodidactus* (ed. Lamoreaux), 12–13.
142. Swanson, "Two Vatican Manuscripts," 192–93.
143. For a response of Mikha'il to Marqus preserved in the *History of the Churches and Monasteries*, see *HCME* (ed. Evetts), 33–43. Also see Swanson, "Telling (and Disputing) the Old, Old Story," 79–80 (for a fresh English translation of Mikha'il's list of Marqus's theological errors).
144. *Al-Sunan allati infaradat biha al-qibt*. See Graf, *Ein Reformversuch*, 35–134 (study), 147–80 (German translation). Mikha'il also wrote a letter addressed to Abu l-Fakhr [Marqus] ibn al-Qunbar; see Graf, *Ein Reformversuch*, 180–92 (German translation).
145. Graf, *Ein Reformversuch*, 154.
146. See Graf, *Ein Reformversuch*, 163–70.
147. See, for example, Martin, "Le Delta chrétien à la fin du XIIe s."
148. An additional factor that might be mentioned here was the international and cosmopolitan outlook developed by some Copts under the Ayyubids. The great Coptic Orthodox scholars of the thirteenth century were ready to learn from scholars from outside Egypt, even from theologians outside the circle of miaphysite orthodoxy.

Chapter Six:
Chaos and Glory

1. The *diwan al-jaysh/juyush* was responsible for keeping the rosters of the troops, and especially for keeping track of the system of land apportionment through which they were paid. See Chamberlain, "The Crusader Era and the Ayyubid Dynasty," 234–36.

2. *HPEC* 3.2, 197–202.

3. See Sidarus, "The Copto-Arabic Renaissance." Sidarus speaks of the "golden age of Coptic literature in Arabic," which he defines as occurring "between the second half of the twelfth century and the first half of the fourteenth"; p. 141. While this temporal delimitation may vary from author to author, there is no question but that the high point of literary production comes in the middle decades of the thirteenth century.

4. For richly illustrated studies of thirteenth-century Coptic wallpaintings, see Bolman, *Monastic Visions*; and Lyster, *The Cave Church of Paul the Hermit*, esp. Chapters 9–10.

5. See Sidarus, "La pré-renaissance copte arabe," 201–204.

6. Den Heijer, *Mawhub*, 1–13.

7. MS Paris, Bibliothèque Nationale, arabe 302 (15th c.).

8. Edition and English translation: *HPEC* 4.1 and 4.2. To call Yuhanna ibn Wahb the author of this text may be oversimplifying matters. A note in the manuscript identifies one 'Alam al-Mulk ibn al-Hajj Shams al-Ri'asah as the "compiler" of the narrative; see *HPEC* 4.1, 6 (of the English translation), n. 2. It could be that we are dealing with an eyewitness account and a later editor. Also, it is not entirely impossible that we are speaking of one and the same person, whose *name* was Yuhanna and who bore the *title* 'Alam al-Mulk, etc.

9. Moawad, "Zur Originalität."

10. *HPYusab*, 178–81.

11. The best summary treatment of Cyril's life is in Arabic: Wadi, *Studio su al-Mu'taman Ibn al-'Assal*, 44–65. This insightful treatment builds in part on the older, invaluable work of Nakhlah, *Silsilat tarikh al-babawat batarikat al-kursi al-Iskandari*. [Hereafter Nakhlah, *Silsilah* (2nd ed.), i. Note that the pagination of the second edition, which is followed here, differs from that of the first.]

12. The literal meaning of Ibn Laqlaq is "Son of the Stork." Names that refer to birds are not uncommon in Arabic; remember that Marqus ibn al-Qunbar is Mark "Son of the Lark." On such names, see Samir, "Vie et oeuvre de Marc ibn al-Qunbar," 129.

13. *HPEC* 4.1, 14 (Arabic text, with its own pagination) / 28 (English translation, with its own pagination). Throughout this chapter, I will cite *HPEC* 4

in this way, giving reference first to the Arabic text, then the English translation; thus, in abbreviated form, *HPEC* 4.1, 14 (text) / 28 (translation).

14. On his name, see Sidarus, *Ibn ar-Rahibs Leben und Werk*, 7–8. I am grateful to Prof. Sidarus for an e-mail conversation about his and others' names and titles, which has saved me from some errors. I am opting here for "Nash' al-Khilafah" rather than "Nushu' al-Khilafah" (as found in Prof. Sidarus's book), based on Maqrizi, *Suluk*, i, 183, as well as the orthography *nun-shin* (without *waw*) found in *HPEC* 4.1 and *HPYusab*.

15. *HPYusab*, 160; Nakhlah, *Silsilah* (2nd ed.), i, 8.

16. *HPYusab*, 160; Nakhlah, *Silsilah* (2nd ed.), i, 8.

17. Which he did in *Kitab al-I'tiraf, The Book of Confession*. See below, note 29.

18. Medieval honorific titles were conventionally abbreviated in this way, e.g., Safi al-Dawlah [ibn al-'Assal] to al-Safi, Mu'taman al-Dawlah [ibn al-'Assal] to al-Mu'taman, or Shams al-Ri'asah [ibn Kabar] to al-Shams.

19. The use of fetters was incorporated into the liturgy for the consecration of the patriarch: *Rite of Consecration of the Patriarch of Alexandria*, 9–10 (Coptic text), 55 (English translation).

20. *HPEC* 4.1, 4 (text) / 42 (translation). Throughout this chapter, English translations from the Arabic text are my own; thus I give the page numbers of the Arabic text first, followed by the page numbers of Khater's and Burmester's English translation for the sake of comparison.

21. For this story, see *HPEC* 4.1, 1–18 (text) / 2–37 (translation); Maqrizi, *Suluk*, i, 183–84; Nakhlah, *Silsilah* (2nd ed.), i, 9–13. Nakhlah reproduces several paragraphs from the manuscript Cairo, Coptic Patriarchate, Hist. 91—which includes some material not found in *HPEC* or *HPYusab*.

22. *HPEC* 4.1, 3 (text) / 5 (translation).

23. Nakhlah, *Silsilah* (2nd ed.), i, 10.

24. The story of the attempt to make the hermit of Abyar patriarch is told in *HPEC* 4.1, 7–8 / 14–17, with other details (e.g., the healing of al-Malik al-Kamil) in Cairo, Coptic Patriarchate, Hist. 91 as reported in Nakhlah, *Silsilah* (2nd ed.), i, 11–12.

25. *HPEC* 4.1, 10–18 (text) / 21–37 (translation).

26. Up to this point in the paragraph, *HPEC* 4.1, 10–18 (text) / 21–37 (translation).

27. It is *HPYusab* that tells us where Da'ud retired: *HPYusab*, 162 = Nakhlah, *Silsilah* (2nd ed.), i, 12.

28. MS Paris, Bibliothèque National, arabe 167. See the description in Troupeau, *Catalogue des manuscripts arabes*, i, 140–41.

29. *The Book of Confession* has not yet been properly studied, despite its popularity (witnessed to by its presence in dozens of manuscripts). For now, see Graf, *GCAL*, ii, 365–67.

30. See *HPYusab*, 162 = Nakhlah, *Silsilah* (2nd ed.), i, 12–13, where the number of bishops remaining is given as four; and *HPEC* 4.1, 65 (text) / 135 (translation), which mentions five bishops, although the bishop of Isna "had become like a dead person."

31. On this powerful family of advisors to the Ayyubids, see Gottschalk, "Awlad al-Shaykh."

32. *HPEC* 4.1, 64–67 (text)/134–39 (translation); *HPYusab*, 162–63 = Nakhlah, *Silsilah* (2nd ed.), i, 13–14, 17. We note the continuing importance of the relic of the head of St. Mark the Evangelist, kept in a private home. It should be noted that the Church of St. Mark in Alexandria had been demolished in June–July 1218, for fear that the tower might be used by the Crusaders then besieging Damietta; *HPEC* 4.1, 30 (text) / 62 (translation).

33. Preserved in MS Cairo, Coptic Patriarchate, Theol. 291 and published in Nakhlah, *Silsilah* (2nd ed.), i, 14–15.

34. Nakhlah, *Silsilah* (2nd ed.), i, 15.

35. Nakhlah, *Silsilah* (2nd ed.), i, 14.

36. *HPEC* 4.1, 67–69 (text) / 139–44 (translation); *HPYusab*, 163–65 = Nakhlah, *Silsilah* (2nd ed.), i, 17–20.

37. Preserved in MS Cairo, Coptic Patriarchate, Theol. 291 and published in Nakhlah, *Silsilah* (2nd ed.), i, 34–37 (to Alexandria), 37–41 (to Damascus).

38. *HPEC* 4.2, 77–78 (text) / 158–60 (translation); *HPYusab*, 171 = Nakhlah, *Silsilah* (2nd ed.), i, 58–59.

39. Nakhlah, *Silsilah* (2nd ed.), i, 59–62. There is now an English translation and study of this correspondence, as well as other letters of Cyril III: Werthmuller, "An In-Between Space." The Arabic text and English translation of Cyril's correspondence with the Syrian patriarch is at pp. 216–23, and see Chapter Three.

40. *HPEC* 4.1, 69 (text) / 145 (translation); *HPYusab*, 165 = Nakhlah, *Silsilah* (2nd ed.), i, 20–21.

41. *HPEC* 4.1, 69 (text) / 145 (translation); *HPYusab*, 166 = Nakhlah, *Silsilah* (2nd ed.), i, 21.

42. On the preparation and consecration of the *myron*, see below, Chapter Seven.

43. *HPYusab*, 167 = Nakhlah, *Silsilah* (2nd ed.), i, 29–30. *HPYusab* is an independent and important source at this point, where it appears to preserve an eyewitness account by the future bishop Yusab. Yuhanna ibn Wahb's account, on the other hand, does not mention the reason for the conflict that erupted between the monks and the patriarch, leaving readers to speculate; *HPEC* 4.2, 74 (text) / 151–52 (translation).

44. *HPYusab*, 167–69 = Nakhlah, *Silsilah* (2nd ed.), i, 29–32.

45. *HPEC* 4.2, 75 (text) / 154–55 (translation); *HPYusab*, 170 = Nakhlah, *Silsilah* (2nd ed.), i, 41.
46. *HPEC* 4.2, 76 (text) / 155 (translation).
47. *HPEC* 4.2, 78–79 (text) / 161–62 (translation); *HPYusab*, 171–72 = Nakhlah, *Silsilah* (2nd ed.), i, 67.
48. *HPEC* 4.2, 81–92 (text) / 166–68 (translation); *HPYusab*, 173 = Nakhlah, *Silsilah* (2nd ed.), i, 68–70.
49. *HPEC* 4.2, 81–82 (text) / 168–70 (translation); *HPYusab*, 173–74 = Nakhlah, *Silsilah* (2nd ed.), i, 70–71.
50. *HPEC* 4.2, 82–83 (text) / 170–72 (translation); *HPYusab*, 174–75 = Nakhlah, *Silsilah* (2nd ed.), i, 71–72.
51. *HPEC* 4.2, 85–87 (text) / 175–80 (translation); *HPYusab*, 175–78; Nakhlah, *Silsilah* (2nd ed.), i, 72–75.
52. *HPEC* 4.2, 97–106 (text) / 199–218 (translation) informs us about the series of meetings.
53. For this meeting at the Citadel see *HPEC* 4.2, 105–106 (text) / 217–18 (translation), and especially Nakhlah, *Silsilah* (2nd ed.), i, 76, 117–21.
54. See Graf, *GCAL*, ii, 398–403.
55. These events include a general deterioration of the position of the Christians after the death of al-Malik al-Kamil in 1238 and a series of aggressions against the Muʻallaqah Church. On the reintroduction of discriminatory *ghiyar* regulations in 1239 for the first time in twenty years, see *HPEC* 4.2, 92–93 (text) / 189–90 (translation).
56. *HPEC* 4.2, 88–89, 104–105, 118–19, 120–24, 135 (text) / 182–83, 214–16, 243–45, 248–55, 275–76 (translation); *HPYusab*, 178.
57. *HPEC* 4.2, 135 (text) / 276 (translation); *HPYusab*, 178; Nakhlah, *Silsilah* (2nd ed.), i, 89.
58. *HPEC* 4.2, 136 (text) / 277–78 (translation).
59. *HPEC* 4.2, 139–40 (text) / 284–85 (translation).
60. Arabic *ghaffarah* = *phelonion*, a cape-like ecclesiastical garment; Innemée, *Ecclesiastical Dress*, 48–50.
61. Arabic *balariyya*, a long, narrow strip of cloth something like a western priest's stole; Innemée, *Ecclesiastical Dress*, 45–48.
62. Arabic *ʻardi*, a kind of scarf worn about the neck; Innemée, *Ecclesiastical Dress*, 50–55.
63. Arabic *al-hujur allati li-l-badlah allati takunu ʻala l-raʼs*, "the *hujur* belonging to the set of vestments, which are upon the head." I do not know precisely what these *hujur* are, but see Innemée, *Ecclesiastical Dress*, 56 on the headcoverings of Coptic patriarchs.
64. *HPEC* 4.2, 136 / 277.

65. Unless one gives symbolic significance to Yuhanna's report that Cyril's body emitted such a foul smell at the funeral that the officiants had to sprinkle rose water over it; *HPEC* 4.2, 136–37 (text) / 278 (translation).

66. Chamberlain, "The Crusader Era and the Ayyubid Dynasty," 239. On "great men," see Chamberlain's section on "Urban Politics," pp. 231–40.

67. Note that Cyril was criticized for not confining himself to traditional Coptic vestments, but making use of *Melkite* ones; *HPEC* 4.2, 83 (text) / 171 (translation); *HPYusab*, 174; Nakhlah, *Silsilah* (2nd ed.), i, 72.

68. See above, at notes 38 and 39.

69. Cahen, "Le régime des impôts dans le Fayyum." See the chart opposite p. 12, and pp. 22–23.

70. Cahen, "Ayyubids," 800.

71. Chamberlain, "The Crusader Era and the Ayyubid Dynasty," 238. After one of the hearings of 1240, the Muslim judges wondered, with regard to Cyril's relationship with his community, "how it was that he lacked the leadership skills [*riyadah*] with which to govern their minds and tame their hearts toward him"; *HPEC* 4.2, 100 (text) / 204 (translation).

72. A somewhat loose translation of *ma kana yubali bi-shay'in mimma yajri*; *HPEC* 4.2, 74 (Arabic text).

73. *HPEC* 4.2, 74 (text) / 153 (translation).

74. Nakhlah, *Silsilah* (2nd ed.), i, 90–92.

75. Nakhlah, *Silsilah* (2nd ed.), i, 90.

76. Nakhlah, *Silsilah* (2nd ed.), i, 91.

77. See, for example, Sidarus, "Medieval Coptic Grammars in Arabic," esp. 65–66.

78. Moawad, "Zur Originalität."

79. See, for example, Davis, *Coptic Christology in Practice*, 238–51, 299–306; Faltas, "Athanasius the Great as Source."

80. See, for example, Griffith, *The Church in the Shadow of the Mosque*, 65–66.

81. Al-Safi ibn al-'Assal, *Brefs chapitres sur la Trinité et l'Incarnation*, esp. pp. 634–48.

82. Or perhaps al-Nash'? See above, note 14.

83. Sidarus, *Ibn al-Rahibs Leben und Werk*.

84. In the previous chapter, for example, see Mawhub's treatment of Patriarch Christodoulos (#66).

Chapter Seven:
Marginalized Patriarchs

1. *HPYusab*, 179; Nakhlah, *Silsilah* (2nd ed.), ii, 5. The patriarchal history attributed to Yusab is our chief source for this contested election; Nakhlah draws from it, and often provides a better text than that of the published

edition. For a brief summary of the history, see al-Safi ibn al-ʿAssal, *Brefs chapitres sur la Trinité et l'Incarnation*, 624–27.

2. On al-Sanaʾ, see Chapter Six. His sister's son was Sharaf al-Din Hibatallah al-Asʿad ibn Saʿid al-Faʾizi, who had become a Muslim about a decade earlier.

3. *HPYusab*, 179; Nakhlah, *Silsilah* (2nd ed.), ii, 5–6.

4. On the work of Ghubriyal (Gabriel) as a copyist of manuscripts (many of them for the Awlad al-ʿAssal and their friends), see MacCoull, "A Note on the Career of Gabriel III." To the list of mss that Gabriel copied (or that were copied from Gabriel's copies), add MSS Dayr al-Suryan, 383 Lit. and 11 Bibl.; Bigoul al-Suriany, "New Elements in the History of the Pope Gabriel III the 77th."

5. On Gabriel's relationship to the Awlad al-ʿAssal, see al-Safi ibn al-ʿAssal, *Brefs chapitres sur la Trinité et l'Incarnation*, 624–31.

6. *Inna bab al-badhl qad infatah*; *HPYusab*, 180; Nakhlah, *Silsilah* (2nd ed.), ii, 8.

7. See above, Chapter Six, for his deft handling of a quarrel between Pope Cyril and the monks of the Monastery of St. Macarius, as well as his role in the reform agenda that was finally pushed through at the Synod of the Citadel in 1240, where he served as secretary.

8. *HPYusab*, 179; Nakhlah, *Silsilah* (2nd ed.), ii, 6.

9. We are not told what arguments Yusab and the other bishops used to make peace between the two factions; *HPYusab*, 181; Nakhlah, *Silsilah* (2nd ed.), ii, 9.

10. *HPEC* 3.3, 228–29. (After the exception of Chapter Six, I now revert to my usual practice of citing the English translation of *HPEC*, unless I state otherwise.)

11. *HPEC* 3.3, 229. From now on I will refer to these two as "John" and "Gabriel," rather than as "Yuʾannis" and "Ghubriyal" (the same names in Arabic).

12. Al-Mufaddal ibn Abi al-Fadaʾil, *Histoire* (ed. Blochet). For the story of Gabriel III and John VII, see PO 14.3, 447–51. The title of al-Mufaddal's work indicates that it is a continuation of the world history of al-Makin Jirjis ibn al-ʿAmid; see den Heijer, "Coptic Historiography," 88–95.

13. On the early Mamluks, see Irwin, *The Middle East in the Middle Ages*; on Baybars, see Chapter Three.

14. Al-Mufaddal ibn Abi al-Fadaʾil, *Histoire* (ed. Blochet), PO 14.3, 449, where the name of the monastery should read Dayr al-ʿArabah, one of the names under which the Monastery of St. Antony was known.

15. PO 14.3, 449, where the sum mentioned is five hundred thousand dinars. The *History of the Patriarchs* mentions a fine of fifty thousand dinars (*HPEC* 3.3, 230), still enormous when we think of the mischief played a few years earlier by Cyril's debt of a "mere" three thousand dinars!

16.   According to *HPYusab*, 182, Gabriel died on 1 January 1271, after which
      John VII returned to the patriarchate. However, the *History of the Patri-
      archs* and Mufaddal ibn Abi l-Fada'il are agreed that Gabriel did not die
      until July 1274. The Ethiopic *Synaxarion* reports that during the last period
      of Gabriel's life he spent a year in ascetic practice in secret in Old Cairo,
      but then was established at the Church of the Apostles, where he devoted
      himself to prayer, the liturgy, and pastoral care. When the time came for
      him to be received into heaven, it was St. Athanasius who came to him with
      the glad tidings. See Ethiopic *Synaxarion* (ed. Guidi), PO 7.3 = No 33,
      316–17; Budge, *Book of the Saints*, iv, 1109–10.
17.   See Chapter One, as well as Davis, *The Early Coptic Papacy*, 115–20.
18.   Ethiopic *Synaxarion* (ed. Guidi), PO 7.3 = No 33, 310–16; Budge, *Book
      of the Saints*, iv, 1106–10.
19.   Conti Rossini, "Aethiopica," 502–505.
20.   On the Monastery of St. Paul, see Lyster, *The Cave Church of Paul the
      Hermit*. I tell the story of Patriarch Gabriel in my contribution to this
      volume: Swanson, "The Monastery of St. Paul in Historical Context," 47–48.
21.   The book in question is the Arabic translation of the *Pandektes* of Nikon
      of the Black Mountain, of which Gabriel made a copy; see Graf, *GCAL*, ii,
      64–66. The Ethiopic translation of the Arabic preserves Gabriel's
      colophon, written at the Monastery of St. Antony in March–April 1267;
      Conti Rossini, "Aethiopica," 502.
22.   Conti Rossini, "Aethiopica," 504.
23.   Conti Rossini, "Aethiopica," 505.
24.   On Ethiopian monks at the Monastery of St. Antony, see Gabra, "Perspectives
      on the Monastery of St. Antony," 176.
25.   *HPEC* 3.3. This part of the *History of the Patriarchs* is an "updating" of the
      work for the years 1235–1894. Note that the patriarchal history attributed
      to Yusab [*HPYusab*], once beyond its detailed description of the patriarchal
      election of 1250, has similarly brief entries.
26.   *HPEC* 3.3, 135 (Arabic text); my translation. (The editors' translation is
      found at pp. 233–34.) 8 Abib, AM 1065 = 2 July 1349; 6 Amshir, AM 1079
      = 31 January 1363.
27.   See, for example, Irwin, *The Middle East in the Middle Ages*, 134–38.
28.   The seminal study is Little, "Coptic Conversion to Islam." See also
      Vermeulen, "The Rescript of al-Malik as-Salih Salih."
29.   A helpful overview, in addition to Irwin, *The Middle East in the Middle
      Ages*, is provided by essays in *The Cambridge History of Egypt*, Vol. 1. See
      especially Northrup, "The Bahri Mamluk Sultanate," and Garcin, "The
      Regime of the Circassian Mamluks."

30. Irwin, *The Middle East in the Middle Ages*, 134–36. Twenty epidemics over a period of 170 years works out to a major epidemic on the average of every 8.5 years! For lists of the outbreaks, see Dols, *The Black Death in the Middle East*, 305–14 (Appendix One), or, conveniently, Garcin, "The Regime of the Circassian Mamluks," 308.

31. Ambraseys, Melville, and Adams, *The Seismicity of Egypt, Arabia and the Red Sea*, 42–44. The Azhar, Hakim, and 'Amr ibn al-'As mosques in Cairo were so badly damaged that they had to be razed and rebuilt.

32. In the entry for Theodosius (#79, 1294–1300), the *History of the Patriarchs* comments: "There occurred in his days high mortality and hyperinflation, and people used to eat one another's dead." *HPEC* 3.3, 134 (Arabic text); my translation.

33. Note the dramatic titles in Jenkins, *The Lost History of Christianity: The Thousand-Year Golden Age of the Church in the Middle East, Africa, and Asia—and How It Died* (New York: HarperOne, 2008), where the author devotes several pages (124–29) to the Copts under the [early] Mamluks in a section subtitled "The Great Persecutions," which is part of a chapter entitled "The Great Tribulation."

34. See above, Chapter Three.

35. Here and throughout this section, see Little, "Coptic Conversion to Islam."

36. See above, Chapter Five, where we learned that Patriarch Gabriel II ibn Turayk had unsuccessfully attempted to suppress this festival.

37. On the Feast of the Martyr and its fate, see Lutfi, "Coptic Festivals of the Nile," 263–68.

38. Little, "Coptic Conversion to Islam," 568–69.

39. Dols, *The Black Death*, 295–96; compare his summary of European Christian persecution of Jews, pp. 288–89.

40. Northrup, "The Bahri Mamluk Sultanate," 265–73.

41. The disturbances of 1301 arose after the visiting *wazir* of "the king of the Maghrib" denounced the significant roles and respected positions of Jews and Christians in Egyptian society; Little, "Coptic Conversion to Islam," 554–55.

42. Little, "Coptic Converts to Islam during the Bahri Mamluk Period," 265–66; on the extremity of Ibn Taymiyya's Sunnism, see Northrup, "The Bahri Mamluk Sultanate," 266–68.

43. Little, "Coptic Conversion to Islam."

44. *HPEC* 3.3, 134 (Arabic text); my translation. (The editors' translation is at p. 231.) Mid-Misra, AM 1019 = 8 August 1303; 5 Nasi, AM 1021 = 28 August 1305.

45. For the mention of Barsum in the litany of the saints in the Coptic Orthodox psalmody, see *Coptic Orthodox Psalmody: Tasbihat nisf al-layl al-sanawi:*

al-ahad wa-l-ayam, 68; Italian translation in Brogi, ed., *La santa salmodia annuale della chiesa copta*, 23. On Barsum, see Crum, "Barsaumâ the Naked"; al-Mufaddal ibn Abi al-Fada'il, *Histoire* (ed. Blochet); Voile, "Barsum le Nu"; the entry for Barsum in the Coptic *Synaxarion* for 5 Nasi; or, more briefly, Coquin, "Barsum the Naked, Saint," or Wadi Abuliff, "Barsauma il Nudo."

46. Crum, "Barsaumâ the Naked," 206; MS Paris, Bibliothèque Nationale, arabe 72, f. 50v.

47. Coquin and Martin, "Dayr Shahran."

48. See the entry for Barsum in the Copto-Arabic *Synaxarion* for 5 Nasi, e.g., Coptic-Arabic *Synaxarion* (ed. Basset), PO 17.3, 777–81; on his refusal to exchange his white turban for blue, pp. 779–80.

49. Crum, "Barsaumâ the Naked," 202. The *Life* also ends with a prayer for the patriarch, who defends the faith like Saints Dioscorus, John Chrysostom, and Athanasius; Crum, "Barsaumâ the Naked," 203.

50. Peter had been superior of the monastery.

51. *HPEC* 3.3, 135 (Arabic text); my translation. (The editors' translation is at p. 232.)

52. Maqrizi, *Suluk*, ii, 223–24.

53. *HPEC* 3.3, 233.

54. This name is transliterated in a variety of ways, often as al-Nashw. I believe that a *hamza* is either missing or represented by a weak letter, so that the name should be al-Nash' or al-Nushu', an abbreviation for a title such as Nash'/Nushu' al-Khilafah. See Chapter Six, n. 14.

55. *HPEC* 3.3, 135 (Arabic text); my translation. (The editors' translation is at p. 233.)

56. See Little, "Coptic Converts to Islam during the Bahri Mamluk Period," 272.

57. Maqrizi, *Suluk*, ii, 464.

58. A readable English introduction to the preparation of the *myron* is Meinardus, "About the Coction" (and see the bibliography). The most extensive excerpt of a *Book of the Chrism* presently available, with a French translation, is van Lantschoot, ed., "Le ms. Vatican copte 44 et Le Livre du Chrême"; this extends to the making of the chrism by Pope John VIII in 1305. An edition of a *Book of the Chrism*, including the narrative of the making of the chrism by Pope Gabriel IV in 1374, is being prepared by Youhanna Nessim Youssef and Ugo Zanetti.

59. On these traditions, see Zanetti, "Matarieh, la Sainte Famille et les baumiers," esp. pp. 40–44, with an appendix of botanical interest at pp. 59–65.

60. Meinardus, "About the Coction," lists some of these ingredients; or see *Book of the Chrism*, ed. van Lantschoot.

61. The *kallielaion* (or *galileon*) is olive oil blended with aromatic ingredients that was prepared and consecrated along with the *myron*. It is used in pre-baptismal anointings; see Burmester, *The Egyptian or Coptic Church*, 117–18. I am grateful to Fr. Ugo Zanetti for explaining the composition and use of the *kallielaion/galileon* to me.

62. For a description of the service, see Burmester, *The Egyptian or Coptic Church*, 219–36.

63. The holy *myron* was prepared in 1257, 1299 (in Old Cairo), 1305, 1320 (in Old Cairo), 1330, 1342, 1346, 1369, and 1374. For the later Mamluk period, we can add 1430 (in Old Cairo) and 1458 (in Cairo), after which the *myron* was not again prepared until 1703. For lists of the bishops in attendance at each of these occasions through that of 1346, see Munier, *Recueil des listes épiscopales*, Chapter Six, "La coction du chrême."

64. *Book of the Chrism*, ed. van Lantschoot, 211 (and see his French translation at p. 233).

65. *Book of the Chrism*, ed. van Lantschoot, 211–12 (with French translation at pp. 233–34).

66. See Burmester, *The Egyptian or Coptic Church*, 221; the patriarch prays that the *myron* "be now a divine Myron invested with the Holy Spirit, the Paraclete."

Chapter Eight:
A Burst of Holiness

1. *HPEC* 3.3, 136–58 (Arabic text); my translation. (The editors' translation is at pp. 235–71.) Below I shall generally make reference to the English translation.

2. The *Life* may be found in a number of manuscripts, notably two in Paris: MSS Paris, Bibliothèque Nationale, arabe 132 (AD 1629), ff. 32–58, and Bibliothèque Nationale, arabe 145 (AD 1641, from a manuscript of AD 1446), ff. 77–143. We note that MS Paris, BN ar. 145 was copied from a manuscript of AD 1446. The text itself claims to have been written at the urging of Anba Ruways (d. 1404), even before Matthew had died.

3. 5 Tubah, normally 31 December in the Julian calendar. The beginning and conclusion of the homily have been published by Kamil Salih Nakhlah: Nakhlah, *Silsilah* (2nd ed.), iii, 47–53 (the panegyric introduction to the *Life*), 44–47 (its conclusion). Nakhlah used a manuscript of the Church of the Virgin in Harat al-Zuwaylah, Cairo.

4. For Matthew's youth, until his consecration as patriarch, see *HPEC* 3.3, 235–40. Additional stories about his youth are found in the Ethiopic *Synaxarion* for 5 Ter: Budge, *Book of the Saints*, ii, 451–54.

5. See above, in Chapter Five.
6. *Life of Shenoute* 3, in Besa, *Life of Shenoute* (trans. Bell), 42.
7. *HPEC* 3.3, 235–36.
8. *HPEC* 3.3, 236–39.
9. *HPEC* 3.3, 240–41. Before his death St. Barsum the Naked cut off part of his tongue, but then went on to recite psalms; Crum, "Barsaumâ the Naked," 201.
10. *HPEC* 3.3, 241–45. When Matthew was imprisoned and fined in 1400/1, "he swore that he had no money, and that he spent all the money that he received on the Muslim poor and the Christian poor"; Maqrizi, *Suluk*, iii, 1040.
11. *Holy Jerusalem Voyage of Ogier VIII* (trans. Browne), 57.
12. *HPEC* 3.3, 246.
13. *HPEC* 3.3, 247.
14. *HPEC* 3.3, 260–62.
15. *HPEC* 3.3, 258–59.
16. *HPEC* 3.3, 250–52; at the behest of "king" Barquq, Matthew wrote to the king of Ethiopia—but not to the reigning king, but rather to his brother, David, who succeeded him. Matthew's correspondence with King David is also mentioned by Maqrizi, *Suluk*, iii, 445 (for the year 783/1381).
17. *HPEC* 3.3, 267.
18. *HPEC* 3.3, 258–66.
19. *HPEC* 3.3, 262–63: Matthew binds the martyr Theodore to deliver a youth from a calamity; he binds the icon of St. Shenoute in order to learn who had stolen the vessels of his church; and he binds St. George to take vengeance on an *amir* who had proposed to do away with the Christians. The youth was delivered, the thief was discovered and cruelly executed, and the *amir* was promptly poisoned. Another story tells how Matthew's prayers to the Archangel Michael led to the death of the *amir* Uzbek (*HPEC* 3.3, 263–64), while another tells how Matthew's charge to the Four Living Creatures kept Yalbugha al-Salimi in prison (*HPEC* 3.3, 255). The *amir*s were emancipated mamluks who had been invested with authority and who served in an (ideally) hierarchical military system: *amir*s of one hundred, *amir*s of forty, *amir*s of ten, etc. In fact, throughout the Mamluk period the senior *amir*s were regularly jockeying for power. See Irwin, *The Middle East in the Middle Ages*, 39–40.
20. The *amir* in question was Yalbugha al-Salimi; *HPEC* 3.3, 254–55, where we also learn of his arrest, torture, and imprisonment in Alexandria—which is corroborated by Maqrizi, *Suluk*, iii, 1163.
21. *HPEC* 3.3, 255–56.

22. *HPEC* 3.3, 257–58. According to Maqrizi, *Suluk*, iii, 1040, the *amir* Yalbugha proposed new *ghiyar* legislation (that is, legislation to mark off non-Muslims by types and color of garments, etc.) on 1 January 1401.

23. On the Circassian Mamluk period, see Garcin, "The Regime of the Circassian Mamluks."

24. *HPEC* 3.3, 252.

25. *HPEC* 3.3, 254. Maqrizi, *Suluk*, iii, 675 gives the date of Matthew's arrest as 23 November 1389.

26. *HPEC* 3.3, 254. Maqrizi, *Suluk*, iii, 1040 gives the date of Matthew's arrest as 19 December 1400.

27. *HPEC* 3.3, 267–68; Ibn Taghribirdi, *History of Egypt, 1382–1469 A.D.* (trans. Popper), vol. 14 (Part II), 51–52.

28. *HPEC* 3.3, 267–69.

29. *HPEC* 3.3, 269.

30. *HPEC* 3.3, 270.

31. See above, in Chapter Two and Chapter Four.

32. *Coptic Orthodox Psalmody: Tasbihat nisf al-layl al-sanawi*, 68; Brogi, *La santa salmodia annuale della chiesa copta*, 23.

33. On Marqus al-Antuni, now see Swanson, "'Our Father Abba Mark.'"

34. For a list of manuscripts of the *Life of Marqus al-Antuni*, see Wadi Abuliff, "Marco l'Antoniano" (with excellent bibliography). To Wadi's list may be added MS Monastery of St. Paul, Hist. 115 (AD 1700); it is to this manuscript that I refer below (as *L.Marqus*). While there is no edition of the *Life of Marqus al-Antuni*, a number of Arabic-language summaries have been published by monks of the Monastery of St. Antony; see Swanson, "'Our Father Abba Mark,'" p. 218, n. 5 for bibliography. In addition, see the summary in Nakhlah, *Silsilah* (2nd ed.), iii, 53–61.

35. On Marqus's early years, when he was trained as a monk at the Monastery of St. Paul, see Swanson, "The Monastery of St. Paul in Historical Context," 49–51.

36. On Yalbugha, who ruled without claiming the sultanate, see Irwin, "The Middle East in the Middle Ages," 143–49

37. *HPEC* 3.3, 238–39; *L.Marqus*, Miracle #7, ff. 59r–61r. See Gabra, "New Research," 97.

38. *HPEC* 3.3, 239.

39. *HPEC* 3.3, 240–41.

40. *L.Marqus*, Miracle #34, ff. 89r–90r.

41. See *L.Marqus*, f. 27rv (on Ephronia, who came disguised as a monk) and ff. 61r–63r (Miracle #8: a woman who came disguised as the monk Michael).

42. A number of the miracles in the second part of the *Life of Marqus* have to do with converts to Islam who returned to Christian faith: *L.Marqus*, ff. 64r–65v (Miracle #10: Fakhr al-Dawlah ibn al-Qiss al-Mu'taman, who is also known from *Life of Anba Ruways* and *Life of Matthew*); ff. 80v–81r (Miracle #25: 'Ubayd al-Najjar); ff. 86r–87v (Miracle #31: the *katib* Jirjis); and ff. 87v–88r (Miracle #32: Furayj). See Swanson, "'Our Father Abba Mark,'" 224.

43. See *L.Marqus*, ff. 68v–69v (Miracle #13: Karim al-Din ibn Makanis), and ff. 70v–71v (Miracle #15: Sa'd al-Din Nasr Allah ibn al-Baqari). For the identification of these figures, see Swanson, "'Our Father Abba Mark,'" 223–24.

44. See *L.Marqus*, f. 25rv (Marqus's long intercession for a monk who had died) and ff. 67r–68v (Miracle #12: Marqus's care for a dying Coptic official).

45. *HPEC* 3.3, 236–37. The Ethiopic *Synaxarion* makes Ibrahim the person who introduced Matthew to the monastic life; Budge, *Book of the Saints*, ii, 451–52.

46. Ibrahim is not very well known: there is no article on him in the *Coptic Encyclopedia* while A. Wadi, "Abramo l'Egumeno," consists of two tiny paragraphs. I read the *Life of Ibrahim* in Monastery of St. Antony, Hist. 75 (old catalog number, AD 1700), to which reference will be made below [as *L.Ibrahim*].

47. On his early years, *L.Ibrahim*, ff. 9v–17r.

48. *L.Ibrahim*, f. 17r.

49. *L.Ibrahim*, f. 17r.

50. *L.Ibrahim*, ff. 18v–20r.

51. *L.Ibrahim*, ff. 14r–15v.

52. *L.Marqus*, f. 41r.

53. *L.Marqus*, f. 40v. See Gabra, "New Research," 98, with a plate (figure 5.3) of what may have been the image from which Marqus advised his disciples to flee.

54. *L.Marqus*, ff. 48r–50r; *L.Ibrahim*, ff. 21r–22r.

55. *L.Ibrahim*, ff. 22v–28r.

56. *L.Ibrahim*, f. 28v.

57. *L.Ibrahim*, ff. 28v–30v.

58. *L.Ibrahim*, ff. 6v–7r.

59. On the rise of the monasteries of the Eastern Desert during this period, see Swanson, "The Monastery of St. Paul in Historical Context," 49–50.

60. See Wadi Abuliff, "Ruways," for an excellent bibliography including a list of manuscripts of the *Life*. I have used the copy in MS Paris, Bibliothèque Nationale, arabe 282 (AD 1650), ff. 82–139, to which reference will be made below (as *L.Ruways*).

61. On Anba Ruways's early life, see *L.Ruways*, ff. 91r–99v.
62. *L.Ruways*, f. 108v; Anba Ruways showed them his tattooed cross and made the sign of the cross upon himself.
63. Among Anba Ruways's prophecies was the terrifying advent of Timur-Lenk, but also the consoling word that he would not reach Egypt; *L.Ruways*, f. 106rv.
64. E.g., he saw cherubim and seraphim above a baptismal font; *L.Ruways*, f. 98r. He communed with the saints in heaven; *L.Ruways*, f. 99r.
65. See the following story. In another story, Anba Ruways travels to Syria and back—in the space of an hour; *L.Ruways*, ff. 118r–121r (Miracle #5: Bint al-Zuhri and her husband).
66. *L.Marqus*, f. 29v.
67. *L.Ruways*, f. 103r–v.
68. *L.Ruways*, ff. 112r–113v (Miracle #1): in an encounter with Ishaq ibn al-Adib, deacon at Dayr al-Khandaq, Anba Ruways prophesied his own death there thirty-three years later. Anba Ruways died in 1404, which places this encounter in 1371.
69. *L.Ruways*, f. 105v: "Then he left off traveling throughout Egypt and returned to Cairo...."
70. *L.Ruways*, ff. 113v–123r, Miracles #2–6.
71. *L.Ruways*, ff. 123r–125r, Miracle #7.
72. *L.Ruways*, ff. 128r–130v, Miracle #10.
73. *L.Ruways*, ff. 130v–133r (Miracle #11: on Abu l-Faraj ibn Quzman, a deacon much admired by the wife of a high Muslim official); ff. 133r–135v (Miracle #12: on Sadaqah ibn 'Ajin, a scribe who became enamored of a high-born Muslim lady, and later, as a monk, became Patriarch Matthew's servant).
74. *L.Ruways*, f. 96r.
75. E.g., Matthew bore witness to the miraculous healing of Wahbah from Naqadah; *L.Ruways*, ff. 126r–128r, Miracle #9.
76. *L.Ruways*, ff. 121r–123r, Miracle #6; *Life of Matthew* in *HPEC* 3.3, 245–46.
77. *L.Ruways*, ff. 104r–105v.
78. Al-Masri, *Qissat al-kanisah al-qibtiyyah*, iii, 367.
79. *L.Ruways*, ff. 116v–118r, Miracle #4, tells the story of how Anba Ruways healed a deaf, dumb, and blind boy even after his death.
80. See Chapter Seven for the suppression of the Feast of the Martyr. Tamer el-Leithy reviews a variety of Coptic Nile festivals and their suppression under the Mamluks in his important dissertation, "Coptic Culture and Conversion," 116–26.

81.   See Chapter Three above for another "crisis of cohesion" in the life of the medieval Coptic Orthodox Church.

82.   *HPEC* 3.3, 271. Translation slightly modified.

83.   On the martyrdoms during Matthew's patriarchate, see el-Leithy, "Coptic Culture and Conversion," 101–39 (= Chapter Three, "Martyrdom and Apostasy in the Late Eighth/Fourteenth Century").

84.   See, for example, MS Paris, Bibliothèque Nationale, arabe 145, ff137v–141r; Nakhlah, *Silsilah* (2nd ed.), iii, 44–46. The list is also found in the patriarchal history attributed to Yusab: *HPYusab*, 200–202. It has been published elsewhere, e.g., al-Masri, *Qissat al-kanisah al-qibtiyyah*, iii, 376–78; or, in a European language with commentary, Wadi Abuliff, "Quarantanove martiri."

85.   See the Appendix, nos. 20–23 in the list of martyrs. In addition, Wadi suggests that the seven soldiers of nos. 24–30 may have been members of a Latin military order; Wadi, "Quarantanove martiri," 867.

86.   In the Appendix, nos. 19, 13, and 43 respectively.

87.   In the Appendix, no. 42 (Mikha'il, formerly "Mamadiyus").

88.   In the Appendix, no. 31 (Hadid or Jadid) and no. 41 (the monks Mansur and Da'ud) appear to fall into this category

89.   In the Appendix, no. 39 (the monk Ya'qub) and no. 42 (the monk Ibrahim al-Suryani) come under this category.

90.   Presumably many of the monks and priests in the list would come under this category.

91.   See the Appendix. The martyrs for whom we have dates are not mentioned in every edition of the *Synaxarion*, but see Copto-Arabic *Synaxarion* (ed. Forget), ii, 60 (Rizq Allah, 3 Barmudah), 79 (Da'ud al-Banna', 19 Barmudah), 111 (Arsaniyus al-Habashi, 9 Bashans), and 122 (Sidrak and Fadl Allah, 15 Bashans).

92.   Maqrizi, *Suluk*, iii, 372–73.

93.   Maqrizi, *Suluk*, iii, 373. Al-Maqrizi notes that there was some controversy over the beheading of the women.

94.   Maqrizi, *Suluk*, iii, 373.

95.   Maqrizi, *Suluk*, iii, 373.

96.   Maqrizi, *Suluk*, iii, 373. In the following paragraph, al-Maqrizi mentions one more would-be martyr: a cavalry officer who declared his apostasy from Islam and asked to be "purified" by the sword. He was beaten and imprisoned; we are not informed of his ultimate fate.

97.   Rizq Allah, no. 5 in the list of martyrs (see Appendix), was executed at about the same time as Ya'qub Abu Muqaytif. It is not impossible that he was one of the original martyrs mentioned by al-Maqrizi.

98. From the martyr list in Nakhlah, *Silsilah* (2nd ed.), iii, 44.

99. *L.Marqus*, ff. 27v, 62v.

100. See *L.Marqus*, f. 27rv (Ephronia, who visited the monastery disguised as a monk); ff. 61r–63r (Miracle #8: a woman who came to the monastery disguised as the monk Michael—is this a doublet?); f. 63rv (Miracle #9: the Ethiopian servant girl Ghazal).

101. Note that Marqus became very ill in 1384 and died in 1386. The four Latin priests, nos. 20–23 in the martyr list, are probably to be identified with the Franciscans Nicola Tavelic and companions, martyred on 14 November 1391; see Matanic, "Tavelic, Nicola e III compagni." According to al-Maqrizi (*Suluk*, iii, 792), the news of the execution of four monks in Jerusalem reached Cairo on 5 November, 1393.

102. E.g., *L.Marqus*, ff. 64r–65v (Miracle #10: Fakhr al-Dawlah ibn al-Qiss al-Mu'taman), or ff. 86r–87v (Miracle #31: the *katib* Jirjis).

103. E.g., *Life of Marqus*, ff. 80v–81r (Miracle #25: 'Ubayd al-Najjar), or ff. 87v–88r (Miracle #32: Furayj).

104. See previous note; there was a real possibility that each of the stories told there could have ended in martyrdom.

105. We note that Ya'qub Abu Muqaytif and his disciples are quickly followed in the martyr list by six monks from the Monastery of St. Antony; see the Appendix, nos. 7–12.

106. See, among other works, Coope, *The Martyrs of Córdoba*, and Wolf, *Christian Martyrs in Muslim Spain*.

107. For interpretations of the meaning of the martyrdoms, see el-Leithy, "Coptic Culture and Conversion," 125, 130–31; also Swanson, "'Our Father Abba Mark,'" 226–27. El-Leithy stresses the importance of Mamluk suppression of Coptic festivals, and the voluntary martyrdoms as a reclamation of public space: 116–26.

108. For another debate about voluntary martyrdom within the *Dar al-Islam*, see Swanson, "The Martyrdom of 'Abd al-Masih," esp. pp. 125–29.

109. *L.Ibrahim*, f. 17r.

110. *L.Marqus*, f. 29v: Marqus had to come to the defense of Ya'qub Abu Muqaytif.

111. Cf. el-Leithy, "Coptic Culture and Conversion," 112–13, where it is suggested that Matthew himself instigated or inspired many of the martyrdoms. This suggestion can be reexamined in the light of the evidence from the *Life of Marqus al-Antuni* and the *Life of Ibrahim al-Fani*.

112. *Life of Matthew*, Nakhlah, *Silsilah* (2nd ed.), iii, 46.

113. *Life of Matthew*, Nakhlah, *Silsilah* (2nd ed.), iii, 47–53; Mark and Ruways appear toward the end of the unit (p. 52).

Chapter Nine:
Humility in Action

1.   *L.Ruways*, f. 139r.
2.   See previous chapter, and the report in Maqrizi, *Suluk*, iii, 1040.
3.   See, for example, Ibn Iyâs, *Histoire des mamlouks circassiens*, II, 278, 362, 370, 482. Christians and Jews were squeezed for funds to support military operations—as was everyone else.
4.   For background on the period, see Garcin, "The Regime of the Circassian Mamluks."
5.   Such instances may be collected from the chronicles of the period, e.g., in English translation, Ibn Taghribirdi, *History of Egypt, 1382–1469 A.D.* (trans. Popper), vol. 17 (Part III), 67–69; vol. 18 (Part IV), 5; vol. 23 (Part VII), 56.
6.   In the entry for 12 Muharram 868 (26 September 1463), Ibn Taghribirdi both admits that the regulations did not stay in effect for more than a year and observes that many "people of the covenant who were bureau administrators were converted;" *History of Egypt*, Part VII, 56.
7.   *HPEC* 3.3, 272–74 (a fraction over two pages); *HPYusab*, 203–204 (just over a single page).
8.   *HPEC* 3.3, 271.
9.   = 1 January AD 1427.
10. Maqrizi, *Suluk*, iv, 760. The final sentiment is rhymed: *fa-ma adrakna batrakan akhmal minhu **barakah**, wa-la aqalla minhu **barakah**.* For another (free) translation of the paragraph, see Samir, "Gabriel V," 1131.
11. Maqrizi, *Suluk*, iv, 247. The reassessment took place immediately after Sultan al-Mu'ayyid Shaykh took power.
12. Maqrizi, *Suluk*, iv, 505; he dates the theft to Sha'ban 822 = August–September 1419. Latin sources date the theft of the body of St. Mark by the Venetians to AD 827; see Geary, *Furta Sacra*, 88–94. The Copts were not unaware of this tradition. The fourteenth-century encyclopedist al-Shams ibn Kabar reports that while some said that the Venetians had the body, the Copts had the head; Ibn Kabar, *Misbah al-zulmah fi idah al-khidmah*, vol. 1, 89. *HPYusab*, 163 mentions that some people thought that the relic in Alexandria was the head of St. Peter (Peter Martyr, the seventeenth patriarch), since the Venetians had undoubtedly taken St. Mark's head with his body.
13. PO 1.4, 499–500; see Chapter One.
14. *HPEC* 2.3, 264–67.
15. *HPYusab*, 158 (Patriarch Mark ibn Zur'ah, who took the relic to his breast while reading and giving praise); 163 (Patriarch Cyril III, who wrapped it in a sumptuous new covering).

16. In a thirteenth–fourteenth century liturgical encyclopedia: Ibn Sabbaʻ [ibn Sibâʻ], *Pretiosa margarita de scientiis ecclesiasticis*, 284–87 (Arabic text), 541–43 (Latin translation). In a fourteenth-century liturgical manuscript: *Rite of Consecration of the Patriarch of Alexandria*, 46 (Coptic text), 83 (English translation). The ritual is also described in Maqrizi, *Suluk*, iv, 505.

17. Maqrizi, *Suluk*, iv, 505. Did al-Maqrizi have his facts straight? In any event, the head of St. Mark seems to disappear from the sources for the next three centuries; see Meinardus, "An Examination of the Traditions," 375. We again hear of the head at the time of Patriarch Peter VI (#104, 1718–1726); Nakhlah, *Silsilah* (2nd ed.), v, 8.

18. Edition, Italian translation, and study: *Book of Ritual* (ed. Alfonso ʻAbdallah). Samir gives a good outline: Samir, "Gabriel V," 1132.

19. On the influence of these reforms on the subsequent development of the Coptic Orthodox liturgy, see *Book of Ritual*, 67–73. Samir comments that Gabriel's liturgical reforms are "comparable to those made by Pius V for the western Latin Church"; Samir, "Gabriel V," 1131.

20. For orientation to these complications, see Bcheiry, "Lettera del patriarca copto Yuhanna XIII," 385–88.

21. For this entire paragraph, see Bcheiry, "Due patriarchi?" Kamil Salih Nakhlah (Nakhlah, *Silsilah* (2nd ed.), iv, 6–7) reported on this consecration, but he was led astray by the existence of parallel patriarchates in the Syrian Orthodox Church, and ended up misinterpreting the consecration as that of Patriarch Ignatius IX Behnam (wrong patriarch) in 1412 (wrong date). Nakhlah has been followed by many writers, but Bcheiry sorts through the confusion.

22. Bcheiry, "Due patriarchi?" esp. p. 264.

23. Nakhlah, *Silsilah* (2nd ed.), iv, 7; Bcheiry, "Due patriarchi?" 260–61.

24. For the occasions on which the holy *myron* or chrism was prepared in the earlier Mamluk period, see Chapter Seven.

25. On the importance of the chrism in Syrian Orthodox tradition, see Varguese, *Les onctions baptismales*.

26. Nakhlah, *Silsilah* (2nd ed.), iv, 11; Bcheiry, "Due patriarchi?" 260–62.

27. Maqrizi, *Suluk*, iv, 1007, 1098, 1170–71.

28. Maqrizi, *Suluk*, iv, 1034.

29. See Coquin, "Dayr al-Maghtis." For an account of the Virgin's recurring appearance, see Cerulli, *Il libro etiopico dei miracoli di Maria*, 195–99.

30. Marie-Laure Derat, "Dabra Metmaq."

31. Maqrizi, *Suluk*, iv, 1024.

32. Al-Sakhawi, *Kitab al-tibr al-masbuk*, i, 164–70. The Ethiopian king's threats are found on p. 168.

33.   Al-Sakhawi, *Kitab al-tibr al-masbuk*, ii, 81 (20 Jumada I 852 = 22 July 1448).

34.   There is a fine study of this exchange, with an edition of the letter of Patriarch John XI to Pope Eugene IV: Luisier, "Lettre" and "Jean XI."

35.   The edition of the letter, with French translation, is at Luisier, "Lettre," 115–29. Luisier points out that the date of the letter is significant: 12 Tut, the commemoration of the Council of Ephesus, remembered as the triumph of Cyril of Alexandria over Nestorius; Luisier, "Jean XI," 553.

36.   John praises Eugene in the most fulsome terms, but reminds him that he is pope "of the great city of Rome and all its provinces" (Luisier, "Lettre," 120–21, line 34); earlier John had specified his own jurisdiction. As for the incarnate Christ, John speaks of "the mediating essence between the two essences of God and Humanity before the union" (pp. 118–19, lines 10–12), which appears to be fully in accord with the miaphysite confession of "one nature of the incarnate Logos."

37.   See Luisier's discussion, "Jean XI," 561–62.

38.   Luisier, "Jean XI," 561–62.

39.   See Bilaniuk, "Coptic Relations with Rome."

40.   See above, note 7.

41.   Samalut, Naqadah, and Sidfa, respectively. To find all these towns, see the map of Egypt on the National Geographic website: http://travel.nationalgeo-graphic.com/places/maps/map_country_egypt.html (accessed 9 June 2009).

42.   See Swanson, "The Monastery of St. Paul in Historical Context," 52–53.

43.   Another monastery to be mentioned here is Dayr al-Qalamun, the Monastery of St. Samuel the Confessor, to the south of al-Fayyum. Patriarch Gabriel V (#88, 1409–1427) had been a monk there.

44.   Nakhlah, *Silsilah* (2nd ed.), iv, 33–34.

45.   Future archival/documentary research on the Coptic Orthodox Church in the fifteenth century will undoubtedly fill out what is now, based on the literary materials, quite a sketchy picture.

46.   Samir, "Gabriel VI," reports that two manuscripts in the Coptic Patriarchate record Gabriel's canonical answers to questions concerning marriage and the service of the altar.

47.   Bcheiry, "Lettera del patriarca copto Yuhanna XIII."

48.   The passage of the letter under consideration here is found in Bcheiry, "Lettera del patriarca copto Yuhanna XIII," 404–407 (paragraphs 38–40).

49.   Bcheiry, "Lettera del patriarca copto Yuhanna XIII," 404–405 (par. 38); my translation.

50.   Bcheiry, "Lettera del patriarca copto Yuhanna XIII," 404–407 (par. 40); my translation. Bcheiry calls attention to the importance of this passage in his commentary, p. 389.

Epilogue

1. As well as the references to Severus of Antioch at the beginning and end of this book, note the references to him as the patriarchate goes into "exile" away from Alexandria; see the end of Chapter Three.

2. Davis, *The Early Coptic Papacy*, Chapter Four.

3. See Chapter Two on the portrayal of patriarchs as near-martyrs, and note the common use of "crown" language; Patriarch Matthew I (#87) was said to have received a crown like the crown of martyrdom (Chapter Eight). For the development of the idea of the Church "of the Martyrs," see Papaconstantinou, "Historiography," and Bagnall and Worp, *Chronological Systems of Byzantine Egypt*, Chapter Eight, "The Era of Diocletian and of the Martyrs," esp. pp. 67–68.

4. Perhaps the best example of this is Patriarch Abraham ibn Zur'ah (#62); see Chapter Four.

5. One lament over the "death of Coptic culture" is MacCoull, "The Strange Death of Coptic Culture."

6. See Coquin, "Dayr al-Maghtis"; Armanios, "Coptic Christians in Ottoman Egypt," Chapter Two, "Visiting with Kin: The Hagiography and Shrine of Saint Dimyana during the Ottoman Period."

7. Girgis, Shelley, and van Doorn-Harder, *The Emergence of the Modern Coptic Papacy*.

Appendix

1. See Nakhlah, *Silsilah* (2nd ed.), iii, 44–46; Wadi Abuliff, "Quaranta-nove martiri."

Index

This index of names and subjects provides page references to the main text. References to the bibliography and notes are not included.